D0875766

WAR BIRD

War Bird

THE LIFE AND TIMES OF

ELLIOTT WHITE SPRINGS

BY BURKE DAVIS

The University of North Carolina Press

Chapel Hill and London

© 1987

Springs Foundation, Inc.

All rights reserved

Manufactured in the

United States of America

Library of Congress Cataloging-in-Publication Data

Davis, Burke, 1913–

  War bird.

  Includes index.

  1. Springs, Elliott White. 2. Springs Industries—

History. 3. Cotton textile industry—United States—

History. 4. Industrialists—United States—Biography.

5. World War, 1914–1918—Biography. 6. Novelists,

American—20th century—Biography. I. Title.

HD9880.S67D38 1987   338.7′67721′0924 [B]   87-5934

ISBN 0-8078-1752-X

91 90 89 88 87   5 4 3 2 1

FRONTISPIECE

Elliott White Springs in a
studio portrait shortly after
World War I.
Courtesy of Anne Springs Close

To the Colonel's daughter, Anne

Contents

Sections of photographs follow pages 70 and 182.

Acknowledgments

I acknowledge with gratitude contributions to this book by Anne Springs Close of Fort Mill, South Carolina, the daughter of Elliott White Springs; by Frances Close Hart of Columbia, South Carolina, his granddaughter; by Marshall Doswell of Fort Mill; by Anne Skipper McAden and the late James T. McAden of Columbia; and by Katherine Wooten Springs of Matthews, North Carolina.

I am also grateful to Joseph M. Bryan, Mrs. Benjamin Cone, Sydney M. Cone, Jr., and Mrs. Richard G. Newell of Greensboro, North Carolina; Helen Cowley of the Patrick County Library, Stuart, Virginia; John Gates of Winston-Salem, North Carolina; Dr. Charles P. Graham of Wilmington, North Carolina; and Peggy Thompson of Fort Mill.

Particular thanks are due the following, who granted extensive interviews and shared their recollections of Elliott White Springs: Dr. Haynes Baird, Charles Crutchfield, Harry L. Dalton, Dr. Monroe Gilmour, Walter Mallonee, Cecil Neal, the late Gus Travis, and Mrs. Gordon Watt of Charlotte, North Carolina; V. A. Ballard, Anne Springs Close, the late H. William Close, Palmer Freeman, Mr. and Mrs. John Hallett, Lunsford McFadden, the late Elizabeth Mack, and F. H. Martin of Fort Mill; Lavoy Bauknight, James Bradley, the late Joseph Croxton, Eunice Hite, James B. Lasley, Herbert Mathewson, Henry Montgomery, and Peg Smith of Lancaster, South Carolina; Righton Richards of Liberty Hill, South Carolina; Julian Starr of Morehead City, North Carolina; J. William Medford of Tryon, North Carolina; Earl Crenshaw of Gastonia, North Carolina; Herbert Elsas of Atlanta, Georgia; Peter Kriendler and Mary Wilson of New York; John Roddey of Rock Hill, South Carolina; and Henry Schniewind, and Maxie and the late Julian C. Stanley of Locust Valley, New York.

My wife, Juliet, acted as coauthor, translator, interviewer, psychologist, consultant, and computer operator.

A Note on Sources

Elliott Springs left a vast collection of papers covering every aspect of his life, almost as if he anticipated biographers. Letters, diaries, scrapbooks, school, college, and army records, files of periodicals and books, photographs, and a miscellany of documents comprise the Springs Papers of the South Caroliniana Library at the University of South Carolina in Columbia. The collection was organized and cataloged by Barbara Fenix in 1970–71.

Though most of the material is personal, the extensive business files document Elliott's role in creating the modern Springs Industries. Except where otherwise noted, this biography is based upon the Springs Papers.

Notable exceptions are interviews by the author with friends and associates of Elliott White Springs. Other interviews were made available to the author through the generosity of John Gates of Winston-Salem, North Carolina, who made an earlier study of the Springs Papers. Supplementary interviews, taped over the course of many years, were also used by the author.

The only writers who have previously had access to the Springs collection are Helen Vassy Callison, whose unpublished doctoral thesis at the University of South Carolina surveys Springs's literary activities; and Louise Pettus, author of the corporate history of the Springs firm.

Though Springs corresponded widely throughout his career, his letters to his father, Leroy, and to his stepmother, Lena, are the most remarkable and revealing. These letters and those to his wife, during their courtship and during his mental illness twenty years later, were key sources for this biography.

The published works that I consulted are listed in the chapter notes following the text. Among these are the works of Springs himself, almost all of which are autobiographical. *War Birds*, the purported diary of an "unknown" aviator killed in France in 1918, was especially valuable in interpreting the vivid personality of Elliott White Springs.

WAR BIRD

Prologue: August 1918

From the southwest the wind, the prevailing wind, quartered up the Channel across the French coast and inland toward the German border. It bore six frail canvas-covered planes across the battle lines into enemy territory in Belgium and northern France. B Flight of the 148th (American) Squadron of the Royal Air Force had risen from an airdrome at the village of Bertangles, a few miles north of Amiens, near the western flank of the front where millions of infantrymen were locked in the final struggle for France. The tiny biplanes, hardly more than powered kites, were Sopwith Camels, swift and agile but unstable in some respects, inferior to the new German fighters—yet today, as ever, B Flight sought the enemy in whatever strength he might be found. All were eager to add to the score of the most deadly of American squadrons.

Even these combat craft were far advanced over those that had begun the war—the first fighter pilots had armed themselves with butcher knives and shotguns. The armament of B Flight, though still light, was a miracle of wartime development—.32 caliber bullets fired from Vickers or Lewis machine guns, at the rate of about one thousand per minute.

The roaring engines of the Camels drowned all other sounds so that the war on the ground seemed to rage in silence with the brief bright wink of exploding shells fired from invisible guns upon invisible targets. On the scarred plains below, the last great Allied offensive was slowly pressing the invading German armies northward. This month, in the fourth year of the war, the tides of the conflict had changed. Russia had withdrawn from the eastern front and was locked in a revolutionary upheaval. The French army was only now recovering from its mutiny of 1917, and the British army, numbed by devastating casualties, had thrown the last of its reserves into battle. More than two hundred thousand American troops were now arriving in France each month.

The leader of B Flight, who had just passed his twenty-second birthday, was Elliott White Springs, the son of a wealthy South Carolina cotton mill owner, already known to his companions as one of the most fearless of combat pilots—and the most accomplished bartender in uniform. Springs was a stocky, sandy-haired youth whose handsome face still bore the marks of a recent crash. His eyes were red-rimmed and raw, but though he complained that his eyelids were often savaged by the wind, he refused to wear goggles in combat. His face was smeared with rancid whale oil as a protection against intense cold at high altitude, but he wore only a heavy fur-lined flying suit of British issue with a pair of silk pajamas underneath.

To his right and slightly to the rear, Springs saw his wingman and most intimate friend, Larry Callahan of Chicago, the fun-loving, piano-playing "gypsy" of the flight. The imperturbable Callahan was Elliott's favorite companion in dogfights, for even after the most trying patrols, when no other pilot of the squadron could "get a glass to his mouth with one hand," Larry remained unaffected. "He has no nerves," Springs said. "He's made of cheese." The two had slept little the night before and were so troubled by nightmares that a tentmate "had to get up and find his teeth and quiet us."

Springs, whose repressed inner tensions had contributed to his suffering from abdominal pains since boyhood, carried in his cockpit a bottle of milk of magnesia tablets and a flask of gin. "If one doesn't work," his theory went, "the other will." He also carried a good luck charm—a garter from the left leg of a purported virgin (American).

Springs would become the fifth-ranking American ace of the war, though, like most of his contemporaries, he had been given scant training at home. A year earlier, after a lively career as a ladies' man that had won him campus fame as "Cave Man," Springs had become a student pilot at Princeton University, an ecstatic novice captivated by the perilous new world of flight. "I had control of the plane yesterday for twenty minutes," he had written his disapproving father. "I'm afraid I'll never be happy on land again."

Through a miscarriage of army orders Springs and his companions had been cast away in England, subjected to the whimsical but highly effective training methods of the Royal Flying Corps—and exposed to the riotous nightlife of wartime London. During eight months that had claimed scores of lives, Springs and other young colonials had set new standards of undisciplined exuberance in flight. They also stirred consternation in London's cafe society and particularly in its theatrical world. Elliott emerged from the English experience with admiration for the accomplishments of the American neophytes with British actresses: "If these boys can fly two-bladers like they can fly four-posters, there'll surely be a shortage of Huns before long."

Springs had fought for only three months in France but was one of the most observant of the hundreds of men who courted death in the skies. He was moved by each glimpse of the devastated landscape beneath him. To his uncomprehending parents back home he wrote:

> I know every tree, every village, every road, every canal, every little wood, every little change of color . . . for twenty miles on either side of the lines, from Boulogne to St. Omer to Arras, to Roullers, to Amiens to Montdidier on our side . . . I've spent a couple of hundred hours above it, looking first down and then up, searching . . . I can close my eyes and my mind becomes a huge map whose accuracy has been tested hundreds of times.
>
> I've flown between the piles of ruins of Nieuport, Dixmude, Ypres, Bailleul, Arras, Bapaume . . . and their memory will always be a sear. . . . You almost need a map to tell where they are . . . simply pushed to one side and flattened. . . . For miles around there is a flat brown expanse of mud and dust which from above seems to be boiling. . . . The Menin road once lined with poplars has a few stumps to mark it.

Yet he confessed that he found in combat an irresistible fascination from which he would never recover: "No matter where I go or what I do the best part of me will always remain between Zeebrugge and Armentières, and in front of Cambrai. There I lived a life, a long lifetime, there lie my companions, and many adversaries and there also lies the biggest part of myself."

In recent days Elliott had acknowledged that he, no less than the ravaged French countryside, was a victim of war. He had lost the exuberance with which he had begun. Now, he conceded, he had begun to lose control. "I'm all right in the air, as cool as a cucumber, but on the ground I'm a wreck and I get panicky."

He had also become depressed by the deaths of many comrades. Few veteran pilots remained, and Elliott was shaken by the loss of so many friends. "It gives me a dizzy feeling every time I hear of the men that are gone," he wrote. "And they have gone so fast I can't keep track of them; every time two pilots meet it is only to swap news of who's killed."

After less than half an hour of flight on this hot, clear August afternoon, B Flight encountered the enemy, nine of the new Fokkers, accompanied by a new two-seater, a Hannoveranner. Springs gave the signal to engage and dove after the larger plane. He forced it to low altitude, but his bullets seemed to have no effect, and he discovered that the Hannoveranner had few blind spots. The guns of the pilot and his observer covered most approaches. The fabric of Elliott's plane was stitched with bullet holes before he could break away. He was separated from his companions.

When he saw more Fokkers some three thousand feet above him, Springs climbed to lure them into the range of Allied planes he expected as support, but he found himself alone when the Germans pounced in "the worst scrap" of his career.

Two Fokkers attacked him in the first wave. Elliott nosed toward the ground and waited to be overtaken. "As soon as one of them opened fire, I pulled up in a long zoom and turned. One Hun overshot and I found myself level with the other one. He half rolled and I did a skid turn and opened up on him. He wasn't much of a pilot because I got about 150 rounds into him. He went into a dive."

The more accomplished enemy pilot then ripped one of Elliott's wings with his opening burst and stalled beneath him to spray tracers about the cockpit. Springs rolled away, searching the sky for reinforcements. There were none. Three Germans swooped at him in a display of unfamiliar tactics—one plane on his tail and the other two coming in on his flanks. "They were all three firing and all I could do was to stay in a tight bank and pray. I thought I was gone. One of them pulled up and then came straight down to finish me off." Springs managed to evade this German. "As soon as I saw his nose go by, I put mine down, for I saw it was time to think more about rescuing the decoy than holding any bag for the rest of them."

Springs dove at his top speed of more than two hundred miles per hour but found an enemy plane close behind him. "As soon as his tracer showed up close I pulled straight up. He tried to pull up but overshot and went on by, about fifty feet from me. I was close enough to see his goggles and all details of his plane, which was black and white checked with a white nose." Elliott waved to his enemy. The other Germans watched as Springs and his lone opponent repeated these deadly maneuvers again and again. "The rest of his crew didn't seem to be in a fighting mood and only picked at me from a distance so I got away."

He fled homeward at low level, exchanging fire with German troops below. He did so in the face of the wind, which slowed his plane and made him more vulnerable to enemy planes, antiaircraft fire, and small arms fire from the ground. There was also a danger that his straining engine would run out of fuel before he reached safety.

"Before I got back," Springs said, "I was shivering so I could hardly land. And I haven't been feeling right since. My heart seems to be trying to stunt all the time."

That night, in the grip of violent nightmares, he fought Germans for two hours. He confessed the next day, "I don't know which will get me first, a bullet or the nervous strain. This decoy game is about the most dangerous thing in the world."

As he wrote of this encounter, he returned to a favorite theme—his scorn for back-home "patriots." He noted that he had now filled three volumes of his combat accounts and assumed that they could not be published. "It will never do to let the people at home find out the truth about this war. They've been fed on bunk until they'd never believe anything that didn't sound like a monk's story of the Crusades."

From the moment of his landing near Dunkirk three months earlier, Springs had recorded his impressions of war. Companions who knew him as a wild, reckless prankster were unaware that he made notes daily, sketching themes for stories of men in combat. Elliott's letters home were a remarkable blend: he seldom failed to hurl defiant challenges to his stern father, but followed these with detailed and vivid accounts of war in the sky that were reminiscent of scenes from a novel. To his father, these striking letters came as messages from a distant planet.

Since early boyhood Elliott had sought, and had been denied, the approval of his father, the imperious, opinionated, hard-drinking, and quarrelsome Leroy Springs of Lancaster, South Carolina. In the resulting conflict the son had often been more than a match for his father.

For months, Leroy badgered his son to send a photograph of himself in his aviator's uniform. Elliott resisted, realizing that his father would pass the picture among his friends and publish it in newspapers so that he might boast of his son's career. Leroy finally wrote to Elliott's commanding general and forced the rebellious ace to send home a photograph but discovered that he had won an empty victory. He unwrapped the picture to find that Elliott had scrawled across it in ink, "Here's looking at you, you old drunk."

Elliott reacted angrily when he learned that his letters were being published in South Carolina newspapers. He wrote to Lena Springs, his stepmother, "Word has reached me that my letters are being quoted. There's honor among thieves but darn little among families."

In response to gratuitous advice from home he wrote shortly afterward, "The opinions of you and Father on how to fly and how to fight are doubtless valuable but . . . I wish you would send them to someone else . . . and you haven't told me a thing about how to use my compass. I shall probably be lost though before you get the information to me. Think it over."

Almost against his will, Elliott Springs was to survive the war in the air and to record his experiences in *War Birds*, a unique novel that became a popular and influential American war book of his generation. Sholto Douglas, the future British air marshal, praised this book as a "classic," and T. E. Lawrence, the historian and hero of the desert wars of the Middle East, declared it to be "immortal."

Springs was also to expand his family business beyond recognition and shape it into a major American textile corporation. In reaction to the tasteless vulgarity of advertising of his era, Springs aroused the trade with a memorable series of rollicking, risque ads that caused a furor and raised his Springmaid sheets to the status of a national institution. Though he lacked experience, Springs revolutionized the advertising industry and rid it of many of its inhibitions. As one of the most creative American industrialists of the day, Springs devoted his time, energies, and varied talents almost exclusively to his business. He kept his own counsel, resisted the conventional wisdom of the majority, and achieved his goals in face of the skepticism of those who failed to detect the brilliant executive behind the facade of the playboy-prankster.

Despite a long, unique, colorful, and phenomenally successful career, Elliott Springs remained a War Bird at heart, and a part of him, he confessed, always remained in the French skies of 1918. A decade after the Armistice he looked back to the war he could not forget:

It was the greatest sporting event in the history of history . . . a big game hunt, the like of which had never been seen before.

It was the most dangerous of sports and the most fascinating. It got into the blood like wine. It aged men forty years in forty days. . . . No words can describe the thrills of hiding in the clouds, waiting on human prey. . . .

What human experience can compare with it. . . . The average life of a pilot at the front was forty-eight hours in the air. . . .

Is it any wonder that pilots became fatalists . . . that those who survive fear a drab and boring existence more than they ever feared Hun machine guns? No man who has ever pressed triggers above the bright blue sky will ever be happy keeping books.

I / "As Smart As He Could Be"

Elliott White Springs was born in the small town of Lancaster, South Carolina, on July 31, 1896 into a family prominent in the affairs of the Carolinas since the Colonial era. His father, Leroy, born during the first year of the Civil War, was an acquisitive, irascible entrepreneur who laid the foundation of the family's fortune and had scant time for companionship with his son.

Young Elliott's mother, Grace Allison White, was the daughter of Captain Samuel Elliott White, a much-wounded Confederate veteran, prominent landowner, and founder of a small cotton mill. She was also a rarity in the upland South Carolina of her day, an educated woman; she had attended a finishing school in Baltimore, Maryland, and Charlotte Female College (later Queens College) in Charlotte, North Carolina. A devout Presbyterian given to good works, she financed local charities privately, often anonymously, and became a beloved figure in the community. This gentle, dignified woman, whose personality contrasted so strongly with that of her husband, passed to their only child the more ingratiating traits of her lineage—good humor, wit, tolerance, and a certain tenacious stability. She was the center of Elliott's life. Perhaps as an antidote to Leroy's insensitivity, she lavished love and attention upon her son.

Through his mother Elliott descended from an Englishman, John White, lord of an Irish estate granted by Oliver Cromwell and a member of the celebrated Long Parliament in the reign of Charles II. Around 1742, John White's descendant, Moses White, migrated to Pennsylvania with his wife, Mary Campbell. Their seven sons joined the swarm of settlers to the Carolinas, where Elliott's grandfather, Samuel Elliott White, was born in 1837.

The Springs family traced its American heritage to an original settler of New Amsterdam, Gertrude Springsteen, a widow, who arrived from her native Holland with her three children in 1652. Her children and grandchildren married into families destined to become well known in the new nation—Vanderbilt, Van Alstyne, and Van Bleecker. One branch of the family drifted southward into Delaware and Maryland, and by the time of the Revolution, to Mecklenburg County, North Carolina, and thence into upper South Carolina, where they acquired large land holdings and Americanized their name as Springs.

Through both of his family lines Elliott was related to vigorous families who had supplied the leading citizens of the backcountry Carolinas—Brevards, Baxters, Moreheads, Craigs, Davidsons, Hutchinsons, Erwins, Russells, Phifers, Caldwells, Holts, McKamies, and Alexanders. Elliott inherited two notable facets of his personality from these progenitors: like the Springs men, he was to be sternly authoritarian and frequently abrasive, but like the Whites, he was also to be sensitive, warm, charming, and vivacious. He became in manhood the most remarkable of his line.

Elliott's father, Leroy Springs, attended the University of North Carolina for little more than a year and began his career as a salesman for his brother Eli, who was a merchant. Leroy travelled the primitive roads of the region in a buggy, selling supplies to country grocers, frequently sleeping in the haylofts of accommodating farmers. He had outgrown this role by the age of twenty-one, when he opened a branch store in Lancaster with capital of $5,000. He surpassed the parent firm within a brief period—but he assumed such heavy debts that his partners withdrew. Once, it was said, he borrowed the entire capital and surplus of a large bank "and then frisked the president's pockets for his change." Leroy continued expansion of his company and also added a cotton export and shipping company with seven branches. Springs became a legendary figure in the cotton trade by his reckless gambling in cotton futures. In a day when New York Cotton Exchange contracts required delivery of cotton in the city, Leroy broke a corner in the market by shipping three trainloads of cotton by express that arrived just six hours before the end-of-month deadline. "These gyrations," as one historian said, "were profitable to the stockholders, but they made a whirling dervish out of Mr. Thomson [the treasurer], misanthropes out of the customers, and panhandlers out of the speculators." In the process Leroy also became the largest shipper in the Southeast and one year was "the largest shipper into Liverpool."

He also became known as a fearless, even violent, man. In June 1885, he shot and killed a young man, John R. Bell, during an altercation on a Lancaster street. Bell, a bartender and carpenter who was "somewhat inclined to drink," accused Springs of slandering him. Leroy denied the charge, but the two—both armed—met the following day and fell into an argument. Bell struck Leroy and then reached for his pistol.

Leroy drew swiftly and shot Bell in the heart. The "large, powerful young man" died almost instantly. Springs surrendered to the local sheriff and was briefly placed under guard in his hotel room but was released and never tried. Though Leroy was declared to have fired in self-defense, he said he was "deeply affected" by the death of Bell and insisted upon paying his funeral expenses.

By 1892 Springs had achieved his goal—he was worth $1 million. He married Grace White in that year.

Three years later Leroy took the decisive step to wealth by organizing a cotton mill in Lancaster, an enterprise that provided a durable industrial base for the community. Leroy proved to be a nimble executive in this era of recurring financial crises. He acquired all of his equipment by convincing machinery manufacturers to accept preferred stock in lieu of cash. He also persuaded a few investors to buy stock to build his plant, and within a brief time Leroy's mills were prospering.

Leroy was merely one of hundreds of pioneers who created the Southern textile industry in the last quarter of the nineteenth century by capitalizing on plentiful water power, vast cotton crops, and an inexhaustible supply of cheap labor. In the two decades before 1900, more than four hundred cotton mills sprang up in the Piedmont region between Danville, Virginia, and Birmingham, Alabama. Few of these enterprises were more successful than those of Springs.

In 1896—the year of Elliott's birth—Leroy bought at auction the bankrupt little Cheraw and Chester Railroad for a mere $25,000. This line, shortened and renamed the Lancaster & Chester Railway, became a factor in Leroy's rise to riches. He bought out his partners, borrowed from the infant Southern Railway to improve the line and provided traffic from his textile operations. Though this was his first experience with railroading, he was following a strong family tradition. His father had been a contractor on what became the Southern's main line from Charlotte to Columbia, and his grandfather was a director of the nation's first operating railroad, the South Carolina Canal and Railroad Company—one of whose pioneer locomotives was called the John Springs.

The timely boom brought by World War I had a dynamic effect upon Leroy's little railroad and especially upon his Lancaster Cotton Mills, which he had expanded into the world's largest under one roof. He also directed a farming operation on his twenty thousand acres, most of which he rented to neighbors; one hundred fifty tenant families worked his remaining eight thousand acres, producing cotton as their chief crop.

Leroy drove himself to the limit and expected his employees to match his efforts. In order to give maximum time to business, he slept only four or five hours each night. W. C. Thomson, his vice president and treasurer, often left Springs in his office at midnight and the next day found him "out at six in the morning trading mules."

As he achieved prominence, Leroy served on various official state boards and committees, including a term as Colonel on the staff of a South Carolina governor; he was known thereafter as Colonel Springs. He was also a delegate to several Democratic national conventions.

Leroy survived the financial panics of the 1890s that ruined scores of Southern textile mills. He was once summoned north by his banker to negotiate foreclosure on one of his plants, but rather than surrender the keys of the mill, Leroy sold the banker some stock in a promising new mill he had opened in nearby Kershaw and returned home to lead his growing empire into the new century and to permanent security. He bought still more mills in neighboring Chester, South Carolina, and also took over the Fort Mill Manufacturing Company of which his father-in-law, Samuel White, was founder, president, and a major investor. These mills were acquired just in time to enjoy full benefits of the first great boom in twentieth-century America.

From his first year the precocious, bright, energetic Elliott won the hearts of his mother's parents, and to Captain Sam's wife, Esther Allison White, he was "the idol of my heart." He was taught the alphabet and elementary arithmetic before he entered the first grade and during his opening year became a volunteer teacher for his classmates in the local Franklin Academy. He became one of the leading students in this small school, but was remembered longest for his debut as an author-publisher: he wrote, arranged, and bound a story and presented it to his teacher in the form of a complete book.

Elliott suffered the usual ailments of childhood, including measles and whooping cough, but in 1905, at the age of nine, he also had typhoid fever, which apparently affected his health for life.

The scanty record of his early years suggests that Elliott spent an otherwise idyllic childhood as the scion of Lancaster's leading family. He was once photographed on a farm wagon, perched atop a load of watermelons and surrounded by grinning black playmates of about his own age, some of the servants and companions who tended him throughout his early years.

When he was six years old, Elliott was given a pony and cart, which was described by the local newspaper, "The tiniest turnout ever seen in these parts is owned by Master Elliott White Springs, the bright and manly son of Colonel and Mrs. Leroy Springs. It consists of a decidedly diminutive Shetland pony hitched to a cute little cart. Almost any afternoon Master Elliott can be seen taking some young Miss out to ride."

The rig provided diversion for young Elliott during summer vacations when the Springs clan gathered in the North Carolina mountains. His pony and cart were carried along as part of the family caravan, and he staged reckless races with his cousin Julia Scott, who became his fast friend and admirer. There were also trips to Camden, South Carolina, to visit the family of Ralph Shannon, one of Leroy's business partners. A troop of children frequently roused the town with noisy games of cops and robbers, usually instigated by Elliott. "He was never quiet," Julia remembered. "He was always good company." But there were exceptions, for Elliott was sometimes moody. "He had a habit of chewing on his fingers. He was thinking then. As smart as he could be."

The first traumatic shock of his life came to Elliott at the age of seven, in May 1903. His grandmother, with whom he spent much of his time, had promised to take Elliott for a walk before supper on the warm spring evening. The sixty-year-old Esther was second only to his mother in Elliott's affections. He was unaware that she suffered from "gastritis" and heart disease and feared that she was near death. Earlier in the day, indeed, she had told her husband, "I hope the end comes suddenly."

The boy waited outside the White home in Fort Mill about five o'clock that afternoon and, when his grandmother failed to appear, entered the house, called from the entry hall in vain, and climbed the stairs to her bedroom.

She lay dead on the floor.

Elliott's reaction was unrecorded but some relatives noted his impenetrable reserve at this time and judged that the tragic moment had a lasting effect on him.

Elliott won a reputation for exceptional maturity before he was ten. He and his mother were riding a fast passenger train of the Southern Railway when its engine derailed near Greensboro, North Carolina, and several crewmen were seriously injured. Of all the passengers and bystanders at the scene, it was only young Elliott who thought of reporting the mishap. As the *Lancaster News* commented, "He went to the newspaper office and gave a remarkably intelligent account of the accident."

His maturity was soon tested by another personal tragedy. Three years after the death of her mother, Grace Springs became seriously ill of an undisclosed ailment (probably cancer) and was taken to Kelly's Sanatorium in Baltimore, where she endured intense "pain and suffering" for seven months. She died April 30, 1907, at the age of thirty-three. In Leroy's absence, Elliott was told of her death by Julia Scott's mother, his Aunt Bleecker, of Charlotte. Though he gave little outward sign of distress, the loss of his mother was the most devastating blow of Elliott's life and one from which he never fully recovered. In later life, his daughter recalled, he never spoke of his childhood nor of the death of his mother.

Grace Springs was buried in a family cemetery plot in Charlotte. Her funeral was an especially trying time for Elliott, for it was delayed about three hours until the train bearing her corpse arrived from Baltimore and the service could begin. Ten-year-old Elliott sat with the mourners through those hours until his father arrived at last, the casket was transferred to a waiting hearse, and the horses in their black trappings plodded off to the First Presbyterian Church. It was near dusk when the party left the cemetery. Elliott, who evidently maintained his composure throughout, concealing his emotions from the crowd, was described by an observer: "He is as bright and accomplished as if he were five years older. He has fallen heir to his mother's fine qualities of heart and head."

His boyhood had ended with his mother's death, for the stern, preoccupied Leroy, at a loss as to how to deal with his son, turned him over to Grace's seventy-year-old father, who now spent much of his time in Leroy's home in Lancaster. Elliott came to love and admire his grandfather, who was one of the local war heroes. Though Captain Sam founded a cotton mill and a bank and became well known in the region as a public speaker, the central interest of his life was the Confederacy and its role in the Civil War, a topic which fascinated young Elliott. Not only did the Captain bear scars from his wounds, two of his five brothers who also fought for the South died in the war.

As head of the Jefferson Davis Memorial Association during the 1890s, Sam White erected in Fort Mill one of the first monuments to Confederate soldiers and funded other memorials in the town to Confederate women, to faithful slaves, and to the Catawba Indians of the region who had fought in the Confederate Army. Elliott's whimsical grandfather also founded the Sons of Rest, a group of war veterans who gathered daily to gossip, whittle, and drink in a wall tent on Main Street provided by Sam White.

Captain White was painfully afflicted with gastric ulcers during his later years. The old man claimed his stomach trouble was brought on by poor army rations during a terrible winter when Robert E. Lee's army nearly starved and men ate roots and berries from the woods to ward off scurvy. (Leroy Springs, a two-fisted drinker in his own right, laid the blame upon Captain Sam's fondness for liquor.) Local doctors, in any case, gave Captain Sam no relief from his "dyspepsia." They took his temperature and pulse, inspected his tongue, and advised him to report to a clinic in the North.

"Hell's katoot," White said. "The only time in my life I've crossed the Mason-Dixon Line was to chase some Yankees back into Pennsylvania. I've no idea of crossing it again."

Despite pleas of his friends and Leroy's protracted arguments, the captain refused to leave Lancaster. His suffering continued until Leroy finally summoned a specialist from Baltimore to attend the old man. The visiting expert fed Captain Sam a full meal, produced a stomach pump and subjected the patient to a treatment. White said he felt much better but refused further ministrations at the time. The doctor instructed him in the use of the pump and returned to Baltimore.

Young Elliott watched avidly the scenes which followed and occasionally took part in them. Thereafter, when the captain's pangs recurred, usually about an hour after lunch, he "put away his whittling" and went to the back porch. Armed with a tin tub, a quart of warm water and a tube, he called on the cook for help. The old man expertly swallowed the tube and waited patiently while Mammy Lucy clambered onto a chair and poured the water into a funnel and down his tube. The captain squeezed the tube, turned it down into the tub to create a vacuum and thus relieved his pains by regurgitation. Elliott was called upon to pour when Lucy was not at hand, but since he usually spilled water into his grandfather's face, his service was limited to emergencies.

As Elliott recalled it, Captain White kept himself alive for eight years with these rigorous treatments until he "finally died of starvation when he could eat no longer."

Elliott had his first adventures with outsiders during these years. From his bedroom window the boy could look down on the field where neighborhood boys gathered for baseball games—played with homemade bats and balls of tightly wrapped string. Elliott was not only much younger than the boys who played in the field, he was small for his age with short arms and legs. Thus he was not invited to play ball, though he had been given numerous pieces of baseball equipment by his indulgent elders. But there came a day the boys called up to the wistful Elliott, "Come on down and bring your stuff, and you can play with us."

He responded eagerly, providing the boys with a new ball and bat and several gloves. During a lull the players paused for water from a nearby spring, and when Elliott lay flat on the ground to drink, a larger boy plunged his head under water and held him for a moment or so, until he struggled upward, choking and strangling. In a fury he gathered his baseball equipment and went back to the house, vowing that he would never play with them again.

Some time later Elliott discovered a second baseball team, which accepted him—and his equipment—without reservation and elected him captain. Though Elliott was a passable catcher and seemed to play as well as most of his companions, his team never won a game and endured humiliating losses to their rivals at each meeting. Elliott consulted his father about the problem and was given conventional advice, "If you can't lick 'em, why not join 'em?" Elliott resigned as team captain and became a substitute fielder for the dominant team.

Leroy made desultory efforts to teach his son the values of enterprise and money management. Apparently in the hope of awakening Elliott's entrepreneurial instincts, Springs bought a large, brightly painted peanut roasting machine, and on Saturday afternoons, when the town's sidewalks were thronged with farmers, mill hands, and shopping housewives, Elliott was posted before the Lancaster Mercantile Company to tend the roaster.

His piercing cries of "Peaaa nuuts!" were not in vain. Not only was the aroma of the freshly cooked nuts tantalizing, but many customers patronized Elliott because they recognized the freckle-faced towhead as Mr. Leroy's son. The enterprise was evidently of short duration, but Elliott carefully saved the roaster for the rest of his life.

Elliott also revealed an early and lively interest in girls. During a summer holiday at Tybee Beach in Georgia, he annoyed a playmate by thrusting fiddler crabs down the back of her bathing suit and by tying her pigtails to the back of a seat on a train to Savannah. Half a century later this victim recalled that she ignored her mother's pleas to "play nicely" with Elliott and always tried to hide when she saw him approaching.

Another girl who knew him during his early youth recalled Elliott in a strikingly different light. She remembered him as a young Lord Fauntleroy, "jumping out to open the car door for young ladies," the epitome of a well-bred young Southern gentleman. This was a minority report. A more detailed and convincing story of Elliott in youth involved a pretty Lancaster girl whose identity is unknown.

One of Elliott's favorite haunts was the vast, cool cavern beneath the back porch of his father's house, where a servant, black Aunt Carrie, hung smoked hams from the rafters. Here, on hot Sunday mornings in spring and summer, Elliott turned the crank of a large ice cream freezer. This scene was once an irresistible lure to a pretty red-haired girl who lived in a cottage on a back street nearby. She was in her early teens and was, as she later recalled, "just beginning to need a bra."

When adults were safely in church and she heard the grinding of Elliott's freezer, this young lady walked up the alley past the Whites' barn, hidden from Aunt Carrie's view by a rose hedge, and joined Elliott. She watched eagerly until he could turn the crank no longer. When he opened the freezer and removed the dasher, richly encrusted with strawberry ice cream, Elliott passed it to his expectant admirer—but as she held it to her face and licked the cream, Elliott joyously began to tickle her breasts and ribs. She struck him on the head with the dasher and raced along the alley with Elliott in pursuit, her red pigtails flying and a leg of her flour-sack drawers flapping about her knees.

That sun-drenched morning was still vivid in her memory some fifty years later when, as an aging Hollywood actress, the redhead wrote Springs of the incident from their childhood, "I have since been tickled by some of the biggest heels in Hollywood, but whenever a man lays a hot hand on me I can still taste strawberry ice cream." She signed herself only as "Auld Lang Syne."

Elliott's relationship with his grandfather soon came to an end. Leroy sent the boy to live in Camden for a few months with the Shannons, but he soon left them too.

In 1908, at the age of twelve, he was sent to Asheville School, a fashionable new academy in the North Carolina mountains that was chiefly patronized by wealthy families from the Midwest. The campus, west of the small resort city of Asheville, was remote and often foggy and dreary. Despite earlier visits with his family to the highlands, Elliott disliked the gloomy hills. But if he suffered homesickness, he concealed it well, as he did the wrenching sorrow over the loss of his mother. His actual state of mind was revealed only many years later when he published a magazine story about a lonely boy sent off to a boarding school after his mother had died.

Elliott was the youngest of the one hundred boys in school and was undersized in addition. The school was conducted by an exacting twelve-man faculty, and Elliott found the work much more demanding than that of his local academy. His confidence was shaken by his first experiences there, and his weekly letters home, written in an almost indecipherable scrawl, were criticized by his father as hurried and vague. Elliott reported several illnesses, for which Leroy expressed regret, but he did not inquire into the nature of these ailments, which may have been more serious than father or son realized. In later years, at least, Elliott felt that he developed an ulcer at Asheville School under the stress of losing his mother and being thrust into a strange environment.

Though Leroy's letters to his son included expressions of affection, these seemed to be less sincere than his admonitions to send "more news" and to make greater efforts in his studies: "We all love you so much you ought to try to please me in having a good report . . . we love to have good reports of you." Leroy continued to badger the boy to make better grades—though Elliott's deportment was rated "excellent" and his industry "satisfactory." Elliott had fallen behind in mathematics, but, when he improved his early grade of "very poor" to "fair," Leroy urged that he boost it to "excellent" and said he would not be content until marks in every subject were of the highest rank. His rather trite offerings of paternal advice became a drumfire of admonitions: "You want to play when you play and work when you work; it makes a boy happy, contented, and wise. . . . It is just as easy to do your work well as it is to do it indifferently and at the same time, have just as much pleasure and be happier."

Elliott's letters from his grandfather, though infrequent, were more cheerful. The old man sent an occasional dollar bill or a box of Texas pecans—but even he urged the boy to write less hurriedly.

Elliott wrote that he wanted to play football and asked his father to send pants and a jersey. Leroy did so but announced his disapproval, "Do try to avoid being hurt. I do not like the idea of your playing football, as you are too small and are liable to get run over." His fears were groundless.

Elliott began playing football on a lightweight team soon after his arrival and won the admiration of older, larger schoolmates as he fought his way to the captaincy of the one-hundred-pound team—a diminutive but ferocious end who obviously enjoyed the rough sport and played without injury. The little star was often urged on by derisive, but affectionate, yells from the spectators: "Stand up high, Springs, and tackle him around the knees!"

During holidays at least, Elliott gave no signs of unhappiness or withdrawal. On a trip to New York in July 1909, just before his thirteenth birthday, he attended the theater ten times in eleven days—the American Music Hall, the Lyric, the Broadway, the Fifth Avenue, and other theaters, as well as several roof gardens. He dined and lunched in several of the city's leading restaurants. This was probably his first exposure to the high life of the city, an experience that helped to form his tastes.

By his second year Elliott had become a popular figure in the school, partially at least because of his fearless play on the football field. Eighty-two fellow students signed his annual at the end of the year with jocular tributes to his athletic prowess, his singing voice, and his all-around standing—"the best in Lower Four," several boys wrote. His English teacher praised him as a "faithful scholar" and the headmaster admired his loquacity: "The Springs that furnish a constant stream of pleasant conversation." He joined the seven-member "Milk Bottles" fraternity, was teased about his girlfriends, and cited by other boys for the effectiveness of the "soothing syrup" with which he beguiled teachers and girls.

By his third year Elliott's writings were published in the school magazine. His first effort (though anonymous) was probably an article "The Gentle Art of Reading in Study," which revealed his technique of reading extracurricular books or magazines while posing as a model scholar in study hall. He also published some short stories.

The earliest surviving examples of his stories appeared in *The Asheville School Review* of 1909. The first was "An Unpraised Hero," a Civil War tale about a boy who slips through Federal lines to carry a message to his father, who is serving with General Lee in Virginia. Though the youth delivers his message, he is injured in an explosion and taken to an enemy hospital from which he escapes and returns home as a hero. A second story, "Where There's a Will There's a Way," is a rather inane story of two boys, one of them rich and the other poor, who are in love with the same girl—who prefers the poor boy. The plot involved dangerous secret meetings in caves and a final rescue from behind Niagara Falls—a contrived and poorly developed story even from the hands of a thirteen-year-old author.

Back in Lancaster, Captain Sam White, who was in declining health, was being treated with morphine to ease his stomach pains, and Elliott wrote home frequently asking permission to return for a visit with the old man, of whom he was very fond. Leroy refused. "I will send for you should your grandfather grow worse." In the event, Elliott missed his final visit with Captain Sam. The old man's suffering came to an end in March

1911, when he died at the age of seventy-four. His entire estate and that of his wife passed to Elliott and Leroy. Elliott inherited the White homestead in Fort Mill and substantial holdings of securities and other property, including an income of about $1,500 per month from the Fort Mill farm and royalties from a gas well in Louisiana. Thereafter he enjoyed a modest financial independence.

A few months after Sam White's death, Leroy sent Elliott to Culver Military Academy in Indiana, apparently because he felt that his son was in need of discipline. Elliott seemed to like his new school from the start, a summer session that featured sailing and other water sports on Lake Maxinkuckee.

Though Elliott's first report card of the fall session pleased his father—his grades averaged about 85, and he scored a remarkable 100 in "Discipline"—his later performance was somewhat erratic. His grade in Spanish dropped from 94 to 58, he barely passed French and Greek, and scored only 73 in "Discipline." He recovered to score about 90 for the remainder of his Spanish course, and, though he struggled through French and "Discipline" to the end of his Culver career, he emerged as an above-average student with his highest grades in algebra and geometry. Except for an unusual interest in writing stories, he failed to distinguish himself in classroom English and did poorly on examinations in the subject.

The stories Elliott wrote at Culver were strongly reminiscent of those written at Asheville School; under the *nom de plume* "E. LeBlanc Elans," he wrote for the *CMA Vedette* short stories in the same vein of youthful romanticism. He published two long, involved narratives with Civil War settings, "By the Banks of the Greenbriar" and "My Lady Jean," both with improbable plots—and with eventual marriage and happiness for the soldier heroes and their sweethearts. These tales were not what his teacher had expected. Long afterward one of his instructors recalled "the little towheaded fellow from South Carolina . . . and his persistence in writing stories when he was supposed to turn in a bit of Baconian or Macaulay-esque prose."

His military superiors found that Springs could be contentious. When he was reported by a cadet sergeant for failure to count off properly and for subsequent insubordination on the drill field, Elliott appealed to the commandant in writing, maintaining that he was the victim of a misunderstanding. The sergeant was upheld and Springs was given a failing grade in "Discipline" for the month. Later, however, he was promoted to the rank of orderly for having the best-kept equipment and the cleanest rifle in the corps.

Elliott and his father were in frequent conflict over money during these years. Leroy felt that Elliott should use his own money for incidental expenses and complained to his son, "Instead of paying cash for things you get, you charge them and the bills are always coming in to me. The money sent you is not for luxuries but is to pay for the things you get out of the commissary. You seem to think you ought to pay for nothing."

Elliott had recurring stomach pains that school doctors were unable to diagnose. Leroy insisted that he had inherited his weak stomach from Sam White, but the boy still insisted, however illogically, that he had developed ulcers at Asheville School and that his condition was worsened by sleeping in an open cabin during a winter at Culver.

His schoolmates seemed to take little notice of Elliott's digestive problems, for, though he was one of the smallest boys in the school, his appetite commanded respect even among the voracious young trenchermen of Culver. A roommate hailed him as "the greatest consumer of graham crackers," and yearbook editors paid tribute to his prowess in devouring waffles—his nickname, in fact, was "Waffles."

Elliott's father wrote, urging him not to eat between meals or consume sweets or "trash" and that he take his prescribed "tonic" and "try to have two [bowel] actions every day." Charlie Pidcock, a young Georgian who roomed with Elliott in the open-air barracks, was "very much annoyed at the continuous rumbling and grumbling" of Elliott's "plumbing system." As Springs wrote Pidcock years later, "In fact, you once accused me of doing it purposely to keep your mind off your very important studies."

In an effort to alleviate his abdominal discomfort, Elliott was sent to French Lick Springs, Indiana, where he underwent a demanding regimen in hope of a cure. Leroy praised him "for taking the treatment so heroically." The boy's health seemed to improve temporarily, though he also had trouble with his teeth and eyes—the latter handicapping him so severely that he missed several weeks of classes and was briefly in danger of failing his French course.

About this time, probably during summer vacation, Elliott was surprised to learn that his father was involved in a serious courtship. Leroy's companion was Mrs. Lena Jones Wade, a young widow who was serving as head of the English department at Queen's College in Charlotte. A native of Tennessee, Lena Wade was bright and ambitious and was active in the Woman's Suffrage movement, which was soon to win American women the right to vote.

Elliott left no recorded opinion of Lena as a prospective stepmother, but he probably found her trying. Her letters to him after he returned to

Culver were filled with saccharine sentiments, and she assumed a posses-
sive, loving tone with him. She also made coy allusions to secret plans for
her marriage to his father and undoubtedly stirred painful memories of his
mother, which he had repressed for so long.

Elliott not only made good grades in his second year at Culver, he also
performed his military duties exceptionally well. He joined the Rifle Club
and rose from the rank of private to that of captain of C Company's
"Second Team." As one of the most proficient riders in the school, he was
also a member of the academy's crack sixty-man Black Horse Troop and
rode with this precision unit in the inaugural parade of President Wood-
row Wilson, March 4, 1913. Two trains carried the horses and riders,
three hundred of the cadet corps, and a band to Washington, where the
boy horsemen from Culver were a sensation with their faultless precision
riding. Training for this event had consisted of a grueling routine—weeks
of marching and riding on a windswept drill field alternatively covered
with deep snow and freezing mud, but Elliott endured this regimen without complaint.

But the climax of Elliott's career came a few days after the return from
Washington when he and about sixty other cadets were aroused at 3 A.M.
one day with news that the nearby town of Logansport had been inundated
by the flooding Wabash River and that about two thousand people were
stranded by the raging fifteen-foot waters. After a strenuous hour or so of
carrying heavy cutters from the lake to the train station half a mile away,
the cadets were off to Logansport.

For forty-eight hours, working in a snowstorm and near-freezing tem-
peratures, the cadets rowed their boats through the flooded town, rescuing stranded families, women with newborn babies, and two elderly
women, who had been trapped in an attic for two days.

One woman, marooned in a building with her ten-month-old child, had
been vainly pleading for help—rescuers were foiled by a savage current
swirling through the street. The captain of a cutter called for volunteers to
attempt the rescue, and Springs was one of the seven who was accepted.
After a three-hour struggle, this small crew saved mother and child. They
also ripped open the roof of a house with bayonets to rescue two young
girls who were trapped in an attic and picked up a man whose head was
sticking through a hole in the roof of his house. Several people were taken
to safety from the second floor of a hotel.

Elliott wrote his father a melodramatic letter about these adventures.
"You can't imagine how hard it was to navigate those big heavy boats in

that current and those narrow streets." He told of a boat which overturned and flung several people into the swift current, one of them a woman: "They weren't fifty yards from us, but we were powerless to help them. I shall never forget that woman's scream. I have dreamed about it every night since. . . . Two men shouted for help, but soon the waves of the river hushed their cries. We turned away and hid our faces." But the men somehow survived, and one reached a telephone pole. When the crewmen began moving toward the pole the boat captain drew his pistol: "Sit steady, we can't help him! It would be suicide to unfasten these ropes." Both men and the woman were eventually rescued, but Elliott's exciting account gave his father and later the readers of the *Lancaster News* a chilling sense of the perils of the flood.

After their rescue of about fifteen hundred people in Logansport, the cadets were hailed as heroes by newspapers and officials and congratulated by Vice President Thomas R. Marshall, the governor of Indiana, and Acting Secretary of the Navy Franklin D. Roosevelt.

Elliott apparently had dates with so many girls as to win attention on the campus. The yearbook of his senior year noted that he was "a perfect dear with the ladies," and added with unwitting irony, "He is the pride of his father's heart."

But he was to be remembered chiefly at Culver as a man of letters: "His ambition is to be a writer of dime novels. He has contributed to the *Vedette* many interesting articles and stories, all of which have been written under a *nom de plume*, so you see he is very modest and unassuming. We have great hopes for his future."

Soon after graduation Elliott expressed to the commandant his appreciation for the school, "Besides growing six and a half inches and gaining forty-two pounds in two years, I think I can say Culver has made a man of me altho I am only sixteen at present. . . . I shall always look back on my two years at Culver as the most profitable in my life."

He added that he would have liked to spend another year at the academy but felt that his father needed him in his business and said he hoped to finish college by the age of twenty-one.

II / "You're Abnormal Anyway"

In 1913, after six years as a widower, Leroy Springs married Mrs. Lena Wade, and their wedding was an important social event of the season. A Charlotte newspaper described the bride as "one of the most beautiful, attractive young women of the South." Readers understood that the cultivated, spirited Lena was an ideal bride for South Carolina's wealthiest man.

The sixteen-year-old Elliott, who was soon to enter Princeton, served as an usher, and a family friend noted that he wore a grim, unsmiling expression throughout the ceremony. He may have disapproved of the brisk, forceful Lena, whose personality was in such striking contrast to that of his mother.

In this year, too, Elliott saw his first airplane, a feature of the county fair in nearby Rock Hill, South Carolina. The boy was fascinated with aviation from the moment he saw the tiny plane take off.

His freshman year at Princeton was by no means a triumph for Elliott. He endured the traditional campus hazing ("horsing") with no recorded protest. He also survived the annual "rush," a furious hand-to-hand encounter between the freshman and sophomore classes that was soon to be abolished because of the death of a freshman in the melee. He apparently flunked a course in English, a field in which he had expected to excel. But Springs won notoriety when he declared on a routine information form that the Bible was his "favorite fiction."

Elliott lived alone in a dormitory room, perhaps because of his persistent abdominal pain. Despite generally robust health, he suffered from the symptoms of ulcers as he first had at Asheville. By the spring the five-foot eight-inch Springs had become weak and listless and weighed only ninety pounds.

In June Leroy took him to a clinic at Baltimore's Johns Hopkins Hospital to spend the summer living on a prescribed diet. "I came out so fat that I had to buy new clothes to get home," he recalled. He left no precise record of the diagnosis of his abdominal complaint, but doctors realized that he was under stress. Their only prescription: "Stay away from your father as much as possible."

He emerged into a new world. War broke out in Europe, and the first great battles raged in France as Germany launched an invasion. Already, Elliott was eager to join the fighting. His hopes were dashed, for his recovery was brief: "In two weeks I was back where I had started." He lost weight, and pain returned. Even so, he returned to Princeton in the fall and made no further complaints of poor health during his college years.

There were no fraternities on the campus, but when he became eligible to join one of the eighteen clubs as a sophomore, Elliott hoped to be accepted by the Quadrangle Club, the prestigious center of campus literary activity. He was not chosen for the Quadrangle, and, apparently out of wounded pride, he refused thereafter to consider membership in any club.

Perhaps as a result of this rejection, Elliott was not active on campus publications as he had been at Asheville and Culver—but his interest in writing and literature persisted. He took a course in the short story under the popular professor E. C. McDonald, and another in nineteenth-century literature under the British poet Alfred Noyes, who was at the pinnacle of his fame. Though most of his grades were high, McDonald gave him little encouragement as a writer. Springs still smarted from this rebuff many years later after a popular magazine had published "verbatim" one of the stories he submitted to McDonald. He commented bitterly on the faculty's lack of response, "Yet I was later able to make a living writing English, or at least 'American.' " Elliott evidently made no further attempts to write while he was at Princeton, nor did he seek literary friendships.

Other incipient authors in his class were the future novelist of the postwar generation, F. Scott Fitzgerald, and the future poet, John Peale Bishop. Fitzgerald, whom Springs knew only casually, dropped out of school for a year because of failing grades and poor health. Elliott apparently did not become friendly with Bishop. Though he was not prominent in other campus extracurricular activities, Springs found numerous diversions off campus.

Elliott now began to devote himself to a career in the nightlife of Princeton and New York and became a familiar figure at the theater and in fashionable bars and restaurants, usually squiring some striking girl. His candid report on his beginnings as a ladies' man described the opening of a new phase of his life. Elliott spent much time drinking ale in a local tavern with his friend Pabst (Fritz) Goodrich of Milwaukee, exploring such pressing topics as their deplorable state of virginity. "After much discussion we decided that virtue was its own reward but that was all. And that our present state was of interest to no one but ourselves and . . . we seemed to be missing a lot. . . . We decided that we would forsake the straight and narrow path."

Their debut as men of the world was delayed by their high standards of feminine beauty ("anything less than a Goddess, we felt would reduce us to the sordid") and by the difficulty of parting from their current, chaste girlfriends. "I would always weaken," Elliott said. "Every time I got to the farewell scene, I'd get vamped all over again." Goodrich was puzzled by the discovery that his girl "failed to register the shock he had anticipated" but "didn't want him to get mixed up with strangers." It was apparently in the spring of Elliott's sophomore year that he and Fritz achieved their social goals, and Springs, at least, pursued women avidly thereafter.

Elliott won the attention of his contemporaries in other ways. One student who knew him only casually recalled years later that there was "lots of conversation" about Springs throughout his career. One year when the University of Virginia "Drinking Team" invaded the campus for a match, Elliott served as captain of Princeton's team—and led it to ignominious defeat in a memorable bout at the Nassau Inn: "The Virginians carried the Tigers back to bed and then proceeded to get drunk."

As if he sensed that his son had begun to taste worldly pleasures, Leroy continued to carp at him by mail. He charged him with forming bad habits in a misguided attempt to cultivate a cynical, sophisticated manner. Leroy offered particularly dire warnings against spending money to entertain girls.

Elliott again made a spirited response. "I am well aware of the fact that the three causes for masculine failure are first, girls; second, girls; third, girls. . . . I could write a little on the subject myself. . . . But . . . somehow I enjoy the theatre more in New York if I have some expensive nuisance along with me, and when I dance I much prefer something fluffy though expensive. . . . It's just in me, that's all. Possibly I get it by inheritance."

Leroy, who made frequent trips to New York, persisted in offering Elliott as escort for the daughters of his friends. He was bested at this game by his son. One evening Elliott was visiting his father at the Vanderbilt Hotel when a woman approached Leroy in the lobby.

"Mr. Springs, I realize you don't know me. I'm Mrs.——— from Nashville, an old friend of Lena's. I'm in New York for a few days with my daughter."

Leroy responded by calling his son to meet the eighteen-year-old girl. When Elliott appeared, expecting the worst, he was elated to see that the daughter was "a little pink and white bit of fluff" that he had been "trailing" for a week or more without success. He was for once a willing sacrifice. As Elliott recounted his triumph with the young woman, "We weren't seen again for several days. We applied a generous coat of red to the entire city. Sweet child!"

Lena arrived and explained to Leroy that though she knew the woman from Nashville by reputation, "I have never met her socially. They are *nobody* in Nashville." A family row resulted.

"You're both snobs," Elliott said. "Besides, it's too late. We're already engaged."

"Father," he reported, "nearly went wild over it. That cured him for a while but he recovered and began again. I have to play around with every daughter of every old friend, and there are thousands of them." Leroy was to cease these attempts at matchmaking only with Elliott's marriage.

Elliott became more restless as the European war increased in intensity, and in 1916, during his junior year, he talked of joining the American Ambulance Corps as a means of entering the war zone. Leroy resisted fiercely and urged his son to seek some safe haven of the service, if he felt that he must volunteer. He proposed the "Pacific Coast Defense." Elliott dropped his efforts to make his way to France, but only temporarily. The United States broke off diplomatic relations with Germany during midterm examinations of his senior year, and the class of 1917 devoted little attention to education thereafter.

He also reported on an athletic triumph, though he gave no details of his personal performance. "We cleaned up on the University of Pennsylvania 32 to 17 in Water Polo last night. Yale's getting nervous and doesn't want to play us."

Elliott's career at Princeton was virtually over. He had not become a popular or influential figure on the campus and seems to have formed no lasting bond to the university. If his nickname of "Cave Man" was based on his masterful ways with women, he was not a campus leader in other fields. Among class superlatives, Springs finished fifth as "biggest bluffer" (but, with seven votes, lagged far behind the winner, who had thirty-four votes). John Peale Bishop was chosen "most brilliant" ahead of Elliott, who finished ninth. Scott Fitzgerald received only two votes in this category.

In his rush to prepare for war, Elliott did not comment on the value of his college experience, but in later years he declared, "education as dished out to me at Princeton entirely unfitted a young man to enter contemporary American life on any other basis than to administer an inherited fortune. . . . The average possessor of an A.B. degree in this country cannot use a screw driver intelligently and yet will be compelled to live in a mechanized society."

By April, when the United States declared war, the campus neighborhood had become a training center. A civilian Aeroplane Corps was formed at Princeton to train pilots—and Elliott was one of one hundred volunteer students. Since only three small planes were available, he felt that his best hope of making his way to France was to join the Aviation Section of the U.S. Army Signal Corps. His father, who was now urging him to enter the Quartermasters Corps if he insisted upon volunteering, denounced Elliott for his failure to consult him. Elliott responded:

"I do try to consult you on all matters, Father, but you won't let me. . . . I spoke to you Christmas about the Aviation Corps. 'It's ridiculous, don't annoy me,' you said. . . . I tried to discuss several matters with you in New York. You went to sleep the first time I tried and the second time you got mad."

When Elliott mentioned his plan to become a pilot, Leroy growled, "I don't care to discuss it."

The struggle continued.

When Elliott reopened the subject during one of his father's later visits, Leroy snapped, "I don't care what you do. You're abnormal anyway."

Elliott later wrote to his father in frustration, "You think I am nothing but a machine and that a father's only duty is to force his son to study. As a matter of fact I have never had to be forced to study and if I was as well developed on other lines as on Academic you might have reason to be proud of me. . . ."

"Every time I ask your advice I get no advice at all but blame instead. . . . After several failures I just go ahead and do what I think best."

He explained that though he had volunteered as an army aviator, his prospects of induction were unpromising, because only about twenty of the Princeton applicants would be taken. If all else failed, he would join the Ambulance Corps, after all.

While he awaited word from the army, Elliott won another protracted quarrel with Leroy—he was at last given a car to use at Princeton. He reviewed the progress of negotiations in a letter to his stubborn father.

"You wouldn't discuss the matter with me at all at first. Then you said I couldn't have it because I was going abroad. Then you said I couldn't have it at all because it cost too much and finally you said I could have it but not until after commencement. In other words, I can't have it until it's too late!"

But, as usually happened, Leroy succumbed. He approved the purchase of the Stutz before graduation. Elliott was exuberant. He acquired the new car in the nick of time to impress a stunning new girlfriend he had found in New York, an "expensive nuisance" whom he identified only as Adahmaye. After taking her to lunch at the Vanderbilt Hotel, where they drank several cocktails, Elliott led Adahmaye to the Stutz auto agency and bought the stylish Bearcat he had coveted for so long. Because he had no credit and the agency was "unaccommodating," he charged it to his hotel bill and later used his father's check to pay for it. He wrote to Leroy, "I can't tell you what a wonderful car the Stutz is. It's the finest car I've ever driven and many, many thanks."

Elliott had the Bearcat emblazoned with his initials and made it a familiar sight on the Princeton campus and along the highway to New York. He attended few classes that semester on the nearly deserted Princeton campus; most of the students were bound for the war. Springs won a place in Princeton's new aviation group and began learning to fly. Though still civilians, they were under military control during their time at the airfield—otherwise, they were on their own and Elliott took full advantage of his leisure hours. For the rest of the spring he "nearly ran the wheels off" the new car to the delight of Adahmaye, who enjoyed the experience at any speed. "The more I'd skid, the better she'd like it." They wandered near coastal areas, Long Beach, Sea Cliff, and Arrowhead, dining and drinking in secluded hotels. Elliott sometimes drank too much, and, as he noted, once "got tight" and was assigned to guard duty when he reported to the flying field in tipsy condition. Occasionally, after a sleepless night of dancing, romancing, and drinking with Adahmaye, he reported to the field and went aloft with his instructor but somehow managed to avoid accidents.

He found Adahmaye the most entertaining of the many young women he courted during his college days. They had met while he was in New York in February during an attempt to enlist in the Lafayette Escadrille. He failed with the French, but his affair with Adahmaye on the eve of war provided the city's cabaret set with an example of flaming youth.

He remembered her years later, "slender, brown hair, freckles and upturned nose. Never without a smile. She could cry and smile at the same time. We were very fond of each other, very, very fond." He felt that they were perfectly matched. Elliott said he was not in love with her, but that he had never been "as fond of anybody without being in love."

"We could dance a week without missing a step," he said. They met at the Plaza each Saturday afternoon at four and danced until 3 or 4 A.M. "We would gather a crowd like rolling a snowball. Usually we would end up ten or fifteen strong."

It was a few days after buying the car that Elliott was accepted by the army's Aviation Section, and his happiness was complete. Flight was even more exciting than life with Adahmaye and the Stutz. The timing was fortunate, for at the end of June, just as Elliott was ready to leave for New York to meet Adahmaye, he had a brief note from her—she was to be married to another man. "O death where is thy sting?" Elliott scrawled in his diary and added, "I wander about to Sound Beach—drink—and try to forget."

His grief was fleeting. He immediately made plans to visit another girlfriend, Olive Kahlo, in White Sulphur Springs, West Virginia, where the Springs family had often spent summer vacations. Olive was willing, and four days after Adahmaye's surprise announcement, he was aboard a train to White Sulphur. The West Virginia interlude was evidently a blissful one: "Spend day in close proximity to Olive. My theory is correct. Physical contact is absolutely essential. I am very much in love with her, and all others are forgotten."

He returned to Princeton overnight and spent the next day drilling, but romance was uppermost in his mind. He telephoned Adahmaye, who took him by surprise: "She says she'll marry me but I back down. It's Olive for me only."

Amidst these comic opera scenes—which were to continue through the summer—Elliott achieved his first triumph in aviation and began a new romance with flight that was to be lifelong.

Many years later he recalled his first solo flight, "With a little luck I managed to get the plane off the ground, flew it around gingerly for fifteen minutes, and got it back down without damaging anything except my head, which swelled up until it was too big to get into Grant's tomb. . . . The boys would be out of the trenches by Christmas . . . I expected to be dropping bombs on Berlin to celebrate the Fourth."

The twenty-four student pilots of his class flew cumbersome Curtiss planes from a field on the Trenton road. The pilots were quartered in a dormitory, where they slept on cots and were drilled and disciplined by a stern young major sent in by the army. But Elliott was in his element. He rose at 5 A.M. daily, was ready to take off twenty minutes later, and flew until nightfall. He found himself running to the plane in his eagerness to fly. "That's how it takes hold of you."

He groped for words to convey to his father the appeal of aviation: "I can't begin to describe to you the wonderful fascination of flying. . . . when I get my hands on the controls and start up, I just begin to live. I think if I knew that my next flight would be my last one, I'd still go up."

He assured his father that he was not neglecting his new car, which had become vital to the war effort in Princeton. "The Stutz is the official Emergency Car and when anything goes wrong you see the Stutz tearing madly across the country . . . I had to plough up a wheat field yesterday to rush some tools to a sick plane."

No sooner had Elliott reported for his training than Leroy gave a story to his local newspaper, depicting his son as a heroic volunteer. Elliott was acutely embarrassed. "I saw with regret the article in the *Lancaster News*. . . . Please instruct and request the Editor to mention my name no more . . . the news gets all broken out with incoherency and the final chapter of *Little Lord Fauntleroy*. No matter what happens I shall be afraid to write to you . . . I had no idea that the general public was to be included in confidence."

Unabashed and bursting with pride, Leroy sought to make amends in his own way with an explanatory release to newspapers. Elliott, he announced, had been made a lieutenant in the Air Service, "having passed all examinations . . . his physical condition having been found perfect. He is one of the first from Princeton University to start flying.

"Mr. Springs is now an Honor Graduate of Princeton [a surprise to archivists of the university, who recorded no such honors]. . . . He is the youngest member of the Senior Class, graduating at the age of twenty. He has also achieved distinction in athletics, being a member of the Champion Water Polo Team . . . which has won every Inter-Collegiate contest in the past two years."

Leroy then interpreted his own attitude toward Elliott's entry into service in terms that outraged his son:

"Because of the extremely hazardous nature of the Aviation Service, Col. Springs strongly opposed the desire of his only son and child to enter this branch of the Army, preferring that he enter the regular Army or Navy. Being a graduate of the Culver Military Academy . . . young Springs was peculiarly fitted to serve efficiently in these branches. However, he was irresistibly drawn to the Flying corps and is gratified at the opportunity to go out as a volunteer among the first U.S. Army Aviators in active service in this war."

Elliott challenged his father by mail, "After you consented to Aviation because you couldn't stop me, you then advised me to stay as far away from the front as possible and become an instructor. . . . You were infuriated because I was not going along with [fellow Princetonians] Brewster, Pyne, etc. Told me I was all kinds of a fool because they were coming back as instructors."

Still, Elliott urged his father to visit him at Princeton, the following Sunday if possible. "We will probably be flying all day and you can watch me take a cloud bath. . . . I am sorry you are worrying about me and I assure you there is no cause for it. With a heartful of love to you and Lena."

With graduation imminent, Elliott almost lost his diploma because of the excesses of his friends. Fritz Goodrich, who was on his way to an ambulance unit in France, appeared with a girl and demanded entertainment. "He got it," Elliott recalled. "I had four rooms over the bank in town and Fritz and Gladys went up there while I was out flying and . . . they got very joyful." As a climax to the ensuing "general mess," Goodrich, who had borrowed the Stutz, drove drunkenly through Princeton, where passersby recognized the car and assumed that Elliott was the driver.

The president and the dean of the college questioned Elliott about the incident. "I was in the Army but I hadn't got my Dip and with the Family and Aunt Addie coming up . . . to see me get it, I had a vision of great trouble ahead." Elliott found allies in the building's maid, janitor, and elevator boy, who offered an alibi and vouched for him so stoutly that "the enemy withdrew to talk it over."

Elliott was hardly rid of Goodrich when another of his drinking companions, identified only as "Gus," arrived from Newport in his new Navy uniform and set off a fresh flurry of excitement by staging an impressive party in Elliott's rooms. Springs returned to find Bill ("Pussyfoot") Coan, the university proctor, staring up at his windows. Elliott went up and found that Gus was "holding a reception and had about half the college up there." Elliott sought to restore calm, but was resisted by one of his girlfriends from New York, one Constance, who tried to stab him with a letter opener out of jealousy over Adahmaye. Constance subdued, Elliott sent the elevator boy to divert Pussyfoot's attention while he hurried his guests out the back way. "There was merry hell to pay," Springs recalled.

He was busy for several days trying to explain to Constance that tales of his exploits were untrue: "Everybody used my car and I got the benefit of every wild party pulled off because they knew my car."

All was well in the end. Elliott graduated with a major in philosophy and entertained Leroy, Lena, and Aunt Addie for a few days at commencement, almost without incident—though Constance, upon meeting Leroy, casually handed him the leash of her Pomeranian and strolled away with Elliott for the afternoon, leaving the old man at a loss for words.

The Princetonians moved from their field to Mineola, New York, where the Army Air Service was assembling men for advanced flight training.

Elliott's affair with Constance, though not serious, was the most taxing of his eleventh-hour romances on the eve of war and inspired the most candid passages in his diary of the period: "Take Constance to dinner, then we drive around park. She insists on being petted so I do. And God how she can pet. Then she fills me up on highballs and I return [to Mineola]. . . . Go into N.Y. and take Constance out again." They rode along the Hudson, "partying like hell all the time," then returned to her apartment. "Oh my God what a passionate woman. Never have I seen her equal. I leave her at 3:30 scarcely able to walk. Return to Mineola. . . .

"Up to see Constance. Completely exhausted. Get a bath and feel much better. Take her to a show. . . . Call Constance. We go for a little party. . . . Go back to N.Y. and see Constance."

The diary was also sprinkled with casual mentions of other girls who passed fleetingly through these days of final preparation for war:

Fly continuously and resist temptation in form of Blanche. . . . Blanche calls. I turn a deaf ear. . . . To Long Beach. . . . Get Phoebe—Phoebe with the golden hair—changed, contrite and altered, not the same at all. Returned at 2 A.M. . . .

See Mildred. . . . She thinks I'm a regular hero. . . . Call Phoebe, then ditch her later for Miss Ethel Harriman and have a very enjoyable tho highbrow party. After all life is short and I'd better make the best of it. A charming lady is she. . . .

Being pursued by a stenographer and a telephone operator. . . . Run into Mrs. Gummere, a friend of Father's who invites me to dinner. Has a daughter . . . the affair progresses. . . . Feel real devilish so write Frances inquiring [as to] the disposition of her letters. Great stuff. . . . Letter from Frances, curious one, too. She wants to come back. . . . Call on Gummeres and take a visiting flapper to ride. Very well.

But there was still Adahmaye, whom he saw in New York in mid-July and bade her "a fond farewell" in a "very touching" moment. About a month later he attempted to make a final date with her, "but her fiance said nix. Such is life."

And also there was still Olive, who appeared in New York despite her family's disapproval. After a telephone conversation with her, Elliott wrote, "She's a dear to put it mildly. Wish I wasn't so wild and blood-thirsty." When he met her in New York the affair continued as before: "Olive seems to really be in love with me this time and if I love anyone, 'tis her. Am afraid I'm pretty well burnt out tho."

Elliott's powers of endurance in these months were impressive, for the hectic round of training included five hours of marching on the drill field and three daily half-hour flights—and in the evenings there were often lectures and special training in mapping, telegraphy, and theory of military aviation. On many days they flew at 5 A.M. and again after supper. Aloft, the students not only had to learn to solo but to practice aerial gunnery, bombing, operating movie cameras—and sending a minimum of eight words per minute by telegraph from an altitude of five thousand feet while directing simulated artillery fire.

The battalion was driven so hard, in fact, that two men fainted one morning, and all of the students except Elliott's squadron mutinied, and ten men resigned. Springs was made sergeant of his squadron. "I thought they would have to finally," he wrote. His men excelled in the final drill and, as Springs noted, "simply won't drill for anyone but me. Great triumph." He was named "drillmaster" for the battalion.

Amidst this demanding routine, and the diversions of romance, Elliott was compelled to deal with his assertive father, who bombarded him with letters and telegrams and made several visits to New York. Leroy lectured Elliott on his extravagance: "You are learning how to spend money before you make it," he wrote. He sent an accounting of Elliott's expenditures for the year and complained: "Don't pick up all the tabs. You'll be called a fool behind your back. I sincerely hope you have not contracted the habit of playing poker at college. I have never seen any good come of any man who played cards for money." The admonitions continued week after week.

"Do not keep anything from me. Realize that I am your best friend . . . a father always is if he's a good father. . . .

"I hope you will drive no more to New York at night . . . please don't go so often. You will jeopardize your promotion." Leroy did not hesitate to advise Elliott, "Don't get too close to the propeller . . . practice shooting.

You'll need it as the enemy aviators will fight. . . . Don't stunt. That's how calamities occur . . . put all you have into the service. . . .

"Protect yourself and come home to us safe . . . I pray for your safe return . . . I think of you all the time and feel sure you will come home safe and be a source of comfort and pleasure to me and be a great help to me in carrying out our life work."

But even as he assured his son of his love and concern for his safety, Leroy would launch upon one of his lectures Elliott found so maddening. After a visit with his son in New York, Leroy wrote a full-page, single-spaced letter to chide him for the poor fit of his army shirt—the sleeves were too long and the torso baggy: "When the Government goes to promote a man, they will take into consideration how he dresses." Elliott was aware that he was to blame for much of the stress in his relationship with his father. During one visit with Leroy and Lena and his Great-Aunt Addie at the Vanderbilt Hotel in New York, there was a family spat. Elliott was disgusted but confided to his diary, "Christ what a rotten disposition I have."

But a few weeks later, when his parents returned for a visit, he took them for a "joy ride" in the Stutz, soloed in a training plane as they watched—and persuaded both of them to go aloft with his instructor as pilot. After Leroy and Lena left for South Carolina, Elliott made a will and made a cheerless entry in his diary, "They seem to feel I'm coming back but I know better."

The new group of some two hundred students in advanced training was under command of Major Leslie MacDill, who was then beginning a distinguished military career. That the debut of these aviators was truly a pioneering effort reflected the lack of the nation's preparedness for war. Even the most advanced of their planes were frail and unreliable. The pilots flew without parachutes—and also without wheel brakes, throttles for rotary engines, gyroscopes, or oxygen. Radio communication was years in the future.

Europeans were developing more sophisticated planes and equipment under the stress of war, but American aviation had made no progress since 1914. The U.S. entered the war without a single combat plane. There were no flying schools except for the most elementary type of training. The war was to rage for four years without the appearance of a United States-built-or-designed aircraft at the front.

The American flying service consisted entirely of the miniscule Aviation Section of the Army Signal Corps, staffed by 131 officers, of whom 35 rated as pilots. Fifty-five training planes comprised the total air strength of the United States—there were no bombers, fighters, or even observation planes. When the desperate Allied nations offered to train American pilots to fill depleted combat squadrons, General Pershing ordered the Aviation Section to send one hundred pilots overseas each month, beginning in July, 1917. The first class was sent to France, where it found frustrating delays and confusion. Major MacDill's trainees were scheduled to follow but were allowed to choose their destination.

Ignorant of European conditions, Springs and his fellow fledglings selected Italy because of its warm climate. The "Italian detachment" of pilots then acquired as its supply officer Captain Fiorello La Guardia, an ex-congressman and future mayor of New York City who had recently learned to fly. La Guardia had brought along two of the city's noted Italian chefs as "interpreters," though one of them spoke no English.

At Mineola, Sergeant Springs met two older student pilots who arrived from the training school at Champaign, Illinois—John McGavock Grider, twenty-five, of Arkansas and Laurence Callahan of Chicago, twenty-three years old, both hard-drinking, lively companions, eager for adventure. Grider, a powerful, stocky man who had been reared on a Mississippi River plantation, had married at the age of seventeen without attending college, was the father of two sons and was estranged from his wife. The urbane, tall and handsome Callahan, a graduate of Cornell, came from a prominent Louisville, Kentucky family. He was brilliant, witty, and engaging, and an accomplished pianist and bridge player. Callahan had soloed after two hours and fifteen minutes of instruction, and Springs rated him "the best pilot I ever knew." The trio became fast friends at once and were known as "The Three Musketeers."

Callahan saw that the loquacious, aggressive Springs was not only soldierly and confident—he was dominant. "Springs practically ran everything, and he was running that training camp." He also found that Springs enforced discipline among his men despite all claims of friendship. Callahan once chewed gum in ranks during drill and was sentenced to peel potatoes for four days. Callahan protested on his final day of travail.

"If you want to chew gum in ranks, you'll peel potatoes for the rest of the day, every time," Springs said.

"I've already been assigned to it for four days."

"Yeah, but you haven't peeled one potato yet, and I'm going to get one day's work out of you if I have to chain you to the stove."

But, as Grider noted, Larry prevailed. "Springs was too busy to watch him and he never did finish one pan of spuds."

Orders for embarkation came to the cadets so unexpectedly that Elliott was forced to rush to the Princeton campus and pack his belongings within two hours. He tossed the contents of his desk into a trunk and sent them home, the accumulated reminders of college life he was not to see again for many years: "lectures from Father, notices from the Dean, cancelled checks, reports, essays, telegrams, dance programs, snapshots, incomplete short stories, an attempt at a novel, enlistment papers in the Lafayette Escadrille, flunk notices, membership cards and reams of correspondence from a little bit of everybody." Embalmed in the papers were the stories of half-forgotten romances, "from the first 'Meet me at the Biltmore at four' to the last 'I hate to have to tell you' or 'I saw you last night at the Frolics, you dirty little bum.'" Leafing through the collection years later he reflected, "Yes, I certainly was a little hellion in those days."

The pilots took their final flights on September 17 and prepared to embark. Leaves were cancelled, but Springs somehow managed to get into New York to say farewell to Olive. They dined at the Vanderbilt, and she wept at the table. "It was very impressive," he said. "I may return to America some day after all." He added apologetically, "It really hurts, too. I love her very much." Later he called Constance and on returning to Mineola found a last letter from Frances. "All well," he said.

As he dashed for the dock to board ship in Hoboken, he left his suitcase at the Vanderbilt, parked his beloved Stutz on 42nd Street and left the keys in a nearby garage for safety. Only after he had crossed the Atlantic did he write to his father, asking that he rescue the abandoned Bearcat.

The pilots, 210 strong, sailed on the British liner *Carmania*, accompanied by 2,000 infantrymen. After a brief pause in Halifax, Nova Scotia, to join a convoy, they left for Italy via England. Elliott was in an ebullient mood as the fourteen-ship convoy sailed eastward. He wrote to Lena, "It's great to be alive. You can't imagine how rosy my existence has become. . . . Every day a new opportunity seems to open itself to me. Why, I wouldn't swap jobs with a Colonel of Infantry! And you wouldn't know me now. I'm just death on efficiency and discipline." He was stirred to greater exertions by praise from Major MacDill. "You're working too hard, Springs, and it's your own fault. You're too damn efficient." No one had ever paid him a greater compliment, Elliott confided to Lena. He added wistfully, "Forgive me for telling you about it. . . . Maybe Father won't think I'm such a bum."

He had been given "the best accommodations in the world" and anticipated a few days' holiday in London and Paris before going into combat. "War is not so bad after all. So far I've enjoyed myself immensely and think it will be even better at the front." He said he now had "unbounded confidence" and promised, "I'm going to finish this thing in the proper style . . . when I sight a Boche I'll not weaken."

Mac Grider began a diary: "This is the damn fool diary of a son of the South & of rest. I hope he don't weaken & forget to write in it." He had little hope of completing his record of events. "I have never done anything constantly except the wrong thing, but I want a few recollections jotted down in case I don't get killed. . . . I want to die well and not be killed in some accident or die of sickness . . . I haven't lived very well but I'm determined to die well."

Mac wrote of superficial matters and without style but left the only detailed account of their Atlantic crossing: nonstop games of cards and dice flourished below. La Guardia and a few others gave the aviators daily instruction in Italian. Their camouflaged escort ships fired a few shots in a brief submarine alarm. Springs discovered the eminent violinist, Albert

Spalding, a private in steerage, and managed to have him transferred to the upper deck, where he played bridge with Elliott and his companions. Grider made his final entry on Oct. 1, the day before they docked at Liverpool—a sparse, unremarkable record covering a period of twelve days. This fragmentary diary was to become the storm center of a literary controversy.

Confusion greeted the contingent in Liverpool. A cablegram from Washington had advised the British that a new training class of pilots had embarked (referring to a unit immediately following MacDill's men), and the Royal Flying Corps (R.F.C.) thus mistakenly claimed the new "Italian Detachment" as its own despite all protestations. Springs and his friends were hurried onto a train for Oxford, fuming with anger at being shunted off to stay in England. They knew little of the accomplishments of British aviation and nothing of the madcap social whirl that awaited them.

Elliott was disgusted, "We aren't going to Italy after all. . . . We've wasted two weeks studying Italian and two months going to Ground School learning nonsense, for now we've got to go through this British Ground School here. And we hear that everything we were taught at home is all wrong." Their mail had been sent to Italy, their wallets bulged with lira, and many of them carried letters of credit drawn on banks in Rome. MacDill and La Guardia and the enlisted men of the *Carmania*, including Spalding, left for France—MacDill promising to have their orders reviewed and to return for them. Springs was left in charge of the cadets, dependent upon the mercies of the British to care for his disgruntled reinforcements.

Springs herded his troops out at Oxford, where they were housed in Christ Church College. He felt a sense of history here. "Our barracks are a million years old," he said. "I know, because it took that long to cool off to this temperature. The stone is crumbling away and the whole place is very ancient. . . . The last time troops were quartered here was in Oliver Cromwell's time." Paintings by Gainsborough, Reynolds, and Romney hung in his mess hall.

Springs was an immediate convert to the British culture. "This is indeed the life," he wrote. "These English people are wonderful. Everyone over here is so damn polite. I know now why they always think of us as savages. This is the most charming country I ever dreamed of."

Elliott admired the cool reserve—and morale—of the British at war. He saw an example of British charisma when he met the legendary British ace Major James McCudden. The handsome fighter pilot, just home from the

front and bedecked with medals, caused a stir in an overcrowded London restaurant, where women "fought to get at him just like they do at a bargain counter back home. He's the hottest thing we have now—fifty-four Huns." McCudden wore a new Victoria Cross and a Distingished Service Order with a bar. "I think there are only five airmen living that have the V.C.," Springs said. "The first thing you have to do to get it is get killed."

Springs felt a compulsive urge to emulate McCudden. "Well, I'm not jealous. I'm going to be hot myself someday."

He visited the poet, John Masefield, in his nearby home, attended lectures on Descartes and idealism at Oxford, and discussed philosophy with the dean of Christ Church at lunch. Elliott was never to forget the impressions of these cultivated, urbane people or the Oxford setting.

Grider and Callahan, concerned with more practical matters, found some girls soon after their arrival. "I tell you this is the home of the brave and the land of free love," Mac said. Springs claimed that Mac "fell violently in love every Monday and Friday. We landed at Liverpool at ten one morning and he was in love with a blonde at Oxford that night." Callahan, so Elliott said, was "too lazy to shift his affections" and he himself was "always too devoted to the liquor" to pursue the English women.

The cadets also discovered British inns and pubs—and, quartered nearby in the university, another contingent of American fliers who had arrived earlier. These trainees were under the command of Lieutenant Geoffrey Dwyer and his first sergeant, a five-foot wild man from Pittsburgh, Bennett ("Bim") Oliver, the son of a senator from Pennsylvania. Dwyer assumed command of both contingents, subject only to occasional intrusions by United States headquarters, London.

Elliott was amused by his role as disciplinarian to the cadets in the first two months before British officers took over their training. He wrote to Lena, "Can you imagine me restricting a man to his room for a week for getting tight? And giving him a good lecture besides? And with a straight face?" Since all his miscreants protested their innocence, he devised a system of judgment, "I ask them what they had to drink. If they can remember, I let them off. Otherwise, bing, on goes the lid."

His men cooperated fully, he said, "But the hard part of it is that I have to be so careful. I hardly dare to take a drink because then I can't hold down the others. And I have to always be the first one at formations, otherwise there ain't no formation, and my shoes and leggings have to glisten like mirrors . . . and my room has to be spotless and, oh, well, I'm just miserable I'm such a model soldier. And you know my real inclinations! . . . I'm a nervous wreck."

The pilots were in a constant uproar with their drinking bouts, and Springs was hard put to control his charges, who included two former cowboys, Robert Kelly and Allen T. Bird, Alaskan sourdoughs, Ivy League football stars—and even a full-blooded Sioux Indian.

Elliott sometimes took a suicidal approach in his effort to maintain discipline. One night when Kelly and Bird put on a drinking bout in a British club and threatened disaster, Springs was called to handle the emergency. Both were powerful, raw-boned men of six feet three or four inches who would "rather fight than eat," and that night they were "well oiled." Springs tried to drink them into a stupor with a round of double brandies. Kelly then ordered triple brandies. Bird called for port as the next round.

"It was a good battle while it lasted," Grider said, but there were no victors. Elliott's companions had to soak him in a cold tub before he could call the roll for dinner. Kelly and Bird were in a stupor until the next morning when they voluntarily—though temporarily—gave up alcohol.

But if cadets failed to appear for morning drill after a wild night, Springs was implacable. When Grider, Callahan, and another cadet staggered into the dining hall at noon one day, Springs put them under arrest and confined them to the campus. "The damn fool made us stay in all afternoon and evening too," Grider complained. "He said if we were too sick to drill, we were too sick to go out and get drunk again. . . . He's just mad because he's missing all the fun."

The men of Elliott's contingent were aviators of uncertain rank. Though still technically privates, the pilots were now called cadets, "the mulattoes of the Army" as Springs said, with "the privileges of neither enlisted men nor officers. And all the trouble coming to both." Though the British were uncertain of the roles the Americans were to play, they provided them with thorough training.

Springs was deposed as leader only when most of the contingent went to Grantham in Lincolnshire for a course in aerial gunnery, and he led twenty picked pilots to join an R.F.C. squadron for advanced flying at Stamford. "I'm glad it's over," Elliott said. "I should have gone mad in another week." He quickly reverted to type. As he wrote Lena, he marked his first flight at Stamford by christening a new silver flask given to him by his appreciative cadets. "I went to 7000 feet and put the joy stick between

my knees and drank a toast to Pegasus and Bellerophon and another to
Daedalus. Then spiraled all the way down."

Flight training began under reckless young R.F.C. instructors. "Classes
are a joke," Springs said, and Callahan added that the British, who were
obliged to produce pilots promptly, "didn't care very much how they did
it."

Springs led his friends in some wild stunting. He flew with Grider and
Callahan up and down the Thames, diving upon terrified guests seated on
a hotel terrace at Maidenhead, knocking over a man who was standing in a
punt, poling his girlfriend along the stream. They then "steeplechased"
homeward over the river, keeping their wheels just above the water. Callahan narrowly missed a bridge, and Springs landed with two hundred feet
of telephone wire trailing from his undercarriage.

Elliott reported that though his companions went "flapper hunting all
the time," he had not "spoken socially to a woman under thirty since I left
New York." His first recorded outing was none too successful. One night
he went to a dance with his friend, Bob Kelly, the Arizona cowboy, who
proved to be as difficult as ever. Kelly refused to leave the dance and,
when dragged outside, threw a bicycle at the insistent Springs in protest.

Elliott's friend, Jake Stanley, appeared and tried to help carry the cowboy to the barracks.

"We'd better knock him out," Springs suggested.

Stanley dragged Kelly to his feet, holding him beneath his arms.
Springs lifted Kelly's jaw and swung savagely with his fist, but the huge
man slipped and Elliott's fist struck Jake on the nose. The three fell into
the ditch as another cadet, May Dorsey, appeared and jumped on Springs
in an attempt to halt the fight.

"Before we knew what was happening, Springs had a black eye and
Dorsey was working on the other one."

Springs then rolled atop Dorsey and "nearly killed him. He was
bumping his head on a piece of cement when they pried him loose." Kelly
was finally carried into the barracks on Elliott's back, under the escort of
two policemen.

By January 1, 1918, the contingent was moved to a field at London
Colney, only twenty miles from London, and plunged into a social whirl
none of them would forget. The cadets met many London actresses and
began rounds of parties at hotels, restaurants, and bars in the city. Most of
these spirited English women were to be identified only vaguely in Elliott's
diary and correspondence, but a few of them became well known in the

theatrical world. Beatrice Lillie and the cast of her current show, *Cheap*, visited the cadets in their hotel suite. Another of their frequent companions was Billie Carlton, the beautiful star of *Fair and Warmer*, who was the object of salacious London gossip. There were also a few American girls who had somehow made their way to wartime Britain, among them Halley Whatley, a charming young Georgian.

After meeting Miss Carlton, Elliott wrote, "Oh, la la, what a knockout!" Billie and Mac Grider, he noted, "got on like Antony and Cleopatra. How that woman can dance! . . . She is about twenty-three and has been on the stage since she was eighteen. She sure is witty. She kept us laughing all evening." After the party Grider took Billie home to her luxurious flat where supper was served by a maid. Billie "slipped on a negligee and looked like a million dollars." Grider found her irresistible. Within a few weeks they were engaged and planned an April wedding. Springs and Callahan persuaded Mac to postpone marriage until he returned on leave. "Billie is lousy with money and you have nothing but your pay as a shavetail." Reluctantly, the love-struck couple agreed to wait.

The roster of lesser-known women friends of the cadets in London included a Spanish woman named "Dora," "The Long, Lean, Lanky Devil," "The Chinless Wonder," and a girl of huge proportions known only as "The Handley-Page," after a lumbering British bomber. There was also "The Queen Bee," a "tomato" who had served as the bait in a trap to help an Englishman bilk a maharajah of £200,000—but was paid off with a rubber check and became the star of a sensational London trial. Springs found another woman known only as "The Doll," of whom Grider said, "My Gawd, what a beautiful thing she is. But she's so stupid it's ludicrous." Elliott claimed that he was suffering a reaction. "The last one had too much brains." Another of their striking companions was hard-drinking Pearl O'Frere, a musical comedy star rated by Springs as "a bottle-and-a-half woman."

Elliott defended their new girlfriends: "Some of our guests may be a bit unconventional in their mode of living, but they had certainly all been ladies around here . . . these London women are in a class by themselves. They are good sports, good looking, good dancers, well educated, act like ladies." He added in a more candid vein, "and they don't sit around and worry about their honor all the time."

Even during a German air raid on the city, Springs and his friends made their way backstage in a theater and met the company. Callahan played the piano, dancing began, and the entire cast was soon abducted by the

Americans. These parties lasted all night, and the cadets frequently reported to the airfield in their cups. Many of their conquests had accompanied the titled Britons or visiting generals or admirals who joined their parties but could not compete with the exuberant Americans. "It's getting to be a disgrace the way we welcome our friends and then put them out and keep their girls," Springs wrote. "Well, they ought to know better!"

In contradiction to his earlier claim of celibacy in London, Elliott was to remember himself in these days as a legendary lady-killer. England at war, he boasted, was meant for him, "a handsome youngster with wings on his chest, money in his pocket, and a cocktail in his hand. He flitted about like a care-free bee, lingering only while the blossom was fresh and playing no return engagements."

Elliott's career in London society ended temporarily when he was abruptly assigned to an aerial gunnery school at Turnberry, Scotland, to be given "the final polish" for combat. For ten days he and his mates flew in the wintry cold, practicing machine-gun fire at imaginary foes for ten hours each day.

Though Springs had been a leader of the London carnival, he returned to training with a relish. He spent more hours in the air than any other cadet of the contingent, going aloft in bad weather when no one else wanted the planes, frequently doing without meals in order to spend a few more hours in flight.

Elliott and other cadets were checked out in some rickety, antique, American-built Curtisses and were then advanced to British Sopwith Pups, small high-performance trainers. Springs and one other pilot were ordered by American headquarters to loop and spin the Pups, which were being considered for manufacture in the U.S. "They couldn't get any of the instructors to go up," Elliott reported. "They knew better." In his first flight in a Pup, he did ten loops in succession and landed safely but another cadet who followed him, one Ainsworth, plunged to his death when the plane's wings fell off. The experiment with Pups was halted by the British commander at Stamford, and for a month Springs was limited to ferrying planes between bases.

Inspired by the British youngsters who taught them, the cadets once more began to harass civilians with their lunatic flying. Elliott particularly admired one young British pilot who hunted by plane—flying low over the fields to "stir up" rabbits, which he then shot with his machine guns. Springs joined another boy aviator in an exuberant display of dangerous stunting near the airfield, zooming over the ground with wheels barely touching, then rising to taxi across the hangar roofs. Springs was not content with that but got into a Pup and chased a machine gun class "in and out of the firing pit." In the midst of the party he "lost his pressure and . . . pancaked in a flower garden." These escapades did not go unnoticed.

The British Commander summoned Elliott to his office: "They need fools like you in France. Pack and get going." Springs soon found himself at neighboring Ayr in Scotland in a pilot's pool of combat replacements.

Springs was not deterred from his daredevil flying. After a hectic twenty-gallon eggnog party for the assembled pilots in Ayr, he took his first flight in a French Spad, carrying a quart of eggnog for sustenance, and staged a "steeplechase" on a nearby race course. He dove to the ground to run his wheels across the flat and took off once more. On one of these maneuvers he caught a wing in some wires, zoomed straight upward for three hundred feet, stalled, and fell onto the flying field. "God certainly took over the controls," Elliott said. He emerged unhurt from the wreckage but fumed at the loss of his eggnog, which he had tossed out before the crash.

Other cadets were not so lucky. During this spring of 1918, young men began to die with sickening regularity in crashes on or near their field. Springs noted them briefly in his diary: Joe Sharpe, Roy Garvey, Clarence Fry, Fred Stillman, Doug Ellis, Stratton, Middleditch, Pudrith, Nathan, Degamo, Bulkley, Carlton, Montgomery, Ludwig, Ortmyer, Dealy, Waite, and several nameless Australians, Canadians, Englishmen, and New Zealanders. Springs attended a dozen funerals and lost two of his roommates within two weeks. He blamed "bad flying weather, some bad planes, and some bad mechanics." Pilots used good luck charms and chose girlfriends carefully. "It was a general superstition that a virgin's sweetheart was seldom killed." One day in mid-March 1918, he wrote, "There's a big party going on here in spite of the wholesale funerals."

Elliott assumed a casual air when he wrote home of his companions who died in crashes: "They've been going fast this week . . . young Montgomery . . . one of the best of the whole bunch, good pilot and a prince of a gentleman. . . . Also our best bridge player here went west last Friday. . . .

"But lest anyone at home get . . . the idea that there's something wrong . . . there isn't. It's absolutely unavoidable. To teach men to fly fast planes you must expect to lose a fair percentage." The training planes used in the United States, he said, were safe, "almost foolproof," but in fighting planes, "every time a man goes up, he's flirting with the undertaker." He described narrow escapes of his own and tried to prepare Leroy and Lena for his own death in a crash. "When you get the news about me, I don't want any weeping and wailing. Just keep in your mind the fact that I went down happy and smiling and that the game has been worth the candle. . . . I've lived a whole lifetime since I sailed. And what a glorious life. . . . So I'm ready and waiting."

He seemed to be deliberately defying death in the last weeks of training. He reported to Lena, as if he expected her to grasp its significance, that he had learned to loop his plane directly off the ground—and that he was skilled at aerial acrobatics. "I've got a new stunt now. First I loop but, instead of completing the circle when I get to the top and am on my back, [I] do a full roll ending on my back again and then dive out of it . . . you wouldn't believe it possible until you've seen it done." He described an even more dangerous stunt, "an upward roll, a roll level and then spin out of it." Another pilot tried this maneuver and, as Springs noted, "It cost me five shillings for flowers."

Elliott had brushes with death almost daily. One day when he and Larry Callahan were stunting together over their airfield, they came within a few feet of crashing into the ground. Grider greeted them on their return with tears in his eyes. "The only reason you fools are alive," he said, "is because Hell is packed with aviators."

In fact, the pilots seemed less concerned about who would die next than they were for their prospects of overseas duty. They were also troubled about their rank. Ayr was filled with rumors. General Pershing had abolished flying pay in the United States Army and urged that pilots be ranked as sergeants, not as officers. Elliott and two others were offered rank as United States second lieutenants but refused and asked for discharges so that they could join the British as regulars. "Everybody here wants to get out of the U.S. Army and join the R.F.C., where they'll get a square deal," Elliott wrote.

"We certainly have gotten a raw deal from the U.S.A. and the British couldn't have treated their Field Marshals any better. . . . The U.S. Army is a great institution. I have been treated like an enlisted man for ten months tho I was never supposed to be one. . . . Washington was too busy to give us our commissions. . . . We lost our seniority and our pay. . . . If we had to choose between fighting the Prussian Guard and the West Point Alumni Association, I know where at least 210 aviators would assemble."

The only two American officers who had treated them decently, Elliott said, were Leslie MacDill and Geoff Dwyer. The latter, since his transfer to U.S. headquarters in London, was trying to help Springs and his friends to reach the front with a British unit. Dwyer's actual role in helping them to elude the U.S. Army was to remain a secret.

The Three Musketeers were saved by Major Billy Bishop, the legendary Canadian ace, who had returned from command of his 60th Squadron at the front, where he had shot down forty-nine Germans. Bishop was now in England forming a new squadron on an emergency basis. The German spring offensive, which threatened to overwhelm Allied armies and engulf Paris, had decimated British air units—both Army and Navy—which were now combined into the Royal Air Force and expanded for a final drive toward victory. Captain Spenser B. ("Nigger") Horn, one of his veteran flight leaders, who had been teaching Springs, Grider, and Callahan, recruited them for the new unit.

Bishop had won fame after an unpromising career. He narrowly avoided expulsion from Canada's national military academy and, with a reputation as an incorrigible roughneck, had been shipped to England, where he was assigned to a Home Guard unit. Somehow the Canadian boy had charmed officials and made his way to France, where he learned to fly.

An inept pilot, Billy had crashed his Nieuport virtually at the feet of a party of visiting dignitaries, one of whom was his commander, a brigadier general. Bishop was booked for a return to England—but undismayed, he went up the next day with a few companions and met a flight of superior German planes, new Albatrosses, which outperformed Nieuports at every turn. Bishop merely flew straight for one of the enemy planes in a reckless head-on attack. The astounded German was forced into the ground and died in the flaming wreckage. Bishop barely managed to glide to safety 300 yards within the British lines.

He had found his calling. He began downing Germans as if they were targets in a shooting gallery. He was apparently invincible. By the end of the summer of 1917, he had scored forty-seven victories. "I had found the thing I loved above all others," he said. "To me it was not a business or a profession, but just a wonderful game."

Bishop was allowed to choose any men he wished for the 85th, since his new assignment in France was to be the destruction of Manfred von Richthofen's Flying Circus, the most feared of German air groups, now commanded by Hermann Goering. The Red Baron himself had been killed on April 21, but his vengeful pilots fought on, the scourge of the French front in their red-and-orange-striped planes. The Flying Circus, as expanded under Goering, was still a dazzling sight in the sky. The predominant color of its planes was red—but some craft had yellow wings and green noses, silver wings and gold noses, and others had red fuselages with green wings and light blue fuselages with red wings.

Except for the Three Musketeers, Bishop chose mostly combat-tested men for the new 85th Squadron, all of them from England or the Dominions. Bishop opened his quest by walking into American Army Headquarters in London and asking Colonel Dwight Morrow's permission to enroll the trio in his squadron. Morrow refused flatly, and Bishop led the Musketeers away. The U.S. officers gaped at Bishop, who wore the Victoria Cross, Distinguished Service Medal, and Military Cross on his faultlessly tailored tunic. "The whole staff nearly lost their eyes," Springs wrote, "staring at us when we strolled out, arm in arm with the great Bishop." Headquarters officers were stunned a few days later when Bishop completed his maneuver for, with the covert aid of Geoff Dwyer at headquarters, Bishop and Horn thwarted American plans to transfer the Musketeers to U.S. units in France.

When Springs, Grider, and Callahan received last-minute orders to leave for France and reported to Hounslow airfield, Bishop's conspirators took action. Springs, who knew nothing of Bishop's subterfuge, was outraged when a U.S. officer said he had failed his flight training and must have more instruction before leaving England. "I'm a damn good pilot and I'll prove it," the enraged Springs said. "Show me the son of a bitch who says I can't fly. I'll wring his neck." Grider grinned and pointed to Bishop, "He did it," he said. It was only then that Elliott learned that Bishop had sent in the fabricated report and "kidnapped" him for his 85th Squadron, R.F.C. They roared with laughter. The process was soon repeated for Grider and Callahan.

Content with his three Americans, Bishop sought to fill out his squadron with men of comparable capacities. As Callahan recalled his methods: "Billy, who was highly congenial . . . decided he was going to organize this group on an entirely new basis, one of congeniality and personality. He . . . went to barrooms in London and . . . finally showed up with an assortment . . . that were highly congenial and had been through many tests [and] . . . could be depended on to stand by under trouble." In addition to his three untried Americans, Bishop had recruited six Englishmen and six Canadians and added Scots, Australians, New Zealanders, an Irishman, and a South African. In addition to Horn, the flight leaders of the 85th were Arthur ("Lobo") Benbow, who wore both a monocle and a Military Cross, and C. B. A. Baker, a soft-spoken youth who had won the Military Cross and the French Croix de Guerre.

Springs scoffed at the idea that Bishop or Captain Horn had chosen the three Americans for their ability to handle planes. "Such was not the case. The captain had the greatest mistrust of our flying, mine in particular. I hung him upside down in a loop one day when neither of us had on a safety belt and he never forgave me. Here we were, hanging by our toes and fingernails, and he was cussing a blue streak at me through the speaking tube." The two survived only because Horn's cushion slipped, jammed the stick and forced the plane into a roll. "No, it wasn't our gentle touch on the controls that got us into that select company of ruffians." He was convinced that what impressed Bishop and Horn were his own talents as the greatest bartender in Europe, Callahan's gifts as a pianist, and Grider's genius at organizing parties and hypnotizing women. The Musketeers were given free rein by Bishop, whose new squadron was the "despair" of his bride, a wealthy Canadian girl who had until now led a sheltered life. Worn out with the endless drinking bouts of the squadron, Mrs. Bishop once asked her husband plaintively, "Don't they ever sleep?"

Bishop warned his three Americans to avoid U.S. headquarters until the date of departure. Their friend, Halley Whatley, the Georgian, found a house for them in London. Miss Whatley's influence made a profound impression upon Springs, "She picked up the phone and called Lord Athlumney, the Provost Marshal, and in an hour we moved into a four-story house in Berkeley Square complete with servants, a cellar, and hot and cold callers." The Musketeers immediately staged a spirited dinner party, a triumph despite all obstacles. Though they lacked rationing coupons to buy meat, they served soup and fish, with substantial alcoholic supplements—a large tub of eggnog with pitchers of robust mint juleps and cocktails in addition. There was a bottle of port and one of champagne at each place at the dinner table. "Our guests arrived about six and we started doing bottoms-up in rotation. It was a riot."

Springs served from the head of the table, and, when the butler appeared with the tray of fish, Elliott solemnly lifted each one by the tail and tossed it to one of his guests "as if they were seals." At the end of the fish course, as Grider recalled it, he was alone at the table. "The rest were chasing each other all over the place."

A woman who lived next door complained of the uproar to the landlord, who demanded an end to the disturbances. Springs went to mollify her but was absent so long that Grider and Callahan assumed that he had found another charming young girl. Elliott finally appeared to report that a kindly old lady had welcomed him like one of her family. "Her son was killed last year in the battle of the Somme," Springs explained. He told her the American boys were awaiting orders to go to the front and "were just trying to have a little fun before they left." The woman sobbed, "That's just how my son felt about it before he went out the last time." She offered to give a dinner party for the Musketeers.

"I want to invite some nice girls for you to meet."

"We know too many of them already," Springs said.

She withdrew her complaint, the pilots agreed to play the piano no later than midnight, and peace was declared. "You can't beat these English women," Springs said.

Springs also staged less strenuous bouts, "Princeton reunions," with another young pilot, Hash Gile, a husky Chicagoan who had played tackle on Tiger football teams. One night during a party which found all the pilots "tight as a nun's corset," Grider found Springs and Gile closeted. "Springs has something wrong with his left eye and when he drinks too much it closes. I . . . found Hash holding Springs's eye open . . . so he could have another drink to Old Nassau. When they meet in hell, these two will organize another Princeton reunion."

There were other adventures as the Musketeers prepared to leave England for France. Elliott astonished his companions by rejecting a beautiful girl, a redhead he met at a dance. "She gave every indication of being ready to burn my fingers so I left while the door was still open . . . she sure is a goodlooking woman. But my grandfather told me never to get mixed up with a redheaded woman who wears black underwear." He was without a girl when the Musketeers went to Maidenhead for a weekend with two British women in a cottage on the Thames. They spent Sunday exploring the "regular fairyland" of the river in a canoe. During dinner in a waterside restaurant, Springs made a date with a girl at a neighboring table and blundered into an international squabble when he returned later to meet her.

Seeking his girl in the bar, Springs encountered British Guard officers who were critical of the American army—particularly "a long, tall bird" whom Elliott found offensive. "I've been reading in the papers until I'm bloody sick of it," said the Guardsman, "about the number of American troops that have come over. But what I can't understand is why none of them will fight. Paris is full of them. London is full of them, but they all jolly well stay away from the front. None of them will fight."

"Well," Springs said, "here's one of them that will." He knocked the Englishman to the floor and retreated when another swung at him. Elliott jumped into his boat and pushed out to safety in the Thames—but, since he had forgotten the paddles, he floated down the dark river and missed plunging over the falls only "by a miracle."

Mac Grider was mystified as to how Springs found his way home to their lodgings. "He's got more lives than a cat and needs all of them."

The squadron spent its last days in England on the bustling airfield at Hounslow near London. Here the 85th was equipped with new planes—Dolphins, which were taken away from them at once to equip another squadron being rushed to France. The 85th was given S.E.5's instead, swift, agile little fighters which they coveted, though they rued the delay in being sent to the front.

Elliott was "like a child with a new toy" tinkering with his British S.E.5, which he called "Mint Julep." He treasured it as the first plane he could call his own: "It's a beauty and the best part is that it's mine—no one else will ever fly it and no one else has ever flown it." He spent days cleaning and oiling and synchronizing his machine guns, tuning the motor and testing the rigging.

He then flew the new ship. "I went up high and did a spinning tailslide. Nothing broke so I have complete confidence in it. It cost about $12,000." He wrote proudly of the array of controls, gauges, switches, and indicators in the cockpit. "How's that for something to keep your eye on?" he wrote to Lena.

It was all for naught. He crashed a day later and, though Elliott was unhurt, the plane was a total loss, and he had a new—and better—"Julep" an hour later. He had a frosted glass of the traditional Southern drink painted on his fuselage.

Springs and Callahan were at the airfield that day, Elliott filthy from overturning his plane in a mud puddle, when Major Bishop's wife and another woman appeared. Mrs. Bishop invited them to tea and insisted, despite their protests that they were improperly dressed. The unknown woman, Elliott said, was "most agreeable but we didn't pay much attention to her," though she was "the most patriotic person I've met over here because she was always talking about the King."

When Springs assured her that all Americans were pleased to be fighting with the British, she said, "I'm sure the King will be glad to hear it." Even that did not prompt Elliott to wonder about her identity, though he said later, "That sounded a bit far-fetched to me."

He enjoyed the visit. "We got on fine with her and we told her some funny stories and she died laughing."

When Mrs. Bishop's friend said she must go into London, Elliott offered to take her in a taxi he had waiting, but she said she preferred to take a bus and get the air. "Besides, it will take me right past the Palace."

Elliott did not understand this and was further puzzled to see Mrs. Bishop curtsy when he took the woman off to catch the bus.

When the woman had gone, Callahan asked, "Who is that old babe?"

"That's the King's daughter, Princess Mary Louise."

"Quite a surprise, to say the least," Elliott said. He and Larry tried to remember whether they had "cracked any jokes about the King." Mrs. Bishop told him soon afterward that he and Callahan had "made a great hit" with the Princess. "God knows why," Elliott responded.

Billie Carlton invaded the house of the Musketeers one night, bringing with her a girlish actress named Babs Helm. Billie's jokes about Elliott's "cave man" tactics with women inspired Springs to action. "If that stuff will work with one, it ought to work with another," he said. He seized Babs, who entered the spirit of the game by cracking Springs over the head with an empty wine bottle. "She was no sylph," Grider said. "And it didn't do a thing but knock him cold." After Springs regained consciousness and found a lump on his skull, Babs spent the rest of the evening sympathizing with him and trying to comfort him.

The next morning Elliott sent Babs a brick wrapped in tissue paper, followed by an imposing spray of orchids.

The departure of the 85th for the front from Hounslow became an unscheduled spectacle. "I don't think there ever was a squadron that got the send-off we did," Springs said. An assortment of their women friends appeared, including a bevy of actresses, some of whom were not on speaking terms with each other. There were also "nice girls." Captain Horn's fiancée was there with her family. And Mrs. Bishop had come with Princess Mary Louise. There were many others. The airdrome, as Springs said, was covered by a cloud of pink parasols.

Billie Carlton and Babs Helm stood at some distance, beaming. Dora and several of her friends, veterans of 85th's parties, were in another group, and nearer the waiting planes were the Horns and Mrs. Bishop and the Princess. "We nearly broke our necks running from one group to another and pretending that we didn't know anybody else," Elliott said. "Naturally, nobody mixed." Farewells were brief and strained, but Grider seemed to feel no embarrassment in bidding goodbye to Miss Carlton, though, Elliott wrote, "As Billie was the most famous and notorious woman in London, everybody was watching her and Mac."

Mrs. Bishop exacted promises from the three Americans that they would keep enemy planes off the tail of the Major's plane, and Elliott noted with admiration her complete self-control, keeping a "stiff upper lip," though she realized that the odds were against Bishop's safe return to her. Springs presented her with an orchid spray like the one he had sent to Babs Helm.

Princess Mary Louise was effusively cordial. "I told the King about you," she said. "He was very pleased to hear that American pilots were so enthusiastic about flying with the R.F.C. He hopes he will have an opportunity to decorate one of you."

To the dismay of the Musketeers, a smartly uniformed party from U.S. London headquarters appeared in the midst of this leave-taking, among them General Biddle and Colonels Dwight Morrow and Billy Mitchell. With them was a smiling Geoff Dwyer, masking his secret role in sending the trio to France with Bishop's unit. "We hadn't expected them," Elliott said. "We tried to get in the ground but couldn't find a hole. . . . That was one morning when I would rather not have been so conspicuous." Springs imagined that Bishop's conspiracy with Dwyer to prevent the Musketeers from flying with the U.S. Army was in danger of exposure because it became obvious that Dwyer was on intimate terms with the trio and with women who had come to see them off as well.

After final farewells, Bishop formed his pilots near the planes, which were waiting in formation, engines warmed up and ready for the flight to France. General Biddle made a short speech, and Bishop gave them last-minute instructions.

"Lympne will be our first stop. And don't forget to check the condom and land straight into the wind." The condom, as Elliott said, was the familiar name for the windsock "when there are no ladies present." Bishop ducked his head in embarrassment at his inadvertent vulgarity, the ladies lowered their parasols, the Princess stared in shocked disbelief, and the Major dashed for his plane. Springs broke from the ranks and ran back to give Dora a passionate kiss. "They put on a burlesque tragic parting that was a scream. Everybody nearly died laughing."

The nineteen planes then took off "and blew a cloud of dust and cinders over our distinguished friends." Bishop led the squadron in a turn around the field, and they dove upon the crowd below, dusting them once more and ruffling the massed parasols.

They rose in unison and, as Elliott said, pointed their "noses toward the Promised Land." He studied the landscape beneath him as if he were glimpsing it for the first time. "It was probably the finest day I ever spent.

England, a mile below, raced by us all covered with flowers and trees and tiny postcard-like golf courses."

Callahan dropped out of formation with motor trouble after a few miles and planed downward toward an airfield south of London. The squadron flew on without him.

One pilot cracked up in the landing at Lympne but somehow found a new plane. All "got pickled" at lunch in nearby Folkestone and two more men, MacGregor and Canning, crashed and were unable to continue. The squadron, now reduced to sixteen planes, climbed into the clear air over the Channel. Two or three pilots carried pet dogs in their cockpits; Springs flew with a huge nickel-plated cocktail shaker strapped to his wing struts, a gift from his accomplished mechanics. The waters below were "covered with tiny boats."

Mac Grider's motor began to sputter, and he watched the vessels beneath him with care, picking out British destroyers and trawlers near which he might make an emergency landing. Now, he saw, there was a smoky haze eastward, and he had a lonely feeling despite the proximity of the other pilots. "There is no horizon and you feel exactly as if you were flying into limitless space," he said. A few moments later, "The dim yellow line that marked the coast of France was a very welcome sight."

Springs motioned Grider to come alongside his plane and, as they flew wing to wing, raised his flask and drank Mac's health. Grider could not respond—his bottle of champagne was stored in his tool box. Springs felt a surge of elation as they crossed over French soil. "I shouted for joy. Of course there was no one within 100 yards of me but I yelled anyway. Both guns were loaded and I . . . felt as safe as in bed in London." The final weeks of training had given Springs complete confidence, and, though he was not sure he would survive, he was eager to get into combat in France. "I'm either coming out of the war a big man or in a wooden kimono," he said. "I know I can fight, I know I can fly, and I ought to be able to shoot straight."

He expected their new commander to teach him how to coordinate these skills in battle. "If I can just learn to do all three things at once, they can't stop me. And Bishop is going to teach me to do that."

He was aware of some fierce compulsion to succeed burning within him—perhaps the resolve to prove himself to his father. "I've got to make a name for myself, even if they have to prefix 'late' to it." Today, as they neared a landing in France, Elliott's only worry was the absence of Callahan.

They landed about 6 P.M. at Marquis, near Boulogne, where two more pilots crashed but survived. After getting "orders and more liquor," they flew a few miles further to Petit Synthe, an old Royal Navy station two miles south of Dunkirk and three miles from the coast. "We finally landed pretty tight," Elliott recorded. "Brown sideswiped a wing."

Two other British squadrons based on the field greeted the 85th to the war with a band concert and a rousing party. Springs, who was entrusted with the bar, went with Grider into the countryside on motorcycles for eggs and cream and produced a huge tub of eggnog, a novelty to the British, whose clamor of approval drew a large crowd for "a regular binge." The eager newcomers were assured that prospects of battle on this quiet front were remote. The sector from Nieuport to Ypres, patrolled by the 65th Wing, was merely a training ground for new squadrons. Their neighbors were a squadron of day bombers that struck German submarine bases at Zeebrugge and Bruges each morning, two squadrons of night bombers, and one of British fighters. Combat seemed far away on this evening of good food and drink and boisterous companionship.

Because their gear had not arrived, most of Bishop's squadron slept on the field. A few German bombers came over during the night and gave them a noisy greeting, and the men of the 85th, watching the show as antiaircraft shells burst harmlessly among the raiding planes, did not trouble to take cover in the sandbagged dugouts. Their war had begun.

L iving was easy for the 85th in its coastal airdrome, and
in the excitement of reaching the front, the pilots did
not miss the comforts of their London town house.
The corrugated iron Nissen huts were roomy, the dugout shelters were
said to be bombproof, there was a canal at hand for swimming, and
supplies of liquor and fresh food were plentiful. Gramophones played
continually, wailing tinny renditions of British and American popular
songs. Springs, who was assistant mess officer in charge of the bar, bought
a freezer in Boulogne and a stock of wine and liquor in Dunkirk.

"I don't think Bishop is sorry he brought us along," Grider said. "We
are the only outfit at the front that has ice cream for dinner every night.
Springs has taught the cook to make Eggs Benedict and we breakfast
well. In fact, although 'in the midst of life we are in death' we manage to
have a lot of fun—chicken livers en brochette, champagne and Napoleon
brandy." At Elliott's insistence the bar was open at all hours, and its policy
was liberal. "We decided it was too much trouble to sign chits for drinks in
the mess, so all drinks are to be free and each man will have to see that he
gets his money's worth."

To the relief of Springs and Grider, Callahan reappeared on the second
day—he had wrecked his plane near Croydon and merely returned to
London for the night, where he found his girl in the Criterion bar and
resumed the endless party as if he had never left. Larry crossed the
Channel in a new plane the next day and rejoined the squadron.

Springs found a piano, and Callahan played his Chicago jazz each
afternoon during the cocktail hour.

The course of the war in France in this spring of 1918 was unpromising
for the Allied cause. The British Army was shaken by four hundred
thousand casualties. During counter-attacks on the Germans, 380 massed
British tanks had proved ineffectual against enemy infantry—and German
planes had destroyed one-third of the English planes flying air cover.
Fresh American troops had not yet been put into battle, because General

John J. Pershing squabbled with his allies, insisting that his Doughboys fight only under U.S. commanders.

The men of the 85th found that even on their quiet northwestern front the war adhered to a rigid schedule. Each morning at 10:30 a long-range German naval gun at Ostend fired an opening round on Dunkirk and dropped in ten more shells at one-minute intervals. The civilian population retreated into cellars during these salutes and also by night, when sirens frequently wailed. On moonlit nights the town and its airfields were bombed at 10:14 and at 11:45 an enemy observation plane appeared, to photograph results from an elevation of about twenty thousand feet, beyond the reach of Allied fighters.

Though he was ordered to keep new pilots out of action for the first two weeks, Bishop allowed volunteers to fight—but only after several days of intensive training. His flight commanders took their men aloft daily, developing tactics to prepare for combat, when discipline and close support would be essential. The squadron also became intimately familiar with the performance of its S.E.5's.

The planes carried two guns, a Vickers, which fired through the propeller, and a Lewis, mounted on the upper wing. Elliott set the sights of both his guns so that a stream of bullets would converge 200 yards ahead of his plane. "You simply point the nose toward an enemy plane and fire and the guns take care of themselves." To reload the Lewis in mid-flight pilots pulled the gun down a track, removed the empty drum and inserted a fresh one—a procedure which "almost broke your wrist." "We've practiced changing until we can do it in our sleep," Elliott said, but even so he found the Lewis a trial. "The Vickers is the best gun by far."

Captain Horn drilled his flight in close formation, flying until combat maneuvers became second nature to them and his prearranged signals were quickly understood. To order turns or dives, Horn dropped his wing to one side. To close the formation, the Captain shook his wings—and if he spotted Germans, he shook the wings and fired his guns.

The flight cruised at three-quarter speed to enable a pilot who spotted enemy planes to fly forward and warn Horn with a burst of machine gun fire. Horn also trained them to obey his signal flares fired from a Very pistol. In case Horn was shot down or forced to return to the airfield, Malcolm McGregor, a veteran New Zealander, was to take over. The Musketeers justified Horn's faith in them by adjusting rapidly to these tactics, working in harmony with more experienced pilots to form a cohesive unit.

Springs, like most other pilots, tinkered with his plane. He had heavier wire installed to support the stabilizer and fin and devised new controls so that he could fire both guns with a press of his thumb. He also decorated his cockpit "so I won't be bored upstairs." He worked closely with his ground crew, "I have three expert Aviation Mechanics, who do nothing else but look after my bus and do my bidding . . . so far, I've managed to keep them pretty busy." But he realized that he must get into combat to preserve their morale. "Unless I bring down a Hun in a few days, I'm afraid they'll get fed up with their jobs." He also was growing restless. "I'm going to get a Hun this week or bust," he wrote his father.

All of Bishop's flights went on two-hour patrols twice daily, morning and afternoon, flying from the coast near their base to Courtrai, some fifteen miles east of Ypres. Elliott was depressed by the sight of the ruins of the French countryside after four years of war. "It made me sick. There's not a wall standing. . . . And there's a stretch of country forty miles square that's as flat as a piece of paper—no trees, no houses, nothing!" He saw tiny traces of barbed wire, like pencil marks across the earth, the continual flashes of big guns, and the smoke and dust of exploding shells.

"The devastation of the country is too horrible to describe," he wrote. "It looks from the air as if the gods had made a gigantic steamroller, forty miles wide, and run it from the coast to Switzerland, leaving its spike holes behind as it went."

Though Bishop had forbidden his new pilots to cross into enemy territory, he often went hunting himself, always alone. By the end of May, he had shot down eight more Germans. His pilots were excited by his laconic reports of victories, and after ten days of uneventful practice Springs could bear it no longer. In defiance of orders he took off alone on May 31 and spotted an enemy plane five or ten miles behind the line, a lone Albatross flying some two thousand feet below him, apparently easy prey. Elliott made straight for the German, "all ready for action, trying to remember everything I had been taught."

Suddenly the sky was full of enemy planes, silver-bellied Albatrosses whizzing about him, firing furiously, some so near that he could see the faces of enemy pilots. Only then did he realize he had been trapped by a decoy. Elliott lost his head and continued to climb straight ahead toward Germany. "I hadn't the faintest idea what to do," he said, but he was aware that he would lose altitude if he turned and would descend into the midst of the enemy. "I fled, ignominiously, but how I did it I really can't remember . . . for a while I was busy as the . . . bee. Somehow I dived away."

He plunged toward the earth, "wondering mildly how long before my wings would fall off." A few moments later he saw that the Germans had turned back. As one historian concluded, Springs had escaped "by sheer luck and by violating all lessons learned in the aerial fighting school at Ayr"—unorthodox tactics that confused the enemy and saved his life. Elliott's reputation for courage was augmented on this day. As Callahan said, "Springs . . . had colossal determination and was almost like an Indian. He had very little sense of fear."

A few days later, in preparation for a reported German offensive, the pilots were roused at 3 A.M. and waited at the hangars with motors running. The planes were fitted with twenty-pound bombs for low-level attacks on infantry. The squadron flew from Ballieu to Armentières at about two thousand feet but found no enemy planes and no signs of the rumored offensive. Springs dropped his four tiny bombs on a train loaded with German trucks.

He flew through a heavy barrage of antiaircraft fire and landed on his home field, his plane riddled with bullet holes and the fabric torn from the top of his wings by the force of a steep dive. He landed heavily and crashed into Bishop's parked plane.

Springs climbed from his cockpit to confront the grim-faced Bishop, who had come out to survey the wreckage. Elliott approached jauntily and ran a finger over the bars and ribbons on the Major's chest. "You see those decorations?" he asked. "Well, you're welcome to 'em." Bishop laughed, and Elliott went into the bar. The Major felt that the unpredictable Springs improved squadron morale with his wild exuberance and wry humor, and he had no intention of disciplining him. But he also noted that Elliott occasionally suffered from "moods so black" that he had to be restrained from "committing some reckless act."

Bishop sent Springs back up after Germans as soon as his plane had been repaired. The next day Elliott, Horn, and McGregor met Bishop aloft just before dusk and followed him several miles into enemy territory, where they found six Pfalz scouts awaiting them near Lille, in the area where Springs had been surprised the day before. Three of the Germans were flying low with three others high above them, poised to pounce upon unsuspecting Allied fighters. "This time," Springs said, "their scheme did not work."

He and Horn climbed to engage the cover planes while Bishop and McGregor dove toward the lower ones. After a brief dogfight, with "the sky full of lead," Bishop and McGregor each shot down a Pfalz, and

Springs fired a long burst into the fuselage of another and saw it going down out of control—his first victim. Conflicting sensations filled Elliott as he watched the doomed enemy plane falling—the elation of victory and survival, accompanied by faint nausea at the vision of the young German pilot meeting violent death. It was a moment he would long remember.

As Springs followed his flight home, three antiaircraft batteries—"Archies"—opened on his plane, and "the whole sky turned black." He tried to recapture the experience in a letter to Lena a few hours later—a sketch in dramatic narrative form, as if it were intended for other readers:

> Scared—of course I was scared—scared stiff. Heavy clouds below. . . . Where are our lines, quick. Ah, the sun . . . sets in the west. Then our lines must be *there*. Pooof! Pooof! right under my wing tips goes Archie and my heart beats 200 higher. . . . He's got my range again . . . this won't do, I'll run for it. So down goes my nose and . . . I make for the lines, diving about 200. Archie's bursts are behind me now. He is not giving her enough deflection. Yes he is. Up we go—fine, he's half a mile ahead now—there he comes back.
>
> After an age he stopped, so I caught my breath . . . it was getting dark.

Unable to see the ground, he dove through clouds until he found Allied trenches, then steered for his home base. The wind had shifted, and he was forced to land in a crosswind. A railroad train was on a siding when Springs came down, and he glided just above the boxcars and attempted a slow landing—but his undercarriage gave way, and he slid to a halt. He had cracked up three British planes in two days.

Bishop greeted him, "Springs, I want you to fight on our side for a change and quit bringing down S.E.5's."

Springs only laughed. By now he was filled with euphoria, savoring his first victory in the air. "A new chapter in my life began," he wrote to Lena. "I am now a changed man. I got sensations I never knew existed before."

Mac Grider had similar reactions to combat. "God, it was Great!" he wrote to his sister Josephine after his first dogfight. "Sherman was all wrong. He was unlucky enough to be in the wrong branch of the service." Grider sought to reassure his family, "We have nineteen Huns to our credit and nobody missing. . . . It's as safe as a church if you know the game, and I am learning under past masters so don't be uneasy about me." Springs and Grider became closer friends in these days.

During a raid by German bombers one night in early June, Elliott and

Mac left the squadron's stuffy dugout shelter and crawled beneath a freight car on the railroad siding, where they were safe from anything short of a direct hit. Their talk turned to home as they awaited the All Clear.

Mac longed to return to his family home in Grider, Arkansas. "I want to sit on the porch of Sans Souci and just rock and whittle the rest of my life. . . . I only hope I can stick it out here and not turn yellow." Springs was in a somber mood. He talked at length of South Carolina and his father with none of his usual badinage. "I've got to get killed," he said. "I can't go home. If I get knocked off, Father will have a hero son and can spend his money building monuments to me and make himself happy and proud.

"But if I live through it and go home, Father will fight with me the rest of his life. No matter what I do, he'll say it's wrong and worry about it!"

"You're crazy," Grider said.

"I mean it. That's a family trait. I just want to last long enough to make a name for myself, so Father will have something to build a monument to.

"I want to get bumped off with a lot of fireworks, the last week of the war. I don't want to go home and have Father make me work five years in a cotton mill as a day laborer and live in the mill village—he's always talking about my starting at the bottom. And any little mistake I'd make would break his heart."

Grider asked Elliott what he wanted to do.

"I want to write, but Father's hell-bent to make a superintendent of me."

Mac realized that Springs was already trying to become a writer: "He's all the time scribbling now . . . always stopping something important to jot down a plot, as he calls it, for future reference. He's got a briefcase full of them already—plays, short stories, poems, sketches. He's tried to read some of them to me several times." Mac saw that Elliott's continual scribbling of stories about the squadron was a more serious concern than he had realized.

"If we get through, I want you and Cal to come and live with me," Springs said. "I've got plenty for all three of us. I've got a big brick house in Fort Mill that was built by my great-grandfather and a plantation of 3,000 acres to go with it. I want you to run the farm.

"I mean it. I've written a will leaving you and Cal enough to get started after the war."

Grider blinked away tears. "I can't leave you and Cal anything," he said. "But if anything happens to me, I want you to help yourselves to my stuff.

I've got that diary. I want you to have it—and I want you to tell people how it was, here and in London. I want my folks to know I was somebody in London. Do it, Springs—and I'll do the same for you if you go first."

A parachute flare lit the field with a brilliant white glare, and a phosphorus bomb exploded on the hangar of a neighboring squadron. Enemy planes droned overhead and launched a heavy attack—thirty-two bombs burst on an airfield just across the canal. One bomb killed forty officers and men in a dugout, and the neighboring field was so pocked with craters as to make it useless for the night. Elliott and Mac were unhurt, though nose fuses from bombs crackled about them and shrapnel clanged against a wheel of their boxcar. Springs recalled it as the "worst raid I've seen."

By now Grider had a clear idea of Elliott's relationship with his father: "Springs is all right until he gets mail from home then he gets into a terrible rage and wants to fight the . . . world. He and his father seem to carry on a feud at long range. He's got so now he doesn't open any letters until after he's had a few drinks and some of them he doesn't open at all. His father writes him full details and instructions in triplicate about how to do everything and finds fault with everything he does. He showed me a couple of them and they certainly were nasty. Springs is no saint but he certainly isn't nearly that bad. I don't see why he cares what's going on at home. . . . Why he should worry over it when he's three thousand miles away is beyond me. . . . He must be awfully fond of his father to care what he thinks about things he doesn't know anything about."

In mid-June, with scant notice, the squadron moved southward into the active war zone beyond Ypres, an old French airdrome near the village of St. Omer. They were told that a major battle was expected and that the 85th was assigned to help support the infantry and tanks.

Springs found the new quarters comfortable despite the lack of a place to swim. "We are on a beautiful, wooded hill overlooking the field and there's a pretty sylvan glade on the other side where we can . . . snooze in the breeze." The squadron's dogs also enjoyed the new base—and there was already a small menagerie: four young Chows flown over from England by one of the pilots, an Alsatian, an Airedale, a pit bull, and others of uncertain ancestry. Bishop added to this collection by picking up stray animals, including a goat and a cow.

The Musketeers joined a patrol the next morning, and Springs saw signs of the ferocity of the struggle as British and French troops advanced to blunt the German offensive—the last of the war. When he flew low the horrors of trench warfare became clear: "Shells were bursting everywhere. . . . Here and there were tanks, some belching lead and some a mass of flames or a misshapen wreck, hit by field guns. I was right down on the ground but saw very few dead bodies but any number of dead horses. The ground was all pockmarked and what little vegetation remained was a light straw in color from the gas. . . . I saw the Huns using gas, a thin layer of brownish green stuff was drifting slowly along the ground from a trench. . . . But no men were to be seen anywhere. Only dead horses and tanks."

Springs shot down his second German plane on June 17 on patrol with Callahan and McGregor. After an hour's flight without sighting an enemy, Elliott spotted a lone two-seater about two miles inside the German lines. He dove at his victim's tail, "I opened fire at about twenty yards' range and after about fifty rounds he burst into flames just back of the pilot's seat where the petrol tank was. So I pulled away, but not before I could feel the terrific heat of the flame."

McGregor had been firing at the enemy plane from above, and he and Springs shared credit for the kill when they returned to their base.

It was about this time that the 85th lost its first man, Lobo Benbow, who was one of Bishop's favorites. The veteran flight leader, though a stout fighter, had been a source of merriment to the squadron. Benbow, too, disdained the use of goggles while flying and wore only his monocle, as he did during every waking hour on the ground. Benbow also went off alone into German territory, just as Springs had done.

In search of "a nice, fat Hun," Benbow spotted a flight of German scouts, climbed above them, and dove out of the sun upon the rearmost enemy plane. His guns jammed as he tried to open fire at close range, and the enemy flight chased him back home "amid a hail of bullets." He climbed from his plane red-faced and bellowing profanely. "Most comical he was," Springs said. "Still had his monocle on and was raging mad." Swearing vengeance, Benbow spent the rest of the day oiling and adjusting his guns and flew back the next morning to even the score. He did not return. Other pilots came in from patrol and waited a couple of hours before it was obvious that Benbow had gone down.

"Engine trouble," someone said without further discussion. The next morning brought no news, but in the afternoon a British antiaircraft battery reported to the 85th that Benbow had fled back to Allied lines with five Germans in hot pursuit but was shot down a few yards from safety. Springs wrote of Benbow's end, "He was buried where he fell, 'So what the hell, boys, what the hell!' He died with his boots on and his grave is marked with a cross made from a propeller. . . . He was certainly a fine fellow."

Bishop refused to allow his pilots to attend the funeral and responded curtly to accusations of callousness: "It's the first time they've lost one of their own in battle. It might be too unnerving. I hope if they stew a bit about it they'll go out and knock down a few Huns."

Elliott was impressed by the casual behavior of British pilots, who mourned deeply but gave scarcely a hint of their sorrow at the loss of Benbow.

> Of course we all felt perfectly bad about it, [Springs said,] but there was no hullabaloo and the subject has not been mentioned since.
>
> No rotten sentimentality about it and yet you'd be surprised how deeply these Englishmen feel things. . . . Everyone thinks of [them] as having a phlegmatic disposition. Nothing could be further from the truth. It is considered extremely bad form to display the slightest emotion.
>
> An Englishman will get news of the death of his brother, son, or father, or the elopement of his wife, be awarded the Victoria Cross or lose a leg, and merely raise an eyebrow. And ten minutes later sit down to dinner and show no trace of any emotion. But they feel anything more than any other race.

Lost in admiration for these stoical gentlemen-warriors, Elliott (perhaps consciously) assumed their attitudes as patterns for his life.

The pilots insisted that they were not superstitious, but Grider never flew without carrying aloft a piece of the first plane in which he had crashed, a Columbian half-dollar, a sixpence, and a woman's stocking to tie over his nose. An American woman had sent Springs a pair of good luck charms—miniatures of the famous German shepherd war dogs, Rintintin and Ninette. But as Elliott told a friend, while carrying the charms "I've lost five men, been shot down twice myself, lost all my money at blackjack and have gotten only one Hun. From that I figure she's been unfaithful to me." He said he had discarded the dogs and was looking for a new lucky piece. "The best one is a garter taken from the left leg of a virgin in the dark of the moon."

"I know they're lucky," Grider said, "but I'd be afraid to risk it. If something happened to her, you know, you'd be killed sure."

The pilots had become expert in collecting tokens of affection from the young women of St. Omer. The squadron mess was now decorated with an impressive display of colorful garters, each bearing the name and address of some local belle. Since Bishop was perhaps the most lenient commander in the Royal Air Force (R.A.F.), pilots spent many nights away from their barracks—but all were expected to be ready for dawn patrol, whatever their condition. Where combat was concerned, the Canadian ace was an uncompromising disciplinarian.

Bishop was lost to the squadron in mid-June when the R.A.F. ordered him to London to help organize a Canadian Flying Corps. The news came on an evening when he had just scored his sixty-second kill—he had shot down fifteen enemy planes in the last nine fighting days.

The Major was infuriated by his abrupt transfer. "First," Springs reported, "he raised unshirted hell about it," and when his protests failed, Bishop went aloft and shot down two more Germans. When his orders were actually delivered to him the following day, he shot down three more enemy planes.

The day of Bishop's departure was melancholy but inspiring for the 85th. Scheduled to leave at noon, the Major took off at 10 A.M. for his final patrol, alone as usual. He attacked five German fighters, shot down one, and two others collided while climbing to dive after Bishop. The Canadian then shot down another plane. On his way home he also downed a two-seater—and then plunged through fire from machine guns and rifles to strafe German infantry.

Bishop's score was now seventy-two German planes—twenty-five of them downed in the past three weeks. "Pretty good morning," Springs said. "That's something for the boys to shoot at. He's made something of this squadron, too."

The 85th flew with the departing Bishop as far as Boulogne, where they toasted him at a champagne lunch before watching him fly westward across the Channel. "So our Major is gone," Springs reported glumly, "but if ever a C.O. had the respect, admiration and love of his unit, 'twas him. The mechanics even are disconsolate."

The 85th was offered Jimmy McCudden as a replacement for Bishop, but Springs and his friends protested that the British ace was not the leader for them. "He gets Huns himself, but he doesn't give anybody else a chance at them." The pilots asked instead for Mick Mannock, who had been their instructor in England and was now a flight commander in the 74th Squadron. "He's the next best man [to Bishop] in the R.A.F. and we all know him and like him. . . . He's got around sixty Huns." The R.A.F. agreed to send Mannock to the 85th.

Mannock's reputation as a tactician had won Springs. "They say he's the best patrol leader at the front—plans his squadron shows a day in advance and rehearses them on the ground. He plans every maneuver like a chess player and has every man at a certain place at a certain time to do a certain thing and raises merry hell if anyone falls down on his job."

Edward C. Mannock, who was thirty-one that spring, was the son of a drunken corporal who had been discharged from the British Army and had deserted his wife and five children. The twelve-year-old Mick had worked first as a grocery boy and later as a barber's assistant and finally as a telephone lineman. He was so severely afflicted with astigmatism that one eye was virtually sightless—but he had memorized an eye chart at a glance and entered the Royal Flying Corps at age twenty-nine.

An unlikely prospect as a pilot, he was tall and bony with a craggy, seamed face and a melancholy air. Mannock had recovered from an un-promising start—he was nauseated by his first flight against the enemy and fled in disgrace. Only with the aid of an understanding commander had he overcome his fear and become a leading ace. Mannock had trem-bled in terror for hours after his opening combat but controlled himself with an iron will and declared in his odd, stilted way, "Having conquered myself, I'll now conquer the Hun."

As a radical Socialist, the Irishman Mannock's hostility toward British officers almost matched his fanatical hatred of the enemy, but now that he had become a squadron leader, he was like a father to his pilots. When the 85th hunted, he frequently risked his life to drive enemy planes into the fire of his youngsters in attempts to build their confidence. He left no details to chance. "Sight your own guns," he said. "The armorer hasn't got to do the fighting. And you must learn to shoot. To be good fliers is not enough. It's the shooting that kills."

Mannock was moody and highly emotional. On days when one of his companions had been killed he hid in his bunk and sobbed uncontrollably, calling the dead man's name over and over. Afterward he went up to attack Germans even more savagely, eager to send another enemy to a fiery death, which was to him the most terrifying of fates. He habitually fol-lowed his victims to the ground as they fell, strafing them to be sure that neither pilot nor observer survived. When asked why he did this, Mannock replied grimly, "The swine are better dead—no prisoners." Mannock also warned his pilots, "If you ever have a chance to kill one and let him off with his life, I'm going to shoot you."

One day after he had shot down four Germans, Mannock dashed into the mess shouting gleefully, "Flamineroes—four! Sizzle-sizzle wonk!" His friends were increasingly concerned about the impetuous Irishman, who was now haggard and gloomy and talked constantly of a recurring dream that he had been shot down in a burning plane. Mannock carried a revolver aloft, vowing that he would kill himself at the first sign of flames in his plane.

Mannock was especially shaken by learning of the death of McCudden, his former instructor, who had seemed to be immortal. But he went on as before, pale and hollow-eyed, still tortured by his dreams. He made his seventy-second kill on July 22. "I've caught up to Bishop's score," he told a friend cheerlessly.

"They'll give you the red carpet after the war, old man."

"There'll be no 'after the war' for me," Mannock said.

He was up at dawn the next day to lead Donald Inglis, a young New Zealander, into battle. Mick played "Londonderry Air" on his gramophone, smoked his pipe, and went to the field. He heard a bird singing as he climbed into his plane. "He's like me," Mannock said mournfully, "full of the joys of life."

When the two were a few miles deep into German territory, Mannock dove on an enemy two-seater and sent it to the ground, but he was dangerously low. Ground fire struck Mannock's plane, which burst into flames before it crashed. His friends never knew whether he had time to use the revolver.

Inglis turned away and glided to earth inside the British lines, where a rescue crew found him huddled in the cockpit, sobbing.

When they were asked to choose a new commander, the squadron demanded C. M. (Billy) Crowe, a Yorkshireman who had been one of the first British pilots to see action. Crowe had been twice demoted from Major, once because of a drunken brawl and again because of an auto crash in which another officer died. Springs, however, thought him "a great lad" and welcomed him warmly. Life in the 85th was never the same after Crowe's arrival, Elliott said. "No one ever got sober again. Even the enlisted men started drinking. It was a riot."

Elliott admired Crowe's matchless courage. "He was the wildest patrol leader in the world and would stay in a fight indefinitely. Of course Mannock was the best; he got seventy-three Huns; Bish had seventy-two and, with Crowe as the third, 85 had the finest C.O.'s of any squadron."

In the meantime, the 85th suffered another loss—a loss that was devastating to Springs. The ranks of the Three Musketeers were broken.

Springs and Mac Grider went up with their flight near Courtrai on June 18, a cloudy, warm day when enemy activity seemed to be light. At 10 A.M. they were flying at about sixteen thousand feet near the village of Menin when Springs spotted a hostile plane, a two-seater, with the inevitable gunner perched in the rear of the pilot. Springs signalled to Grider and they dove upon the German, Springs attacking first. He held his fire until he was only a few yards from the enemy's plane's tail and he could see the observer standing, firing his guns.

"Then I let him have it," Springs said. "Both guns. Right into the observer's pit—about twenty rounds—I could see my tracer going into him."

When Elliott's guns jammed and he was forced to turn away, Grider followed, at a higher altitude. Below them the stricken enemy plane dove straight into the ground and exploded near the Menin road. It was Elliott's third victim.

Springs and Grider flew into a heavy cloud bank where Elliott's plane went out of control. "We had no gyroscopes and I spun down about 10,000 feet." He looked back once and saw Grider trailing him at a normal distance. It was his last glimpse of his friend. As he wrote home the next day, "After five or ten minutes I got my bearing and got back to the patrol. But that's the last I've seen of him. I decided he'd gotten lost."

Springs went aloft once more in the afternoon, seeking another German victim, in vain. There was still no news of Mac when he returned to the field. Elliott tried to convince himself that Grider was safe. "I imagine his motor cut out—I don't think Archie could have gotten him—I saw no Huns about—and I think I killed the observer so I don't believe Mac got hit."

"Of course many things might have happened," he wrote to Lena.

Mac might have been firing at long range from above and shot up his own prop or gotten a burst in the motor from the observer—or gotten hit by Archie, or lost his way, or attacked another Hun a half an hour later.

That's the worst of the game—the uncertainty of it. But I feel sure that Mac is personally safe wherever he has landed. He's a prisoner all right but no one knows how I miss him. No man ever had a truer friend and the fact that we fought together and in unison and harmony shows the confidence we had in one another. And he was as fine a fighter as ever tripped a trigger.

Elliott also wrote to Mac's sister, Mrs. Josephine Jacobs of Washington, D.C., describing the air battle and Mac's disappearance. To Grider's father he wrote reassuringly, "I feel sure that he is safe and we are anxiously awaiting news from a German prison camp." His final words suggested, however, that Elliott did not expect to see his friend again: "Mac has done wonderfully well. . . . He was the most popular man in the squadron and everyone here is constantly bemoaning his loss."

Privately, Elliott noted in his terse log, "Oh, Christ, am I to blame?"

Springs recalled an incident at Oxford when, as sergeant, he was trying to maintain discipline in the ranks and a titled British pilot had complained of Elliott's severity. An outraged Grider confronted the Englishman, "I'll thrash you if I ever hear you criticize him again."

When he reflected that Grider was probably dead, Elliott lapsed into a scornful, even cruel, vein in his response to a particularly inane letter from Lena.

Mac is gone, but he'll never be forgotten until the Hun's aim improves or my bus [plane] goes back on me—or I pass out from irritation at the doings of the Springs family on the home front.

I hope my ghost haunts you and never gives you a moment's peace. You have all the time in the world to make speeches and run around to hen parties called conventions where they fight the battle of social precedence and waist measurements and yet you have the nerve, audacity and bad taste to write me that you have been abed resting from your strenuous labors.

He had slept only three hours the night before, he said, but rather than rest, "I'm writing you until time to go up on patrol and try to avenge Mac." He added another calculated insult, "May your powdered nose take on the color of an over-ripe tomato and may you never see your feet again except in a mirror. I'm completely fed up with you." Incongruously, he followed this outburst of animosity by closing in the vein he had used since childhood, "A heartful of love to you and Father. Devotedly, Elliott."

Springs shot down another German plane—his fourth—on June 25, this one flown by a brave and skillful pilot who tested Elliott to the utmost in a five-minute dogfight. The enemy dodged every maneuver of Elliott's more agile plane, turning and rolling to give his observer a shot at the persistent American. When the German observer missed him at close range, Springs poured a stream of bullets into the enemy's fuselage: "I think I must have hit his engine or tank for he went into a spiral and never came out." To make sure of a kill, Elliott continued to fire, "and even got so exasperated that I threw an ammunition drum at him. . . . he only dove into the ground from 1000 feet. I hope the pilot is still alive; he certainly was a stout fellow."

In his exuberance over the victory and his survival, Springs joined Captain Horn, Callahan, and McGregor in a mock dogfight over the British lines for appreciative troops who "waved frantically."

Springs did not suspect that this was to be his last flight for several weeks.

Captain Samuel Elliott White, grandfather of Elliott White Springs, was a much-wounded Confederate veteran, textile pioneer, and bon vivant.

Esther Allison White, an ideal grandmother, whose warm, close relationship with young Elliott ended traumatically with his discovery of her lifeless body. She was apparently the victim of a heart attack.

The stern, forbidding Leroy Springs, whose hostile relationship with his son was lifelong. His failure to understand the sensitive boy was a major source of stress in Elliott's life, contributing later to an emotional breakdown.

Elliott's beloved mother, Grace White Springs, whose efforts to lessen the friction between her husband and their only child ended only with her premature death. Elliott was ten years old at the time of this loss—one from which he never recovered.

Lena Wade Jones, a lively schoolteacher who became Elliott's stepmother. Though he aided her generously in later life, Springs could not overcome his resentment of the woman who took his mother's place. An energetic leader of the woman's suffrage movement, Lena Springs was nominated for vice president at the Democratic National Convention of 1924—the first woman to be so honored.

The future War Bird aged two or three, in the uniform of a Naval Reserve officer of the Spanish-American War.

A diminutive football hero at the Asheville (N.C.) School, Elliott (left) was the captain and hard-hitting end on the 100-pound team. Sports activity helped to brighten an otherwise unhappy, lonely experience for the motherless boy. Elliott's companion in this photograph from a family album is unidentified.

The young Elliott, a precocious speed demon, at the wheel of his first automobile, a 1910 Hudson roadster. He was probably fourteen at the time and beginning to evidence his lifelong love of cars.

Elliott in his Stutz Bearcat at Princeton in the spring of 1917, already a cadet in the Army Air Service and a dashing ladies' man. His father first refused Elliott the car, then made vague promises, and finally approved on the eve of his graduation from Princeton.

An insouciant survivor, Springs stands before a Sopwith Camel fighter plane he landed on one wheel after his plane was riddled in combat. This crash by Elliott, one of several, occurred at Remaisnil, The Somme, on September 14, 1918.

The 85th Squadron of the British Royal Flying Corps (on the eve of becoming the Royal Air Force) at St. Omer, northern France, 1918. Larry Callahan and Elliott Springs are fourth and fifth from the left. Both later fought with the 148th U.S. Aero Squadron. The dogs and goats were only a few of the squadron's mascots, many of them collected by Billy Bishop, the outfit's most celebrated commander.

The Three Musketeers of the American cadre in British service. Left to right, *Mac Grider of Arkansas, whose brief diary became celebrated in* War Birds; *Elliott White Springs; and Laurence K. Callahan of Chicago, whom Springs regarded as the most skillful fighter pilot of World War I.*

Pilots of the U.S. 148th Fighter Squadron pose in front of one of their planes on an air strip somewhere in France. This Signal Corps photograph shows Flight Commander Elliott Springs in front center. Behind him and to the right is his close friend, Larry Callahan. The two pilots at left are not identified.

Frances Ley and Elliott White Springs during the 1930s, about ten years after their marriage. Elliott was then in the first flush of success as a major textile manufacturer.

Elliott added to his reputation as a daredevil pilot in the postwar era by flying beneath the Buster Boyd Bridge of the Catawba River in South Carolina in 1923. Though engine failure delayed his arrival until the dedication ceremonies were over and another pilot had preceded him, Elliott's aerial feat was long remembered in the region as the sensation of the day.

The riotous life of British and American aviators at war was a major theme of Elliott's best-selling War Birds. *This illustration by Clayton Knight caught the spirit of the candid story as published in* Liberty *magazine. Despite its success the sensational book only widened the rift between Springs and his father.*

A typically droll Springs joke was this pose of the maverick manufacturer and his wife and children, Leroy (Sonny) and Anne, posing as mill hands. When he used the picture on a Christmas card, a textile manufacturer in Wisconsin protested this use of child labor—a protest that Elliott publicized with gusto.

June 26 was a day Springs never forgot. On a dawn patrol he spotted one of the formidable new German two-seaters over Armentières. His companion, the New Zealander McGregor, dove upon the enemy with rattling machine guns without obvious effect.

Elliott flew beneath the two-seater and opened fire, but his Lewis gun jammed, and as he hung there helplessly, struggling to clear his ammunition drum, the enemy plane climbed. The German observer fired a stream of bullets at Springs from close range. A black geyser spurted from a severed oil line into Elliott's face. He was saved by McGregor, who zoomed in again and shot down the German. Elliott's plane plunged 5,000 feet before he regained control.

He flew homeward at low altitude under fire from enemy infantry, and scores of bullets ripped the fabric of his wings and fuselage. The motor roared briefly but fell silent when the last of the oil drained away. The bearings melted. Springs began a long glide for the Allied lines, his doomed plane wreathed in clouds of black smoke. By now, he said, "the Huns . . . were shooting rifles, pistols and throwing old tin cans at me."

Elliott crossed safely into British territory north of the Forest of Nieppe but there, forced to land downwind, he crashed into the parapet of a machine gun nest, and his plane "rolled up into a ball." He lost consciousness when the butt of his Vickers gun struck his chin, dislodging some teeth and grinding and tearing flesh and bone. Elliott revived only as British Tommies removed him from the wreckage.

"I ran my tongue around my mouth and couldn't find any front teeth." He sobbed.

"Why are yer cryin', sor?" a Tommy asked.

"My teeth. They're gone!"

"Oh, no they hin't, sor. 'Ere they are." The soldier tugged at Elliott's lacerated lips. "Your teeth's all right. They were just on the outside of your face."

Springs writhed in pain until someone brought him the only available anesthetic, a bottle of cognac. The brandy flowed from a hole in his chin at each sip, and Elliott spent most of the morning with his head tilted back while an Irish priest poured the brandy into his open mouth. The pain subsided, "But they brought me another bottle so I kept up the treatment."

A British doctor in a field hospital later gave him both morphine and antitetanus serum, and Elliott was soon on his way back to his squadron, riding in a tender that three of his mechanics had driven to the front. He wore no uniform and was dressed only in yellow pajamas beneath his torn, bloody flying suit. Elliott demanded a halt at every cafe and bar on the route to buy champagne and desisted only when he had spent the three hundred francs he carried in his pocket. At dusk, "all tight as sausage skins," they reached the home field, where Elliott's reappearance set off a celebration. The entire squadron became drunk on juleps garnished with fresh strawberries. Only later, when someone noticed that Elliott's face was in need of "a bit of hemstitching," was he taken to the Duchess of Sutherland's hospital, a portable unit with a competent British staff, which, as Elliott reported, "has the Johns Hopkins backed off the boards." But the doctor who examined him gave the drunken Springs an unwelcome, and erroneous, diagnosis: his head injuries seemed to be serious.

He ordered Springs to stand. "Close your eyes. Now open." His senses whirling from his daylong spree and the oppressive heat of the tent, Springs swayed and fell to the floor. "I thought so," the doctor said. "Concussion. He'll be in bed for a while." He sent the other pilots home. "You can't see him for a few days," he said. "He must be kept absolutely quiet."

"I'd like to see them do that," one pilot said.

Not until the next day did Elliott realize that surgeons had made extensive repairs to his face and mouth.

Springs cringed when he was given a glimpse of his face. "I look like a reflection in one of those comic curved mirrors," he wrote to Lena. "I don't like my new face at all. It's all wrong. . . . I may have to smell thru my ears and eat thru my nose. . . . It's a wreck and the doctor's a rotten tailor. . . . they'll use me after the war as propaganda—'the horror of warfare.' I haven't gotten my mouth open enough to count my teeth but they don't feel right."

But he was resolved to flee the hospital. "If I'm not over the lines in four days again, it'll be because I'm in jail for murdering the doc," he wrote. Springs tried to convince his doctor that he was not suffering from "acute concussion" and managed to fend off an operation to relieve pressure on his brain.

For a few days Elliott had swollen lips and a "mouthful of thread and a couple of black eyes"—but despite his appearance and his bitter complaints, his face had been skillfully restored, his torn lips sewn together from inside so that his scars would be undetectable in later life. He recuperated in style. Springs and a wounded British brigadier had set up a private bar and, "full of champagne," were constantly attended by the Duchess of Sutherland and her staff of eighteen nurses.

In the midst of his convalesence Springs received a telephoned order to return to the U.S. Army. He was to become a flight commander in the new 148th Squadron based at Dunkirk—an outfit fully manned by Americans, though attached to a wing of the R.A.F.

"No!" Elliott said. "Give the job to someone else! I won't move." The desperate Springs telephoned his British commander and shouted despite his painfully stitched mouth, "I won't go with the Americans. I don't care about being a captain. I'm staying with the 85th. I refuse the promotion."

"You're not doing the appointing this year," the colonel said.

When his doctor overheard Springs decline promotion, he ordered him closely confined to the hospital. "I'm sure he's cuckoo," he said.

Elliott wrote to Leroy with an air of resignation. "It looks like I'll have to go tho I can't figure why they'd yank me away from 85 like this . . . I don't want to be a flight commander and lead patrols." But he added, "I would rather lead them myself than follow anyone that I didn't have confidence in."

He escaped soon afterward, simply by strolling out of the hospital and walking several miles back to the 85th's headquarters, wearing only his silk pajamas and fur-lined flying boots.

Elliott's outraged doctor appeared to demand his return—but Callahan and others persuaded the doctor that Springs was not deranged: "After we filled him full of julep he finally said he could stay but that he mustn't fly for a week."

All of this went for naught. Springs was ordered to report to Dunkirk despite the protest of friends that he was then incapable of command.

His new outfit, the 148th Fighter Squadron, was commanded by Mort Newhall, a former Harvard quarterback. In addition to Springs, the flight commanders were Bim Oliver and Henry Clay, with whom the Musketeers had trained in England. The 148th was to fly Camels. Powered by

Clerget radial engines, they were unstable little planes with such an evil reputation as mankillers that Callahan and others when later asked to join his flight at first refused. Callahan protested that the Camels were "very bad shooting platforms," though he finally relented, and the two remaining Musketeers eventually flew together again in the new squadron.

Springs appeared in Dunkirk to assume his new command. He and Bim Oliver, neither of whom had ever flown Camels, realized that their pilots must be schooled in the demanding little planes before entering combat. They solved the problem without consulting their superiors. Elliott and Bim located their planes at a nearby village depot, where they found mechanics to explain the controls of the Camels and, as Springs recalled it, "we finally got up our nerve to try and fly them."

Elliot tried to start his plane while an aviation mechanic sucked on his gasoline line—but a short circuit from a magneto flashed sparks, the motor roared to life, and the body of the luckless mechanic was thrown twenty feet. After the corpse was carried off in an ambulance, Springs, as he said, "staggered off and joined Bim," and the two practiced takeoffs and landings on an abandoned airfield near Calais. "When we thought we were good enough to get on the ground by the third bounce, we went on back to our airdrome."

Elliott found that the Camels deserved their reputation: "They would do about 90 level but you couldn't fly level because they would shake your teeth out in 40 seconds by the clock. . . . Its guns were best at 100 yards. . . . Beyond that you would waste bullets because of the terrific vibration. They would stall at 15,000 feet and lose 1,000 feet on a turn. You had to climb or glide. But they could fly upside down and turn inside a stair well." Anticipating the plane's performance in combat he predicted it would be "deadly below 5,000 feet if you could suck the Fokkers down. . . . The Camel could make a monkey out of a Fokker at tree-top level."

But his return to combat was postponed once more, this time by the aftereffects of the antitetanus serum. He wrote to Lena of his downfall, "I . . . was almost ready to go and have a look at the war when something slipped up behind me and tagged me and I went out cold. . . . You know what a mosquito bite looks like? Well, I look like I had been bitten by a million. . . . From the top of my head to the soles of my feet . . . I am one large bite." His hands, feet and joints were swollen to "double their size," his eyes were closed, and "the remnants of my lips doubled up, my tongue broke out, my face looked like a lump of red putty, I itched all over, my stomach broke out on the inside and couldn't receive even water." He was put to bed again, suffering the effects of "poisoning from a combination of whisky, brandy, anti-tetanus serum and morphine."

Even a week later, when he was able to visit the 85th, his condition appalled his friends. "Springs is a wreck. He's blind in one eye and the other isn't much good. He's got cirrhosis of the liver from that serum." He was also so stooped from a neck injury that he seemed to be deformed, and he walked at the halting pace of an old man.

After a few days of convalescence Springs was bouncing along the roads of his sector in a motorcycle sidecar, trying to direct "B" flight while his deputy commander led it into action. His eyes were still so inflamed that he could scarcely read and write, but he continued to send home long letters describing his adventures and begging Lena and Leroy to treat his reports as confidential. "Please don't pass around the word that I've been sick," he wrote. "The only danger was to my sanity and that's as OK as it will ever be. . . . The doctor expected me to run around with an empty beer bottle shouting 'I'm to be Queen of the May,' but I fooled him. Now for the dentist as soon as I can get my mouth open wide enough."

Elliott lapsed into the bitter mood in which he had previously written to his parents. He was particularly scornful of Americans back home who busied themselves "by doing their bit" for the war effort. "Every time I get a paper from home I either break into a loud laugh or get mad. . . . I see where all the patriotic women are studying public speaking and bird life. I can't see the why of either." He continued to belittle Lena's activities with service organizations, and his anger intensified when he learned that Leroy was still having his letters published: "The Springs family seems to be about as honorable as the German Red Cross. Or possibly you and Father don't understand my wishes in regard to publicity. . . . Well, it's got to stop.

"And if anybody writes me again that 'doubtless you hope to be an ace' I'll send them an infernal machine. I am not an 'ace,' don't want to be an 'ace,' and never will be an 'ace.' We don't have 'aces' here. This 'ace' stuff makes me tired. Call it off. . . . Again I insist my letters are private and secret! See to it!" He told Lena of shooting down a German but threatened that if she revealed the feat he would pray that the victim's ghost would haunt her. (She immediately told Leroy who passed word to his Aunt Addie with the comment, "He . . . is very sensitive about newspaper notoriety, which I think is very foolish, as it is but right that his friends should know he is making good.")

Continually, and in the most insulting manner, Elliott scolded his parents for the dullness and inanity of their letters:

"I got fifteen letters today. Most of them upset me very much. Father doesn't seem to like my letters. You might tell him that I can't say that I enjoy his. Your efforts aren't particularly exciting either," he wrote Lena. "Get busy."

When she replied that she was writing him at least weekly, Elliott retorted, "So you pride yourself on writing once a week, do you? . . . And what poor, rotten, weakly weekly letters they are." He added later, "Of course, wit isn't allowed to flourish in the Springs household, but you might with each letter include a couple of jokes clipped from *Puck* or *Judge* to make up for the deficiency of the text." He begged Lena to dissuade Leroy from dictating his letters, since they sounded like "Letters from a Half-made Merchant to his Idiot Son—only they lack the humor of the original."

He wondered, he wrote Lena, whether his own breezy, rambling reports of life at the front were indeed letters: "I flatter myself that they are letters. Yours and Father's might just as well have been written by a machine to a machine."

Elliott's correspondence bristled with expressions of old animosities toward his father—probably intensified by the stress of life at the front—but each letter, however caustic in tone, still expressed his love for Leroy. Beneath his scornful mask lay his lifelong yearning for his father's approval. Elliott once went so far as to express this by quoting an anonymous observer: "If anything tugged at him [Elliott] it was this fondness for his father in spite of everything."

Financial affairs were still a cause of contention between father and son. Leroy had agreed to send Elliott an allowance of $5,000 per year until he returned home (probably from his inherited assets). But his son's easy generosity in lending money to other pilots without notes or collateral was incomprehensible to Leroy—and he was infuriated by Elliott's casual cancellation of these loans when his friends were killed in combat. "When one of us cashed in," Elliott wrote, "we gathered in the mess, drank to his memory and burned his chits. Then all of us got drunk."

Doctors forbade Elliott to fly for at least ten days and literally forced him to take a leave in Paris. Despite his insistence that his leave be postponed, Elliott was in Paris two days later—and quickly adapted to life in the city. He registered in a luxurious hotel, dined in celebrated restaurants, and staged drinking parties with his cousin Eli Springs of Charlotte,

North Carolina and with Pabst and Lorraine Goodrich of Milwaukee. Eli was in the U.S. Army and Pabst with the French Foreign Legion.

Paris was swarming with Americans, both military and civilian. He saw several old friends, among them a few from the original "Italian Detachment," including the loquacious Captain Fiorello La Guardia.

Elliott wooed some French women with hoarded sugar Lena had sent him from home. Sugar, he claimed, was the currency of romance in Paris: "In the olden days the villain corrupted the beautiful village maiden with promises of jewels and fine silks. To-day you whisper in her shell-like ear that you have *deux kilos de sucre* and she will promptly forget home and mother." He offered no details of his French conquests, if any.

Even in the beleaguered capital, he found that the food was "the best in the world . . . food such as you never knew existed. . . . To a man from the front it is heaven itself. I live on . . . filet of sole à la maison . . . smothered with truffles and mushrooms and covered with cheese . . . and the frogs' legs are fine. . . . The climate and the food are rapidly turning me from a pessimistic invalid into a pink butter ball and I live only from meal to meal." His ability to enjoy food was a mystery, for his lacerated lower lip was still so swollen that he could not close his mouth.

Elliott tried to trace Grider, in vain. The Red Cross had no report of Mac's fate, but Springs sent parcels to him through the organization in hope that he would be found in a German prison. Elliott also sent to Mac all the money he had left, saving only enough to pay his hotel bill.

Not only was Grider mourned by fellow pilots, "every blonde and every brunette in Paris," so Elliott said rather recklessly, wept for Mac. And from London came word that Billie Carlton, his bereaved fiancée, was "more dramatic" over Mac's death than she had been on the stage. Though Springs noted that "She has recovered sufficiently to become engaged to another American officer," there was soon a report that Billie had died of an overdose of drugs. A few weeks later the high-spirited playmate of the 85th's days in London, Halley Whatley, also committed suicide under the stress of war.

Springs feared that he would not be able to resume combat immediately. His eyes refused "to return to normal and I can't see much in a strong light." An ophthalmologist who discovered that he had a slight hemorrhage of a retina from his crash at first said Elliott could not return to the air but finally said grudgingly, "It's up to you. If you are so anxious as that to continue flying, you can probably do so. Night flying will give you no problem. It is the strong light you should avoid."

Elliott was so determined to resume flying that he forgot his disdain for aces and wrote to Leroy, "I only need dark glasses and am sure I can fly. I'm going to get my five Huns if it costs me both eyes." He looked into a hotel mirror on his last day in Paris—three days short of his twenty-second birthday—and mused, "Well, I am an old man . . . no white hairs, but . . . reflection shows unmistakable signs of old age."

The doctor and dentist released him for further combat, and he wrote exultantly to Lena, "I am returning tonight and will be over the lines again Monday. Thank heaven."

Grider's fate continued to prey on his mind. A month after the loss of his companion, Elliott wrote that though many pilots were known to be German prisoners, Grider was not among them. The first report came from a German plane that dropped a message on the 85th's airdrome one night—Grider was dead. (Though the enemy had misspelled his name, it was clear that Mac was the pilot who had been shot down.) Elliott wrote home, "News has been received that Mac Grider was killed in action but we can't figure how. He must have attacked a formation or decided to shoot up the ground." His companions noted that definite word of Grider's death seemed to mature Springs.

A few days later Elliott learned that Grider's plane had plunged to earth during a dogfight, reportedly the victim of a German ace, Lieutenant Carl Degelow. Mac had been buried by the Germans at the village of Houplines, near Armentières.

Elliott began to lose some of his natural exuberance in the first days of his new command. Sholto Douglas, who led the R.A.F.'s 84th Squadron, felt that the strain of combat and the continual losses of his companions had a sobering effect upon Springs. Elliott said as much in his letters home. "My nerves are in rotten shape," he acknowledged to his father. "Don't laugh when I say 'nerves.' It's no joke. Long patrol and ground strafing will get any man in time." He now felt that it was merely a question of time until he, too, was killed. For several days he was in the grip of depression.

> I'm all shot to pieces, [he wrote of these days of late summer 1918]. I only hope I can stick it out. I don't want to quit. My nerves are all gone and I can't stop. I've lived beyond my time already.
>
> It's not the fear of death that's done it. It's this eternal flinching from it that's . . . made a coward of me. Few men live to know what real fear is. It's something that grows on you, day by day, that eats into

your constitution and undermines your sanity. . . . I've lost all interest in life beyond the next patrol. . . . I haven't a chance, I know, and it's this eternal waiting around that's killing me. I've even lost my taste for likker. It doesn't seem to do me any good now.

Life between missions was a nightmare for him. "At night, when the Colonel calls up to give us our orders, my ears are afire until I hear what we are to do the next morning." He was then sleepless during the night— and later, "While I am waiting around all day for the afternoon patrol, I think I am going crazy. I keep watching the clock and figuring how long I have to live." He prowled restlessly to his plane to check motor and guns, took an occasional drink of liquor, or wrote in his journal and tried "not to think." Once ready for takeoff, Springs recovered somewhat. "When I go out to get in my plane, my feet are like lead—I am just barely able to drag them after me. But as soon as I take off I am all right again. That is, I feel all right, though I know I am too reckless."

He described a patrol in which he acted as a decoy to attract enemy planes and confessed, "I actually got frightened in the air and lost my head." Only the sight of ten German planes bearing down upon him restored his courage. He flew recklessly into their midst and shot one of them down—though he claimed only that this victim was "out of control" when he last saw him diving toward the earth and did not add the German to his list of kills. Elliott returned to his base and that night, for the first time in two months, "slept like a baby."

August ushered in the decisive days of the war in France. The final German offensive, long since spent, was followed by a massive thrust against the Hindenburg Line as Allied infantry, tanks, and artillery moved forward on most of the front that stretched from Switzerland to the English Channel. On the British front around Cambrai, where the 148th was soon to join an aerial armada in support, infantry of the Third Army suffered grisly casualties, but the Tommies battered their way forward through a barrier of concrete, barbed wire, and iron obstacles in the face of gas attacks, massed artillery, machine gun and rifle fire, and aerial bombardment. These defenses, more than thirty miles deep, were the strongest line ever built, so the Germans claimed.

The 148th was forced to train for this crucible on the quiet front near Dunkirk where the 85th had been bloodied two months earlier. Though it never supplanted the 85th in his affections, the 148th Squadron was much to Elliott's liking. Beneath the firm undertone of discipline essential to prepare for combat, a spirit of democracy ruled its ranks. Mechanics and pilots were on a first-name basis, and there was a family atmosphere in its barracks. Morale was so high and instruction so thorough that the U.S. high command later chose the 148th as the best-drilled squadron on the front.

Due largely to the influence and generosity of Springs, food was remarkably good—menus featured filet mignon and mushrooms, cauliflower au gratin, lemon meringue pie, crullers, and, even amidst the great allied offensive, fresh ice cream. In the evenings, as Elliott wrote to Lena, "We had a little Mozart, Beethoven and Tchaikovsky on the piano and then toodled off to bed after a game of ball—it's light here until 10:30. Not a bad life."

On August 3 Springs officially became an ace, the squadron's first. He was leading B Flight on a bomber escort mission to Zeebrugge, Ostend, and Bruges at a height of eleven thousand feet, when three Fokkers began hovering high above him. After several feints the enemy plunged down to the attack. Springs reported, "I turned on one of them . . . and he turned directly toward me. I opened fire at 100 yards and after 50 to 75 rounds the Fokker turned on its back . . . and went into a dive and went down spinning slowly. . . . It was last seen close to the ground going down with great vertical speed and apparently on fire." It was the fifth kill for which he was credited, though he had downed several others which were not confirmed.

Though the decoration was not awarded at the time for reasons now unclear, this feat won the British Distinguished Flying Cross for Elliott. The accompanying citation described his most recent victories and added praise: "This officer's work as Flight Commander in this Squadron has been marked by a rare combination of cool judgment and most aggressive fighting tactics."

A few days later the 148th was moved southward, first to a field near Amiens and then to Remaisnil, in the midst of the final battle for France.

Springs found the moves a "nuisance" since he was forced to familiarize his men with the new front in each case: "I go up alone and get all the landmarks in our new territory, then I take a flight up and lead them up and down the lines until they get the compass bearings of all roads and canals, know all the woods and the villages and get the position of all salients and then we are ready for battle. I know Mother France pretty well."

He also saw that the struggle raging on the ground beneath his planes had spread to every road and field and engulfed every village and town for as far as he could see. The battle reached a crescendo on August 8, when the British broke the enemy's hold on Cambrai—"The Black Day of the German Army," said the German commander, Count von Ludendorff.

The mission of Elliott's squadron was now to harry the enemy by low-level bombing and strafing and to shield Allied artillery positions from German planes as well. The 148th was assailed at once by Hermann Goering's new Circus, whose squadrons were known as Orange Tails, Orange Bands, Black Tails, and, most formidable of all, the Blue Tails, a Bavarian squadron led by the future Nazi hero Ernst Udet. The Germans favored the Blue Tails as a striking force, shifting them along the front to counter the most furious onslaughts of Allied ground forces.

B Flight joined battle against some of the less effective pilots of the Circus near Amiens on August 15 and 16, both "good scraps," Elliott said. He set a trap for the enemy and awaited an attack: "They came down like a ton of bricks and sounded like a 4th of July celebration. . . . We started twisting and turning to spoil their aim and then the top flight [A Flight] came in. For about 10 minutes . . . everybody was shooting at everybody else. Twenty Huns and eleven of us." Elliott was sure he had shot down at least one German, but though he went so far as to land between the trenches to seek confirmation, he failed, and he was credited only with another victim "out of control."

On August 22, only three days after arriving at Remaisnil, Springs downed his sixth and seventh confirmed victims in a busy day of dogfighting. On patrol at mid-morning he attacked five Fokkers and shot down one, which crashed in a woodland, and then crippled another, which he claimed only as "out of control." He returned to his field with ammunition exhausted and in the afternoon bombed and strafed enemy troops and trucks. On a third sortie about 6 P.M., Elliott attacked three Fokkers as they dove on a British flight. He shot down one of the enemy and watched it fall into the ruined town of Bapaume. The other two Germans fled to the east.

Larry Callahan, who had just returned from a leave in London, noted that Springs had changed: "He was still supremely confident, even exuberant, but now that he was a flight commander, something that had been fun had become very serious." Other observers attributed Elliott's new attitude to the loss of Grider and theorized that since he felt partial blame for Mac's death, he was now volunteering for numerous missions. (In these forays Elliott shot down or damaged several planes which fell far behind the German front, so that their loss was unconfirmed.) Elliott also faced keen competition. Field Kindley, deliberate, mature and coolly competent, had taken over A Flight when Bim Oliver became ill and was running up an impressive score of kills. Springs felt that the squadron's third leader, Henry Clay of C Flight, was the ablest combat leader on the front.

Callahan also brought word that Elliott's friends in London had been mourning him—he had been reported dead on several occasions, and many tearful toasts had been drunk to his memory. Springs merely laughed at this news. He wrote to Lena of a rumor that he had been posthumously awarded the Distinguished Service Cross: "I am neither posthumous nor D.S.C. The Barflies' Union in Paris shoots me down in flames once a week. One fellow actually described my funeral to me."

Springs fought from dawn until dusk every day, but it was August 27 before he was credited with another kill. He reported briefly to Lena of the encounter against the Flying Circus: "Had a good scrap yesterday. Henry Clay got a two-seater—shot its wing off—and I got a Fokker biplane. Got it confirmed, too, luckily. One of the fellows below saw it spin down and crash and then burst into flames on the ground."

But that was only one of several battles that day, against a flight which had recently shot down several accomplished American pilots: "And now in three days, Tipton, Campbell, Hamilton, Frost, Siebald, Curtiss, Matthews, Todd, and Ritter. I'm feeling really depressed . . . my nerves are worn to a frazzle leading all these patrols . . . one of the most difficult jobs. . . . I want to get Huns and I try to do my work, but at the same time I'm trying to go easy on the lives of the men who are depending on me to pull them thru."

Catastrophe struck B Flight on September 2, a blustery day roaring with thunderstorms. Springs had led his men aloft to protect artillery spotting planes when scores of determined German fighters attacked. Even the support of Field Kindley's A flight could not save Elliott's pilots. "The Huns meant business and so did we," Springs wrote. "As soon as I would get on the tail of one, another would get me and as soon as I would shake him off there would be another. . . . My lower left wing buckled. I went into a spin. I thought the machine was falling to pieces and reflected with pleasure that I had forgotten my pocketbook. I thought of Mac and of how glad he would be to see me." Springs was kept so busy for a few moments that he could not follow the course of the numerous dogfights raging in and out of the clouds, the darkest day in the history of the 148th.

"But my plane held together . . . and I got out of the spin in time to hop a Hun. . . . I don't know how many Huns we got out of it. I'm the only one of my flight who returned."

The next day he was given new machines and new pilots were promised: "It means a lot of work now. I've got to train my flight . . . and it takes time to train a bunch of pilots. . . . My old flight was so good too. Good fellows, good pilots, all tried and true." He clung to the hope that some of the missing men would reappear: "They may have been shot only in the engine or petrol tanks and have landed safely in Hunland. There's always that chance." None of his men returned. As much as he mourned their loss he admired their courage and scorned some pilots of whom he had heard, men who broke under the pressure and escaped by landing inside German lines to reach the safety of prison. "They'd be better off dead," he wrote, "because they've got to live with themselves the rest of their lives.

"I wouldn't mind being shot down; I've got no taste for glory and I'm no more good, but I've got to keep on until I can quit honorably. All I'm fighting for now is my own self-respect."

Though no one blamed him for the loss of his flight, Elliott was depressed about the tragedy. He wrote to Lena, "The General was over here the other day and patted me on the back. Said he didn't consider it my fault that I lost my flight but that it was a good show from start to finish. That doesn't make me feel any better tho, nor bring me back good men. . . . This war isn't what it used to be."

During early September, as intensity of the ground battle increased, Springs and his new pilots were in the midst of furious fighting against the aggressive, but steadily weakening, German air force. Elliott shot down his ninth victim on the seventh of the month, a feat he mentioned only casually in a letter home. More important to him were his recent afflictions: "I occupy a unique position in the squadron. I am the only man who has three different and distinct kinds of itch in addition to the hoof and mouth disease . . . all the trench curses except fleas. . . . The Doc is quite proud of me."

Elliott flew another hotly contested mission against the Germans, a "ragtime patrol," on September 15 and barely escaped with his life as he attacked an enemy two-seater from the clouds. Springs killed the gunner and Starkey, his new wing man, finished off the German pilot by swooping upon his rear. The smoking enemy plane spun earthward.

Elliott noticed that one of his flight, Tubby Ralston, had already turned homeward for no apparent reason—and he now saw another of his pilots,

Jenkinson, break formation and circle, waving one hand insistently: "He evidently wanted to tell me something. I looked about—no Huns." Through gestures Jenkinson made Springs realize that his left wheel had been shot off and that he must make a crash landing.

He went through imaginary drills: "Cut off petrol and switch so as not to catch fire, undo safety belt, take off goggles." A stiff breeze should help him land safely, and if he could keep the wind on his left, it might support his left wing. Still, he thought, his right wheel would buckle, and the plane would overturn, but there was no alternative. Elliott had a brief memory of a pilot who had died a few weeks earlier when he unwittingly landed on one wheel after a combat patrol.

As he approached the home field, Springs met Ralston, who flew alongside, displaying a spare wheel for which he had returned. Springs nodded his understanding. Men on the field beneath him fired Very pistols to attract his attention, and mechanics ran beside the strip holding wheels in their left hands. An ambulance waited nearby. Elliott braced himself for the impact. He was headed into the wind at about 55 miles per hour. "Just before my wing touched the ground, I leveled off vertically and got my wheel and tail on the ground with my right wing low.

"It worked! She was losing her speed and it looked as if I was going to get away with it." But his left axle dug into the earth before he could reduce speed and the plane flipped over, "very gentle." The only damage was a broken propeller and a ruptured top wing.

Elliott climbed from the plane unhurt.

"I'll feel uneasy every time I land now," Elliott said.

On September 24 the 148th joined another British squadron in a melee against fifty-three German planes—"the warmest fight" of Elliott's career, as he recalled it. His plane was riddled and scorched by inflammatory bullets: "I could smell phosphorus and burning petrol and thought I was on fire."

During the ten-minute battle Elliott shot down his eleventh—and final—enemy plane: "I took a Fokker head on and we got off by ourselves. . . . I finally got on his tail and put in about 150 rounds. . . . I watched him crash near a railway."

His battle had only begun. "I went back in and hopped another but another hopped me and I had to turn to fight him. About ten more Fokkers came up and things got pretty hot . . . I decided it was time to get out of it as I saw twenty more Fokkers coming up."

Springs was surrounded by three Germans who peppered his plane, and he was saved only when Henry Clay and two others of C Flight dove to the rescue.

Three pilots of the 148th were forced down during this combat, one of them Larry Callahan. Elliott had "an awful sinking spell" when he reached his field and learned that Larry was missing. "It just made me sick at my stomach to think of him gone." But Larry returned late in the afternoon. He had lost a wing and managed to land behind Allied trenches near an anti-aircraft battery manned by British naval gunners, where he spent the day "swilling rum" with the battery commander and firing at German planes. The other two missing men reappeared later. Elliott mourned his plane as the day's most serious casualty: "My machine is so badly shot up that I am going to get a new one much as I hate to part with it. But I'm afraid it's done its time—I've had to have seven new wings on it in the last three weeks."

Elliott's war was virtually over. He shared a kill with Henry Clay on September 27 and two days later flew into No Man's Land and cut some crosses from the fuselage of the German two-seater they had shot down. Springs mailed the canvas scraps to his parents to be displayed later as souvenirs on the walls of his home—for the first time he had begun to think of his return to civilian life. He urged Lena to have the old White homestead in Fort Mill renovated for his use: "There's a good chance now that I may get to live there. . . . You needn't say why you are doing it but draw on Father for the limit. Mortgage the mills if necessary, and fix it up right." Despite his confident air Elliott must have realized that Leroy would veto this plan and that the old house would remain in disrepair. Then occupied by tenants who had no appreciation of its historic past, the White homestead would await his return for restoration to its former grandeur.

In early October Elliott was hospitalized once more. His old stomach ailment had returned, and he was also a victim of the influenza epidemic which was sweeping the globe. "A beautiful case of grippe," he wrote. "I'm a complete and total nervous wreck . . . a chattering idiot." Again he was sent to Paris for treatment, and though his stay there was brief, he fretted to return to combat. "God, I'm itching to get into it again," he wrote. "I prefer the front to all places I've ever been."

He rejected, for the second time, the post of chief instructor at the U.S. school of aerial combat in France—and was soon notified that he had been given command of a squadron. It was not to be. The withdrawal of German ground troops had now become a rout, and with the first days of November the armies realized that peace was at hand.

Astounding most Americans at home, the war's end came suddenly on November 11 while the armies still faced each other on the torn battlefields. Germany had collapsed from within. The High Seas Fleet mutinied at Kiel, a communist-led revolt paralyzed Munich, Kaiser Wilhelm abdicated and fled to Holland, and a German Armistice Commission was sent to France.

Armistice Day found Elliott in a bitter mood. He wrote to Lena:

Peace! The bells in town began ringing at eleven and the band struck up the Marseillaise and the Star Spangled Banner at twelve. The French are still dancing in the streets.

But I can find no enthusiasm. I went to bed a free man but I awoke with a millstone around my neck called tomorrow which pulls and pulls and will hang there 'til the grave. . . . I only scowl at everyone and demand another war. . . .

There is no longer the 'Front' . . . where every man is known by his merit, where a grim, tho sure, justice prevails. . . .

Peace! I find myself alive. Strange—I hadn't considered that possibility—I must alter my plans. . . .

Peace! We've shoved it down the Germans' throats; now let's find it for ourselves.

He took a particular pride in his squadron, which finished the war with the second greatest number of kills among the American units. The 148th had shot down sixty-six enemy planes with the loss of only eight pilots. This was only three victories fewer than Captain Eddie Rickenbacker's more celebrated 94th ("Hat in the Ring") Squadron, which had been in action three months longer. Considering its brief time in action, the 148th was indeed the "champion" of U.S. squadrons in France. Elliott was incensed that he and his companions who had fought with the British had gained little recognition. He complained frequently, if always in private, that hundreds of U.S. aviators had been neglected because the public had been regaled exclusively with the feats of the Lafayette Escadrille and its American successors on the French front, including Rickenbacker's squadron.

But though the role of his squadron in air combat was to seem glorious in retrospect, the terrors of these violent days would haunt him to the end.

Elliott had lost much of his patriotic ardor. "War is a horrible thing, a grotesque comedy . . . so useless." He also had a prescient view of the future. "This war won't prove anything. All we'll do when we win is to substitute one sort of dictator for another . . . in five year's time the sentimental fools at home will be taking up a collection for these same Huns that are killing us now and our fool politicians will be cooking up another good war."

Within two months, despite delays caused by confused and conflicting orders, Springs was on his way home. His youth had ended. Elliott would always look back to his five months at the front as the most significant time of his life.

VI / "I Have No Use for a Wife"

Elliott returned to New York in early February, 1919, to an amicable dockside reunion with his parents. The war hero seemed surprisingly fit. "He looks well and is happy as a lark," Lena noted. But he had little time for his family.

Elliott telephoned women he had known before the war and made a date with Rosie Quinn, a nightclub singer—a tryst abruptly cancelled when Springs fainted in a theatre on his first night ashore. He spent several days in a New York hospital suffering from pneumonia and "delirium" but recovered rapidly and was soon installed in his old room at the Vanderbilt. He enjoyed nightlife despite the grip of Prohibition, which had been foisted upon the country while he was at war (he kept his room well stocked with bootleg liquor). Elliott wired Larry Callahan to come from Chicago and join the fun: "Fleshpots in good shape," he reported. He lingered in the city for weeks, resisting his father's urging that he return home and begin work in the mills.

The exasperated Leroy scolded his son in letters and telegrams: "Serious mistake for you to stay . . . for so long. . . . I cannot see what you want to loaf around New York for. . . . Your attitude is a great injustice to me." He added more pointedly: "You are spending more than twice your income."

Elliott's responses were infrequent and half-hearted: "Regret expense. . . . Sorry you are worrying . . . but I assure you my intentions are good." One of his intentions (which he failed to mention to his father) was to become an author. Though he did return to Lancaster during the spring, his visits were brief, and New York always beckoned him back.

On one excursion to the city Elliott met two young writers, Charles Nordhoff and James Norman Hall, who were also just home from France. The future authors of *Mutiny on the Bounty* and other tales of Pacific adventure persuaded Elliott to collaborate on a history of American aviation in France. Springs made a false start on the project: "I dictated the first installment of it to the stenographer in the Vanderbilt Hotel. When I got hungry, I took her out to lunch with me, and that was the end of the story. Hall and Nordhoff went off to the South Seas to beach-comb, and I flew . . . in a race."

Elliott merely filed his hurried fragment of manuscript.

A few days later, still in defiance of Leroy, Elliott went to work for the LWF Engineering Company, a Long Island manufacturer of small planes. His first—and last—assignment was to fly an LWF plane in a pioneer cross-country race from New York to Toronto. It was a leisurely, but almost disastrous, race for Springs and Field Kindley, another veteran of the 148th Squadron. They left New York on June 25 and flew to Albany without mishap, but Elliott's brakes failed in the landing, and he veered across a runway and down a cliff, followed by a crowd of spectators. Kindley, who landed moments later, averted a tragedy only by deliberately wrecking his plane as he turned sharply to avoid the crowd.

Springs soon resumed the race in his repaired plane but was forced down on a farm near Batavia, New York, where he left his plane while he and his observer walked several miles to the nearest telephone. They returned to find a crowd of people gawking at the ship. The resourceful farmer had posted a sign: "See the Great American Ace and airplane that fell 2000 feet. Admission 50 cents." This experience apparently prompted Elliott to return and face his future in South Carolina.

Back home, he was called into Leroy's office, where he found his father and Lee Skipper of Lancaster, who was also home from a career as a wartime pilot. The old man told Skipper that he was to become assistant general manager of the Kershaw plant at a salary of $150 per month. Skipper beamed.

"And Elliott, I want you to go down to the card room and learn the business. Without pay."

This ceremony marked the opening of a decade of conflict over Elliott's role in the family business—a period during which Skipper rose steadily to become the key production executive for the Springs textile operations, and Elliott often wandered off to New York, torn between loyalty to his father and his quest of excitement. He had no enthusiasm for his father's plans, especially after Leroy sent a photographer to picture him at his first assignment—the digging of a ditch.

Lee, who had been Elliott's friend (and rival) since childhood, was the son of Charles B. Skipper, an engineer who had built the Lancaster plant for Leroy in the 1890s. During Elliott's school years, Lee studied at the Citadel in Charleston, South Carolina, and then at the Massachusetts Institute of Technology before returning to South Carolina.

Elliott and Skipper lived together in a boarding house in 1919 and 1920, and despite their long friendship Skipper found this the most trying time of his career. "Here I was living with a guy who wanted to get fired while all I wanted was to get ahead in the textile business . . . Colonel Leroy was so anxious for Elliott to learn the . . . business. Elliott never showed any interest. He would be in and out, writing in between."

But Skipper realized that Elliott was not wasting his time even now. He saw that beneath his air of bluster and defiance, Elliott was secretly—or subconsciously—preparing for the day when he must succeed Leroy: "He would grin and say, 'Well, I've been fired again.' All the while he was soaking it up. He learned every little detail. He wanted to know what made things work. He had an imaginative mind. There was never a dull moment when Elliott was around."

Elliott's endless quarrels with his father piqued the lively interest of Springs employees. Elliott seemed eager to satisfy their curiosity about these conflicts. One day while they were squabbling noisily in Leroy's office, the angry Elliott strode to a window and threw it open, so that all employees within earshot could hear his father in one of his most irrational moods.

Elliott was confronted with frequent reminders of the war as he sought to adjust to civilian life during 1919. Newspapers published conflicting accounts of his status as an ace. One claimed that he had shot down eighteen Germans "officially" and ten more unofficially—and that he had killed twenty-four enemy aviators within a span of five weeks. Many months were to pass before the War Department finally credited Springs with eleven kills, which made him the fifth ranking American ace, far behind Eddie Rickenbacker, whose total was twenty-six.

Ten U.S. aces were raised to the status of military aviators during the year, promotions that conferred increased pay, a rise in rank, and the privilege of wearing a silver star. Elliott was promoted to captain, but despite Leroy's urging, he declined to wear his aviator's star.

Later in the year Edward, Prince of Wales, visited the United States and made a formal award of the previously announced Distinguished Flying Crosses to a few American aces who had flown with the British, Springs and Larry Callahan among them. Elliott, Leroy, and Lena went to Washington for the ceremony. The citation mentioned some of Elliott's more spectacular victories in the air and praised his devotion: "This officer has at all times shown the greatest determination and courage."

Afterward Elliott blandly assured reporters that he intended to become a textile executive and would make aviation his hobby.

During his most memorable flight from his father, Elliott sailed with Larry Callahan to Europe in 1921 on a pilgrimage to the scenes of their wartime adventures. Springs was diverted by a shipboard romance during the crossing. The young woman was Frances Hubbard Ley of Springfield, Massachusetts, a recent graduate of Smith College, who was sailing with her grandmother on a European tour. Frances was the daughter of Harold Ley, an industrial contractor who owned valuable commercial real estate in Manhattan.

Frances was an attractive and striking, though not beautiful, brunette. In contrast to girls who had attracted him in the past, she was reserved, quiet, and lady-like, almost shy, elegant in manner and dress. Intrigued by her quick wit and superior intelligence, Elliott soon revised plans to tour the old French war fronts and devoted himself to the pursuit of Frances Ley.

During their stay in England, Elliott took her to Hounslow, the setting of his squadron's memorable departure for France. They also went to Maidenhead where, on the banks of the Thames, they acted out a romantic scene with the cool, sophisticated air that had become so pervasive in the postwar era.

"I love you," Elliott said casually.

"Oh well, what of it?" Frances said. "I love you, too."

They kissed for the first time.

Remembering the moment a few months later, Elliott wrote to Frances in lines that might have been quoted from the newly published tales of F. Scott Fitzgerald's young lovers. Springs wrote of how he had "weakly" declared his love "before the clinch. Unconvincingly? Perhaps. But . . . you know you would have been disgusted if I had tried to do it convincingly. . . . Anyway, you gave me to understand that I could drop the subject, 'twas of no consequence to you, what you wanted was amusement, you could get affection when you had to go home."

Elliott followed Frances across Europe until he and Callahan returned home in late summer, leaving the Leys to continue their tour. Elliott apparently proposed but got an ambivalent reply from Frances, which only increased his ardor. From the first day of their separation and for weeks thereafter he sent her a daily cable, each reading only "Love, Elliott." He continued to send these messages even while she was aboard ship in November on her return to the U.S.

He professed to miss her keenly and said he would "sell some cotton" so that he could return to her: "We could apply red paint to the rest of Europe. But after all, we did lose our taste for splashing red paint, didn't we?" He reminisced about the most memorable moments of their courtship: "A glass of brandy at the Metropole. Losing your hat on the river. Breakfast at the Cafe de la Paix. You ordering cocktails at Claridge's before I got there. . . . Running the elevator at the hotel. . . . Carrying you down the Rue Pigalle."

His unconventional love letters hinted that an intimate relationship had already begun, and he continued to write in this vein after his return to South Carolina, where his loneliness increased: "Yes, you are right. Hellsbells, why didn't we get married in Strasbourg? But don't blame me. . . . how I miss you. Wish you were here with me to make me stop drinking! . . . Wish you were in this country. Wouldn't we be raising hell, though! . . . I know I don't love you nearly enough—but for me this much is truly remarkable. . . .

"I wish you were within reach. I'd . . . dash to wherever you were and take you on a hell of a party and—and—oh what's the use?"

He returned to the humdrum of working in the mill: "Well, here I sit on a pile of cotton waiting for some farmers to come into town. I wish somebody down here had a sense of humor, mine is absolutely wasted." The town, he said, was "hell's wastebasket"—his time was spent in talking with farmers and "trying to dodge the parental wrath."

Elliott seemed to take a genuine interest in the mills only when they were threatened, as they were during 1921 when his father's employees went on strike at the Lancaster plant. Leroy crushed the union movement by closing his plant "indefinitely," dismissing "agitators" and "undesirables" and expelling them from the rented houses in his mill villages.

He avoided the "errors" made by other mill owners who had temporized with unions. Leroy told his workers that they could join any group they wished, including unions, but added, "The mill has a labor union of its own, which is run both by the employers and employees, and they will not stand for any outside interference. I am the President of the labor union here."

The strike passed "without friction," Leroy claimed, because "90% of the people were with us." Operation soon resumed at the old rates of pay and under the same working conditions.

In the same year Springs fell into a bitter controversy with a business partner. Leroy accused Charles D. Jones, who traded in cotton for him, with embezzlement and falsifying cotton transactions. Elliott was drafted to help his father assail Jones in the newspapers. The Lancaster Mercantile Company had gone into receivership, the result of misappropriation of funds by Jones, so Leroy charged. (Jones maintained that he had merely recovered personal funds he had invested in cotton futures for the firm—and that Leroy himself had caused the bankruptcy by his sudden demand for repayment to himself of a loan of $800,000.) Elliott felt increasing tension as the case developed and tried to help his difficult father at every turn. "The horrible part of it is that no matter what I do, Father will say that I did wrong. Our six lawyers are like a bunch of old women and they are all scared to death of Jones. They say he is a dangerous character. . . . This strain is costing me a fingernail a day," Elliott reported to Frances. "Everybody predicts some shooting and I believe I am the only man in town not armed." The comic opera affair kept the town in a turmoil.

Elliott was so concerned for his father's safety that he followed him discreetly wherever he went, hoping to deter any assailant. In return, one G. F. Latimer, the company's cashier, who had sided with Jones, shadowed Leroy day and night, until Elliott foiled him by emerging from the mill office one day and standing silently at his side. Still without uttering a word, Elliott followed the baffled Latimer when he retreated into a drug store and then dogged the spy's footsteps through the town until he gave up and returned to his home in frustration.

Soon afterward Elliott actually defended his father in a fistfight with Jones. He wrote a casual account of this to Frances, "Jones is out this morning with his face all bandaged and they say he looks pretty sorry. My scratches are hardly noticeable but my eyeball scratch shows and my thumb is badly swollen." He became a local hero as a result of this brawl.

The case was aired briefly in a courtroom packed with about two hundred men, most of whom were armed. The jury failed to agree, a mistrial was ordered, and the indictments against Jones were set aside at the request of the county prosecutor. Some years later Jones committed suicide after failure of his bank in Lancaster (he had lost depositors' funds by gambling in the stock market). The unforgiving Leroy received this news grimly and said, "I cannot lose any sympathy on Jones." He continued to castigate Jones as a blackguard. Elliott may have been unaware that the Jones episode revealed his deep loyalty to his father, but he did react to the absurdity of Lancaster's preoccupation with the squabble between the two ill-tempered men. "Sweet child, a word of advice," he wrote Frances.

"Never let anyone persuade you to live in a small town." He then set out to lure her to a life in Fort Mill.

Leroy and his Aunt Addie, apparently alarmed by word of Elliott's courtship, continually nagged him to marry and reminded him of the essential virtues expected in his bride. As he wrote Frances, she must be Southern, Presbyterian and of "Good family, under twenty-five years of age—no skeletons in the family closet. Both grandfathers should have been in the Confederate Army—and she must play bridge. The rest they leave to me. They don't care what she looks like. Thank God for a sense of humor."

Apparently convinced that Frances would eventually marry him, he began renovating the White homestead, expanding the stately old brick house by adding porches. He installed a swimming pool and tennis court, landing strip and hangar, and, though he seemed to scorn latter-day Princeton, he transformed one room into a small replica of the taproom of the Old Nassau Inn.

He searched the region for furniture which had belonged to his grandfather White and borrowed money to buy a stove, ice chest, and Victrola. He obscured his purpose in restoring the house: "I haven't decided which room will be yours yet. As to the permanent character of your visit—we will discuss that further later. Having been turned down once I am naturally timid about it.

"However, we won't cross our bridges until we come to them—or get tight."

He sold some stocks to buy rugs for the house but spent the money instead on bootleg liquor. "Now I ask you. . . . Would you have put that . . . in rugs and carpets or Liquor of the Realm? You know what I did. . . . As I transferred it to my chiffonier I caressed each bottle and realized that I shall most certainly end this life as a *drunkard* . . . I can't stir up any honor or regret. Only joy at the prospect."

He revealed more of his dependence upon alcohol: "Sober, I'm a nervous, serious-minded, conscientious, coldblooded wreck, who lives in the past with my mind amid the triumphs and thrills and noises of the front, still feeling the fears and anxieties. . . .

"But give me liquor, *Ah* . . . and I become a cheerful, optimistic little fellow . . . I get almost human. I get back to the irresponsible childhood that I never knew. I forget my glorious ancestry and the responsibility of the position I am to hold and the rest of the snobbery that has been so carefully taught me from the cradle."

His father, he said, was critical of all he was doing to refurbish the old White home. "You ought to hear the outrageous talking he's doing. No regard for truth or propriety. Says I have made a mess of the house and thrown away $20,000. . . . He talks of little these days but . . . the 'Folly at Fort Mill'. . . . the whole family is about to have convulsions over it." Leroy, who wanted Elliott to live in Lancaster, was so incensed that he vowed never to enter the White homestead.

"God," Elliott wrote, "I wish they'd have another war."

He described his father's behavior to Frances: "His attitude towards me . . . is just one of general hostility. He will oppose any move I make. . . . He has a genuine hatred for anybody that likes me. . . . He hates all my friends—won't let them in the house—insults them . . . I am called a crook and a liar at every meal. I am accused of every scoundrelly vice. If I make a statement he will call in the Negro chauffeur to confirm it. He boasts that if he could arrange it he would turn me loose without a cent just to teach me a few things."

Frances returned from Europe in November 1921, and Elliott hurried to Massachusetts for a brief reunion. He returned to Lancaster in the grip of depression. He was "a worthless bum," he wrote, and insisted that he was unworthy of her. He seemed to yearn for marriage but out of fear that she might actually accept him, threw up defenses by recounting numerous tales of his wild behavior:

"Just because I've paused in my career of crime to make love to you is no sign that I'm going to bust my cocktail shaker . . . I do love you though and I'd like to say that I'd always do as you wanted. But I know perfectly well that I won't. . . . Have I really quit throwing wild parties? Isn't it a shame I can't sell my address book for what it cost me?"

Some of his letters to Frances revealed another source of stress and depression. His memories of France, though frequently lighthearted to the point of hilarity, were occasionally more painful than he had confessed to anyone: "I have been a nervous wreck ever since," he wrote. "I still wake up at night with the sound of screaming wires and the smell of brimstone." He had not forgotten the numbing dread of approaching combat: "I have seen 20 pilots at dinner when the phone rang with orders for the dawn patrol. After the orders not a pilot could lift a glass to his mouth with one hand. Ring a phone at dinner [today] and they still can't."

At the end of a vivid description of war scenes he asked her, "Does all this bore you? I've been under a strain ever since then and have never been myself so whenever I get on the subject it's hard to stop. Sometimes my mind stays back there with Mac and Larry and Bob and Bim for two or three days."

More than once Elliott wrote of the strong physical attraction he felt for Frances and of his longing to see her again: "I shall dash up and have a go at that dimple," and "the picture taken in Germany delighted me beyond words. I don't seem to have realized what beautiful arms you have. I rather liked them and thought them very nice, but I never got their full significance."

His declarations of love, however, were offered begrudgingly: "I never intended to fall in love with you, or anybody else for that matter, but I've gone and done it. . . . if you are going to take me seriously and lose your sense of humor as I have mine, well, I am going to get my hat in spite of hell. Because I love you too much."

He returned frequently to troubled reflections on marriage: "I am certain that I just can't get on without you—that I have no other interest in life but you. I love you so much that I'll never get over it. . . .

"But then I stop and think how shot to pieces I am—restless and subject to these spells of melancholia. And I can't picture myself as settled down and a bona fide husband. I know that someday Fritz or Jake or Larry would wire me, 'Meet me in New York. Have supply of red paint.' And I know I wouldn't go—but it would just kill me not to."

He confessed that he had not given up gambling, drinking, and the pursuit of other women and might be a poor domestic risk. "I'm not regenerated by any means. I'm making rapid strides in that direction, I admit, but I still have a long way to go. . . . I've wasted a year, am broke, internally shot to pieces, with a nervous system like a violin string, no future and no ambition.

"I can't do without you—but I have no use for a wife—quite the contrary."

With an ambivalence that must have maddened Frances, he then advised her to return to Europe as she had planned, but added impulsively, "And maybe when you get back in the fall I'll have everything arranged and all you will have to say is 'I do' and be entertained ever afterward."

He urged her to visit him in the White homestead in Fort Mill but could report only moderate enthusiasm from his parents: "Mother says she'd be delighted to have you come down for a visit anytime. She says she has no confidence in my taste but would welcome a fourth for bridge."

When Frances made a tentative response to this, Elliott wrote, "Of course I'm serious about the Fort Mill invitation. I just called up the contractor and told him to hurry up and I have written for some furniture catalogues." He also repeated his hesitant hints of marriage: "If I didn't think you had a sense of humor, I'd swear that I was building this house for you."

Leroy was disturbed by the prospect that Elliott might marry this Northern girl of whom he knew so little.

"What does her father do?" he asked.

Elliott knew a good deal about Harold Ley's finances but refused to tell his father. He said only, "We're engaged and will be married next year."

"I don't like it," Leroy said. "I don't think you should do this."

He went to New York, where he hired detectives to investigate Mr. Ley's standing and received a succinct report: "Ley can probably buy you out."

Leroy returned home, sought out Elliott, and threw an arm about his shoulders. "Son," he said, "I believe you are doing the right thing. I know you'll be happy."

There was similar activity in the North, for Harold Ley, who saw that his daughter was seriously interested in this unconventional young South Carolinian, asked a friend from Princeton to investigate Elliott. The subsequent report evidently eased Ley's concern:

> He is a very bright young fellow who is good at anything he undertakes. He comes from one of the best families in his vicinity. . . . He was quiet at college and did not mix much with his classmates except among Southerners. Without any apparent effort his scholarship work was good, he having been an honor man throughout his college course.
>
> He was rather fond of raising the devil . . . [at] parties . . . and . . . shone in this particular as he did in other activities. He was not known as being at all wild, but as a fellow who enjoyed his liquor, and was glad to have a party occasionally, without its apparently affecting his balance and gentlemanliness. . . .
>
> One would judge that this fellow is quite a star if his activities are becoming controlled as he gets older.

Frances was accompanied by her father on her first visit to South Carolina, and both of them were shocked to find the White homestead in a state of disrepair from years of occupation by tenants, its renovation barely begun and its grounds an unkempt jungle.

Frances returned for several visits in the next few months, and Elliott reported to her that she had made a favorable impression—his father liked her because she had refused to eat snails which Elliott had insisted upon serving; his old friend Rhetta Blakeney "raved" over her and other friends had congratulated Elliott on his "good taste."

Elliott's tentative, halting courtship ended in the summer of 1922 with the announcement of their engagement.

Leroy surprised Frances with a warm note of welcome into the family and the happy couple married in Springfield, Massachusetts, in September. Except for Larry Callahan, who had observed the courtship but briefly and from the viewpoint of a confirmed bachelor, there was no one to appreciate the marked contrast between the irrepressible Elliott and the genteel, shy, and rather naive young woman who was his bride.

Many years later their daughter said of this relationship, "Mother had a kind of Victorian upbringing. Dad was very dashing, and though he was 'wild,' he attracted rather than repelled her—even though she could not 'participate' in his wildness."

Frances was apparently happy in the village of Fort Mill as she settled into the imposing old house and completed its furnishing during several expeditions to New Orleans antique shops. But she made few friends in Fort Mill, and when the Springses entertained at the homestead, guests came from Charlotte and Camden or from the North. They saw Leroy and Lena but infrequently, usually in Lancaster. Leroy, still offended by Elliott's choice of the White mansion, carried out his threat that he would never enter the restored house. When he visited Elliott he always sat in his car in the driveway until their talk was over.

Whether his feud with Elliott prompted him was never to be known— but Leroy now stunned family, friends, employees, and the textile industry by announcing his retirement and the sale of his mills. The price was $10 million, and Leroy was to retain a stock interest. The new owner was a group led by Edwin F. Greene of Boston, which bought other Southern textile plants at the same time, creating a giant firm operating 362,000 spindles.

Supervisors and overseers held a farewell party for Leroy and presented him with a silver loving cup. Springs and Greene appeared at a banquet in Charlotte, where Leroy said farewell and announced that he would travel and play golf during his retirement. Greene outlined plans to make the newly enlarged firm a regional and national leader.

Several towns along the border of the Carolinas invited Leroy to join their community life. The nearby small town of Rock Hill, South Carolina,sent a delegation of three hundred men in a special train, urging Leroy to move from Lancaster. Springs finally announced that he had bought a large home in Charlotte, where he expected to spend most of his time.

But then, as abruptly as he had agreed to sell the family business, Leroy announced that the sale had been cancelled. After three months of fanfare he refused to execute the final documents—saying only that he did not wish to sell to "an international organization." (Greene's firm included one cotton mill in Nova Scotia.)

In the early years of their marriage Frances and Elliott enjoyed some common interests. She drove his expensive cars at high speed on the country roads of the region and once outran a South Carolina policeman across the North Carolina border and into Charlotte before she was arrested. She also rode horseback for a time and began to fly as well.

Elliott kept two small planes in a hangar a few yards from the house with a landing strip in an adjoining pasture. He taught Frances to fly and found her to be an ideal pupil; she flew unassisted after two hours and made landings after six. "Before she had ten hours," Elliott said with lingering surprise, "she did tailspins, whip stalls and vertical banks. In a plane she is accustomed to, she is as good a pilot as any I know." He also noted that she had no fear of heights nor of crashing; "the only time she was ever frightened in the air was when she found a caterpillar in the cockpit."

Still, Frances abruptly gave up flying after achieving competence as a pilot and flying for four years without serious mishap. For some unknown reason she stopped flying as suddenly as she later gave up horseback riding and driving automobiles. Elliott's recklessness may have prompted his wife's decision. To her dismay, he frequently landed on the lawn, dodging among the giant trees. But she must have been aware of his deep-seated need for flying, which he conceded was a form of therapy during his years of struggle with his father: "When I leave the ground I leave behind me all earthly things. I am a free soul until I decide to return. . . . When the world goes wrong, I go out and get in the plane. As my wheels leave the ground, so do my troubles fall away beneath me. A dive through the clouds, a couple of loops . . . and I am refreshed as if by magic slumber."

Among the vexations for which Elliott sought relief in flight were persistent but rather vague abdominal pains. His friends and doctors diagnosed his ailment as hypochondria, but in 1924 Springs finally entered a New York hospital where a surgeon "fitted me with an artificial duodenum." For some years thereafter he ceased to complain of his poor health.

In any case, Elliott's flying was not affected, and he became widely known in the region as an aerial daredevil, darting under bridges, diving upon buildings, and banking around the smokestacks of mills. He frequently performed aerobatics on public occasions. One Armistice Day he stunted for three crowds in nearby towns and was on his way to a fourth when he was forced down by an engine failure.

In August 1923, an imposing new bridge over the Catawba River near Lancaster was dedicated with great fanfare—the Buster Boyd Bridge, a high-level span built to accommodate the waters of a new lake. The governors of North and South Carolina were to address a large crowd, and Elliott was invited to fly his plane under the bridge. Though he was to be long remembered for the feat, he was not the star of the day, for he was more than two hours late. A barnstormer of the area had flown beneath the bridge before Elliott arrived.

Most of the crowd had dispersed by the time Elliott appeared, but he skimmed down under the bridge, dragging the tail of his plane into the water and then turned to repeat the feat, to the delight of the people still waiting on the bridge "on the chance of [my] hitting a pier or drowning." The small plane dove beneath the span, emerged slowly and limped down the river, narrowly missing another bridge before rising above the river bank to land safely in a pasture. Elliott discovered that a loose wire had caused two cylinders to cease firing. As Springs reported the outcome of this stunt: "Did he get a note of thanks from the committee? He did not." Springs claimed that the governor of South Carolina had cursed him for stealing the show, a palpable exaggeration.

During the next summer, 1924, Leroy and Lena were delegates to the Democratic National Convention, where Lena became the first woman placed in nomination for the vice presidency. Elliott's stepmother, who made friends readily and was widely known for her war work with the Red Cross, Liberty Loan drives, and the Federation of Women's clubs, became a convention favorite. The band added to her popularity by blaring out "Oh, You Beautiful Doll" each time she appeared. But her nomination was merely a gesture. The convention finally nominated Charlie Bryan, the brother of William Jennings Bryan, for vice president, and it was he who campaigned with the presidential nominee, John W. Davis, against the Republican incumbent, Calvin Coolidge.

Frances bore a son in 1924, an event which provoked the first recorded disagreement between the newlyweds. She wanted to name the boy Elliott, but Elliott himself insisted that he bear Leroy's name. They were still locked in disagreement when Frances was ready to go home, but the hospital refused to discharge her until the heir had been duly named.

"All right," Elliott said, "Julius Caesar Springs."

He was forced to apply for a legal change of name later, when he had prevailed over his wife and named their son Leroy Springs II. Elliott may have insisted upon the name as a conciliatory gesture, but it had no noticeable effect upon his father, who still refused to enter the White homestead. Leroy II, in any case, was to be known universally throughout his life as "Sonny."

Elliott later recalled with distaste the decade of the twenties under his father's critical eye, but in fact it was then that he realized a major accomplishment of his life. He began writing to escape the tedium of his unpromising career and within a few months became the author of one of the most popular books of his generation.

Characteristically, he left several versions of his emergence from the mills into the literary world. "My career was like a stop-and-go light," he wrote. "One day I would be Vice-President and the next day I would be office boy. In 1924 I was office boy again and, while my duties required my presence in the office, time was hanging heavy on my hands. So I began writing long letters to old friends to give the appearance of industry and, to make these letters more interesting, I turned them into short stories." This casual account fell short of the truth for, as Elliott wrote on another occasion, his interest in writing was fully rekindled only on June 18, 1925, the seventh anniversary of Mac Grider's death in France. Springs fell into a nostalgic mood as he rummaged through a trunk of his wartime papers, where he found the tiny thirty-nine page diary Grider had kept during the Atlantic crossing of the aviation cadets. Inspired to tell the story of his flying unit, Elliott first revised and expanded the sketch he had written in 1919 for the ill-fated collaboration with Nordhoff and Hall. He worked at home, undeterred by the household's new complexities caused by his year-old son or by the pregnancy of Frances, who was expecting a second child in November.

Moved by memories of the most vivid scenes of his life, Elliott worked at his writing every moment he could spare from his work in the mills, by night, on weekends and holidays. In addition to short stories, which were thinly disguised fictional accounts of the men he had known in France, he wrote a nonfiction narrative called "Back in the Summer of Seventeen."

It was near the end of 1925, about the time of the birth of his daughter, Anne, that he passed one of his war stories, "Big Eyes and Little Mouth," to Percy Pyne, Jr., an old Princeton friend who lived in New York.

Pyne took it to the critic Burton Rascoe, who was delighted with his discovery and showed it to Arthur McKeogh, editor of *McClure's Magazine*. McKeogh bought it at once. At this time Springs also learned that his nonfiction account of training for aerial warfare, "Back in the Summer of Seventeen," would be published serially by the struggling aviation journal *U.S. Air Services*, edited by Earl Findley, a war veteran who had never met Springs but was impressed by his talent as a storyteller.

Encouraged by his early success, Elliott yearned to write a full story of his war experiences. Ironically, it was Leroy's recurring criticism which led to his son's literary triumph. The old man denounced Elliott during one of their bitter confrontations in 1925, "You've never made a dime. If you want to please me, go make some money. I don't care how you do it—I only wish I thought you could. I'll judge your worth by the money you earn."

Stung by this ridicule, Elliott left the mill once more, hired a secretary and began full-time work in his home—a burst of activity that opened January 1, 1926 and lasted throughout the year. He now cast his story in the form of a diary, one ostensibly left by an anonymous pilot who had been killed in combat. His typist was Elizabeth ("Willy") Mills, a twenty-one-year-old stenographer whom he abducted from her job at the Bank of Fort Mill. Frances also typed for him on occasion, took a keen interest in his developing stories, and was especially helpful in reading proof and correcting Elliott's lamentable spelling.

Elliott dashed off the story on legal pads in his barely legible handwriting, and Miss Mills typed daily. He drew upon his own letters and memoranda written in France and the diaries and recollections of a few squadron mates including Bob Kelly and Larry Callahan. He used only a few paragraphs from Grider's diary. He combined these elements into a graphic account of life in wartime Britain and in the skies of France. Elliott was unable to use all of his own papers. For some reason Leroy refused to give him his wartime correspondence, those remarkable letters that had taken the form of combat narratives, perhaps in conscious preparation for this day. Elliott's complaint to Leroy was unusually restrained, "I'm sorry you and Lena wouldn't let me have the letters I wanted; they would have helped me considerably, but I realize how busy you have both been." Leroy finally relented and sent him copies of the letters Elliott had written to his stepmother but apparently refused to provide copies of many letters addressed directly to him. Dozens of letters to Lena (and some few of those to Leroy) appeared, almost verbatim, in *War Birds*.

Miss Mills never forgot the months she spent with Elliott in the breakfast room of the White homestead. "It was the most demanding—and interesting—work of my life. He usually wrote in pencil, and I had to decipher his scrawl, French phrases and all. I got real good at reading his writing, but it was the worst I've ever seen. I couldn't take his dictation. He used too many words I couldn't spell. I typed the first two drafts in triple space for ease of editing and then a final draft with four copies. He was quite particular, especially about margins, and I had to keep to those rigidly.

"He worked the fire out of me," she recalled. "That meant all week, Saturdays and Sundays and many nights until 2:30 A.M. When he was going good he would write on one typewriter, and I would copy on another."

Springs enjoyed himself. He frequently chuckled as he wrote and called to Miss Mills, "Hot damn, Willy, that'll get 'em."

Among several related and repetitious war tales written by Elliott in this hectic year, the final and most important was *The Diary of an Unknown Aviator*, a hilarious, often risqué, but moving novel of the 210 American cadets who trained in both the U.S. and England and then disappeared into France and the relative obscurity of the front manned by the British Royal Air Force.

Though he thought of his nameless diarist as Mac Grider, the narrative was in fact Elliott's own, focusing on the adventures of the Three Musketeers. Because he used Mac's shipboard diary only in his early pages, the action of the book took place over the eleven months following Grider's final entry. Elliott's account, in fact, continued for more than two months after Grider's death and described events of which he could have known nothing.

The spirit of American volunteers who had flown with the British was faithfully reflected in the book, but the technique was a blend of fact and fiction whose elements could never be accurately analyzed. As a later critic theorized, Springs may have been too modest to depict himself as the hero of the saga—or may merely have followed his literary instincts in choosing a doomed pilot as his anonymous narrator. Whatever the case, he obscured the origins of his "diary" by presenting himself as its editor and by frequently mentioning the names of squadron members, including his own, an elaborate deception that made future controversy inevitable.

The book lacked literary distinction in the conventional sense, but it was fresh, direct, realistic, and swiftly paced and a revelation to civilians nourished on heroic accounts of the World War. It was all there, just as it lived in Elliott's memory: the wild parties with uninhibited British actresses, drinking bouts, fistfights, card games, and constant defiance of military authority—and then the passage into the harsh climate of war, the nightmare hours preceding combat, the sickening growth of fear and the life-in-suspension on patrol, the chilling sight of enemy aircraft, the snarl of engines, the stench of burning castor oil, the whine of tortured wire struts, the rattle of machine guns and crack of antiaircraft shells, the plunging of the frail planes to earth, wreathed in smoke and flame. The vivid images of the young men of '18 evoked by Springs seemed more lifelike than the faces in his fading photographs: the gaunt, saturnine, one-eyed gaze of Mick Mannock, the insouciant grin of the baby-faced killer Billy Bishop, Mac Grider's ruggedly handsome countenance, the knowing wink of the urbane Larry Callahan, and a tantalizing glimpse of the complex inner life of Springs himself.

When it was finished, after a burst of concentrated effort, Elliott was undecided as to what he should do with the manuscript. At the suggestion of Frances, it was also sent to her father in New York, who showed it to the publisher, George H. Doran. Doran was encouraging but made no immediate offer to publish.

At about this time, Springs sent Mrs. Josephine Jacobs, one of Mac's sisters, the diary in which Mac had begun to record his war experiences. He apparently told her nothing of the book he had written.

Elliott's "diary" had a discouraging reception at home. Lena dismissed it as "very poor and uninteresting," and his father could view the manuscript only in the context of his endless conflict with Elliott. Though this early version of the manuscript contained no offensive references to him personally, Leroy said he was "deeply humiliated and mortified" by the book and appealed to Elliott not to publish it "just to contrary me." He also invoked the memory of Elliott's mother and asked him to withhold the book out of respect for "the beloved woman that gave you birth."

Leroy said the book was merely a collection of tales of "drunken orgies . . . fliers trying to see who could drink the most liquor, get drunk, how many dissolute women you could . . . prostitute." He warned Elliott that the family of Mac Grider would "naturally resent" descriptions of their martyred hero. He urged Elliott to write fiction, if write he must, and to use "fictional names" throughout. Leroy's real concern was for his own embarrassment in case his contemporaries read the book. "I feel that you have lost respect for me and Lena," the old man wrote. "If you publish such stuff I will understand it's no use for me to offer you any more advice on any subject."

Elliott apparently considered following Leroy's admonition, but, if so, his hesitation was brief. He later told his father, "I almost gave it up. What a book I could have written with your help"—but there was no pause in his production. He and Elizabeth Mills continued their daily work, Frances helped with typing and editing while servants tended the children. For the first few months there were only modest sales of other works to cheer the expectant Elliott. *Air Services* published another article, "Iliad 1917," in January 1926 and a month later began his seven-part reminiscences, "Back in . . . Seventeen." In the spring of 1926 *McClure's* published "Big Eyes and Little Mouth," the first of his stories, and Arthur McKeogh bought two more manuscripts. But there was a stream of rejection slips from major magazines including *Colliers, Cosmopolitan*, and *Century*.

In June the excitement of a major success with *The Diary* broke the routine of work in the old house in Fort Mill. Elliott seemed to be as surprised as anyone by his achievement. In some unexplained manner the manuscript of *The Diary* found its way to *Liberty* magazine. Elliott commented only that this passage was "strange." In any case Captain Joseph Medill Patterson, the new owner of the moribund weekly, saw the manuscript and felt that it would cause a sensation and expand his circulation. He bought *The Diary* for serialization. *Liberty* offered $5,000, but, at Elliott's insistence, that price was adjusted to include extra payment for all text in excess of thirty thousand words. Since he intended to make revisions throughout the period of publication, the length of the manuscript was still undetermined. (His final bill was to be $9,388.70, a new record for an American magazine story.)*

Over Elliott's objection *Liberty* retitled the manuscript *War Birds*, and as such the book was published weekly from August through November 1926, with the subtitle, *The Diary of an Unknown Aviator*. Elliott and the editors squabbled over the opening pages, which included material drawn from Grider's diary. In face of *Liberty*'s protest that this section was dull

---

*Among the revisions made by Elliott during the serial's publication was the insertion of a devastating glimpse of Leroy Springs, rendered by a son who had apparently lost all respect for his father but somehow still loved him dearly and hoped to emulate him. Elliott had obscured the source of this view of his relationship with his father as an observation by the "Unknown Aviator," when in fact the words were his own.

and superficial in comparison with the bulk of the manuscript, Elliott insisted that some of Mac's early entries be retained—but finally revised them to the satisfaction of his editors. (Privately he conceded that only one paragraph as written by Grider remained in the published version.) Springs failed to take *Liberty*'s editors into his confidence, and they did not realize that the "diary" presented was in fact a synthesis based almost exclusively on his own letters and other papers. But these details seemed to be of little importance at the time.

War Birds was a sensation from the appearance of the first installment. *Liberty*'s circulation soared, and editors were deluged with letters from readers, most of whom praised the work as a refreshing new kind of American fiction. One of Elliott's agents declared that the book was "the biggest smash that any magazine ever published," and another agent wrote, "You are now writing the best comedy dialogue of anyone."

Startled by the success of the story, George Doran took a second look at Elliott's manuscript and contracted to publish it as a book. Film rights were sold to Metro-Goldwyn-Mayer for $25,000 to be divided between Springs and Doran.

Critics generally hailed *War Birds* as a major contribution to the literature of the war—and its reception was especially warm in England. T. E. Lawrence, an R.A.F. veteran of almost ten years' service who was on the threshold of his literary career, praised *War Birds* as "a permanent book and a real and immortal part of our war with Germany. The British Air Force of today is grateful to you."

Sholto Douglas, another seasoned British pilot who had known Elliott in France, wrote, "No book can touch that one for its splendid and heartwarming story, and for the rugged manner in which that story is told . . . *War Birds* will always be the great classic of flying . . . [Spring's] disdain for all forms of rank and class consciousness was nothing short of superb. . . . And yet he could be extraordinarily perceptive. There was not a thing that missed the shrewd eye of this dynamic character."

Reaction from the British press was also highly favorable. The London *Observer* called *War Birds* "entirely a masterpiece." The *Daily Express* hailed it as "the finest book on the war that has yet appeared, and a finer will never be written." The *Yorkshire Post* said, "There can be only one possible verdict . . . it is magnificent."

Critical reception of the book in the U.S. was favorable but far less enthusiastic than the reaction of the public. The *New York Times Book Review* praised the "freshness and spontaneity" of *War Birds* but felt that it was hurriedly written. This reviewer, S. T. Williamson, suspected that the anonymous diary was not the work of a callow youth—or even of a single diarist: "Its beginning is naively collegiate, but so much does the writer change during eleven months that it is difficult to believe that the entries for the last few days are by the same hand that wrote the shallow entries of the first pages."

The real strength of the book, the *Times* said, lay in the author's depiction of individuals: "There is a character development . . . that hardly could be better done than if it had the freedom of portrayal of creative fiction."

The Bookman praised the author of *War Birds* as a "lusty, fantastic, romantically elevated young man" of extraordinary perception, wit, and courage. Though the reviewer found the book vulgar, he hailed it as a "tonic" for "these tiresome times." He said, "It stands out from [other] war books by the freshness of its record. . . . the most complete picture . . . of the men who flew in the war." *War Birds* was summarized as "a foolish, vainglorious, offensive . . . wholly unreflecting, unselfconscious book"— but also as one "of profound and most nostalgic beauty. . . brave with the gaiety of death around the corner."

William Alexander Percy, a well-known Mississippi poet, wrote a perceptive review for the *Saturday Review of Literature*:

> So much of the ardor, the . . . idiocy, and the heartbreak of youth [in this book] . . . has captivated the American reading public. . . . its very verve and excess strike us as peculiarly American and our Puritan scruples are anesthetized because the gay and bawdy incidents recounted are danced against a crimson backdrop of terror and tragedy and death. We have always wanted to know what those gallant birdmen of ours thought and felt in the brief, glittering interlude before they crashed, and at last this 'Diary of an Unknown Aviator' seems to tell us.

Percy was not content with this appraisal. He sensed that the book was not "what it purports to be" and wondered whether it was merely an entertaining hoax. "Is this a real diary? Can the name of its author be given?" He somehow learned of Grider's role in the book, investigated and was told by Mac's sister, Mrs. Jacobs, that *War Birds* was "based largely on the actual diary" of Grider. Percy asserted that the first twenty-four pages of the book, with some "verbal changes and a few additions," were drawn from Mac's diary. Apparently on the suggestion of Mrs. Jacobs, Percy went further and theorized that Grider had copied his shipboard diary into a larger book and continued entries through his combat career in France. The inference was that Springs had used a much more complete diary by Grider, destroyed it, and sent to Mac's family only the brief introductory volume. Percy felt that this theory was "strengthened" by the fact that a friend from Arkansas had sent Grider a blank diary book during the war. However, Percy also discovered that Grider had been killed on June 18, 1918, and not in late August, when the unknown aviator of *War Birds* was presumed to have died.

Grider's family was not long in challenging Springs with similar questions. In the midst of the fanfare of success, Elliott had an unsettling letter from Mrs. Jacobs, who claimed that Mac's diary had been the major source of the book. In the first installment of *War Birds* in *Liberty* she recognized the entries she knew "almost by heart" from reading the little diary and wrote to Elliott, demanding an explanation.

"It was not Mac's diary," he replied, and added without further explanation, "When it is finished, you may not want to claim it is Mac's diary. . . . Let the mystery remain dark." Both of Grider's sisters were dissatisfied with this response, and although they did not openly accuse him of plagiarism, Josephine Jacobs charged that Elliott's explanation of the facts amounted to no more than "mysticism."

In later episodes of the *Liberty* serial, Mrs. Jacobs claimed, she also recognized "many incidents familiar to me" from letters Mac had sent from France. "I felt McGavock's personality here and there [in *War Birds*] . . . I hoped and believed that the diary to which he referred in a dozen letters was still extant and that it formed the basis for some of the story." Through an intermediary Mrs. Jacobs asked Springs for a fuller explanation. He responded tersely, declaring that the two complaining women were "certainly not Mac's sisters" in spirit.

About this time a Memphis newspaper interviewed one of the Grider sisters, who claimed that Mac was the diarist and also confirmed the date of his death on June 18, 1918—enough to convince attentive readers that the final, highly dramatic pages of *War Birds* (dated in late August) could not have been attributed to Grider. Perhaps because this report was partial and inconclusive, it did not receive wide circulation—but letters from the Grider family (and allegedly from others) did give editors at both *Liberty* and George Doran & Company pause. They threatened to withdraw *War Birds* from publication "as a literary hoax" if Springs did not clarify the matter.

Elliott placated the editors and publishers by making a full explanation of the complex matter and agreed to write an introduction, signing his name and acknowledging his editorship. Still he refused to reveal his own role in writing the narrative and insisted upon leaving the impression that *War Birds* was indeed the work of a single diarist who had been killed in action. Elliott wrote in his introduction that Grider deserved the right to anonymity: "Would you dig up the Unknown Soldier and identify him to satisfy curiosity?"

That partial and oblique explanation seemed to satisfy both publishers and public. Silencing the Grider sisters was another matter. Springs had offered to turn over some of the proceeds from the book to Grider's family. He had sent Mac's widow $500 and promised to send more and said he saw "no reason why" he shouldn't provide some support—$50 per month—for the Grider boys. When Josephine Jacobs continued to protest and threatened suit, Elliott was tempted to tell the whole story of the book's genesis, whatever its effect. "If the sisters keep up their trouble," he wrote to his friend Preston Boyden, a Chicago attorney,

> I am prepared to prove that Mac gave me the diary. If that is not sufficient, I am prepared to prove that I wrote *War Birds* in 1919 . . . for an anthology of the Air Service, which was never published.
>
> I rewrote it again in 1925 in the third person as a series of short stories which were never published in their original form.
>
> I then rewrote it in the first person again and, for the sake of sentiment, attributed it to Mac. It is based largely on my letters, my diary and my combat reports. I also used Barksdale's diary and supplementary matter given me by Kelly and Callahan. To further favor Mac, I used a part of his actual diary. Both *Liberty* and Doran objected to the use of this as they said it was far below the other in standard and would give it a bad introduction. I insisted on using it and made some changes to satisfy them. However, I managed to keep the spirit of it so that it fooled Callahan and has now fooled the sisters into believing that he wrote the whole thing and I merely tacked on the end. I can readily prove who wrote what but I don't want to . . . I have my letters which were copied verbatim into it.
>
> But why spoil one of the outstanding books of the war simply because two fool women want to bask in glory? I think the thing to do is to ignore them. Why help them tear down what I have built up? If they insist on going to court, that is another matter, but I won't unless I am forced to.

Elliott suggested that Boyden "put these facts" before Judge Jacob McGavock Dickinson, a Grider relative who was legal adviser to Mac's family. Springs offered to consult with Dickinson and to "do anything about it that you and he may decide is reasonable. My original intention was to do something for Mac's boys and it still is. . . . If Judge Dickinson wants to know why I wrote *War Birds* as I did, you can tell him that Mac once asked me to tell the people at home about his triumphs in London Society. He was very proud of his success and outlined to me how he wanted the story to be told . . . I followed his instructions but had to make many changes to sell it."

Elliott was reluctant to reveal any of this:

My prime consideration is that Mac Grider should get all the credit for having written *War Birds* and for having performed the deeds therein described. If the sisters can figure out any way that this can be done publicly, I will be only too glad to shout it from the housetops. But all the critics are ready to tear it to pieces and should Doran or *Liberty* or myself state that Mac wrote it, or that any individual wrote it, we would have to withdraw it from sale as it could be proved a forgery. As *The Diary of an Unknown Aviator* no one can do more than sniff at it. The sisters are going to give the critics some straw for their bricks, ruin it as a book, take away what glory I have given to Mac, and force me to admit its authorship, which I will be very loath to do and would only do it to defend my name against their slander. They have everything to gain by shutting up.

Elliott was in bed at this time, suffering from a severe cold and the effects of an auto accident—broken ribs and a stiff neck. He was otherwise troubled: "My eyes have gone back on me . . . and I'm due down in Lancaster for another row with the old man." He also planned a trip to New York to sue the Hearst Corporation for "breach of contract" on another published serial, which he charged *McClure's* with "mutilating." He added, "However, I'm willing to run out to Memphis and look the ground over."

He appeared in Memphis a few days later, conferred with Judge Dickinson and made a settlement with him—Elliott paid $12,500 for the rights to Mac's diary, and the Grider family agreed to drop its challenges to *War Birds*.

It remained for Mac's son George to put the record straight in a letter of 1971 to a scholar then studying the Springs manuscripts: "I have my father's diary. It covers a period of ten [sic] days, beginning when the ship was in the harbor of Nova Scotia on September 1, 1917, and ending on October 1, the day before his ship arrived in port. I received the diary from my aunt, Mrs. Jacobs. . . .

"In any event, every syllable of *War Birds* dated after October 1, 1917, was written by Colonel Springs."

Elliott returned to one of the most furious confrontations with his father in the course of their lifelong conflict, a quarrel conducted chiefly by mail. In October, *Liberty* published the installment in which Elliott had inserted mention of the officious, meddlesome letters Leroy had sent to him in France. Though the comments in *War Birds* were ostensibly made by Grider, they were in fact Elliott's own, written long after Grider's death: "Springs is all right until he gets mail from home. I don't see why he . . . takes all this criticism to heart. . . . He must be awfully fond of his father to care. . . .

"He said that he had to get killed because he couldn't go home . . . his father would have a hero for a son and he could spend all his time and money building monuments to him. . . . But if he lives thru it, he says his father will fight with him the rest of his life."

Leroy responded to this revelation with a letter of outrage:

When I read the last issue of *Liberty* . . . I literally staggered under the attack—a bitter denunciation from my own son, advertised . . . in every city, town and precinct in America . . . charging me with unkindness, cruelty, lack of ordinary intelligence, a son slave driver. . . .

First, [Leroy wrote] I deny every word . . . I have copies of every letter written to you from the time you went to boarding school. . . . There is no word that can be construed, especially while you were in the war . . . in any other way than to express my devoted love . . . admiration and encouragement for your war career. . . . No bitter, outrageous . . . charges on your part can make me feel for a moment that I have not fulfilled my full duty as a father. . . .

To mildly express it, I am deeply hurt and humiliated and my heart bleeds for us both. I do not know how to appeal to you . . . you have left me at times when a father needed a son most. Your whole life has been self-centered and one of egotism.

Leroy came near to disinheriting his son in this diatribe, "I do not feel that I can ever forgive or forget . . . I would advise you to continue your career as you see fit . . . as I can see no chance of your ever coming into my organization, either during my lifetime or after I am gone." As an afterthought he charged that Elliott and Frances had "attempted to hightone Lena and me and treated us as if you are the prince and princess imperial . . . and your children have been treated as if something superior and that it is a condescension for us to even see them. I think I understand it all now."

Public acclaim for *War Birds* did nothing to alter Leroy's opinion. He refused to accept a specially bound copy of the book unless "the severe and uncalled-for comments against me are deleted."

Elliott responded to the challenge in kind:

About six months ago, you told me that I had never made any money. Since that time I have earned over $50,000 in a new business, by hard and faithful work. Are you fair enough to offer congratulations? No. I get only criticism from you. You are the only person who has yet criticized my work unfavorably . . . I gave you *War Birds* to read and you said it was worse than rotten and advised me to burn it. [Captain Joseph M.] Patterson said it was the most remarkable piece of writing he had ever seen . . . and it's going over big. . . .

I also have a book of short stories which will be out in the spring. Have you ever heard of any other writer getting three books on the press in one year? I never have. If you think it's not harder work than sitting in an office sorting yellow and white invoices, try it sometime.

He also insisted that he was happy as a writer and that entering the mill would actually reduce his income: he was earning as much as seventy-five cents per word—a rate of about ten thousand dollars in a month of twelve-hour days. "For one man working alone with one stenographer . . . that's more than I can make in a year at the mill."

Leroy was not impressed—and he now made no attempt to conceal from his friends his outrage over the book. He carried a copy to a meeting of his bank's board of directors and paced the floor, quoting from the book and cursing Elliott. "He wrote it purely to humiliate me," the old man stormed. And then, so it was said, he burned a pile of Elliott's writings on the main street of Lancaster. Only those who knew Leroy intimately realized that the great hope of his life remained unchanged—that Elliott would still "come to his senses" and assume his rightful place in the family mills.

These controversies with the Griders and his father did not seem to give Elliott pause. He could hardly meet the sudden demand for his work. *Liberty* published two new stories before the end of the year and ten more during 1927. By now *McClure's* had published another Springs war story, "The 18-Carat Angel," and also bought *Clipped Wings*, a short novel. *Cosmopolitan, Blue Book, Redbook, College Humor*, and *Harper's* also bought stories—in all more than sixty of Elliott's stories and articles were to appear within five years, virtually all of them (including three books) written during 1926; with few exceptions all were based upon the adventures of Elliott and his companions in France and England. The *New York Times*, citing this prolific output, hailed Springs as "a comer."

Despite his status as a novice, Elliott was difficult for editors. When *McClure's* shortened his long manuscript of *Clipped Wings*, he protested the "mutilation" and threatened suit. McKeogh chided him for protesting removal of two paragraphs from a story and said, "You're beginning to put too much importance on your work." He also advised Springs that he was expecting much higher prices than he deserved at that stage.

As *War Birds* completed its run in *Liberty* even the editors were loathe to see the excitement ebb. The final installment was followed by a lengthy note of explanation—in which the deception of the purported diary was perpetuated by the editors, with the acquiescence of Springs: "Here the diary ends, due to the death of its author in aerial combat. He was shot down by a German plane 20 miles behind the German lines. He was given a decent burial by the Germans and his grave was later found by the Red Cross—The Editor."

No mention of Mac Grider was made, but Springs appeared as if by magic from the pages of his book:

> *War Birds* is ended [the editor continued]. The young American flyer who, unknowingly, set down in diary form the greatest human document which has yet come out of the war, paid the supreme sacrifice of adventure.
>
> But other War Birds carried on. . . .
>
> Among the latter was Elliott White Springs of Fort Mill, S.C. Springs was the closest friend and confidant of the writer of the diary. . . .
>
> It seems that the public is reluctant to take leave of the little company of Americans whose story *War Birds* has told . . . and none is better fitted to carry on a record of their exploits than Capt. Springs.

Liberty revealed that Elliott had been writing stories from his war notes for years—and that his "first" short story, "Faint Heart—Fair Lady," would appear in the magazine two weeks later.

His secretary recalled that Elliott worked as hard as she did and was "always courteous and considerate" when they were processing his stories. Springs once called her on a Sunday morning to ask if she had completed a story. "Not quite," she said, "but I'll finish it if you need it."

"Well, I'm leaving for New York at 4:45."

"I did all I could but didn't make the deadline. He finished typing the story on the train up to New York."

Near the beginning of 1927 Elliott urged his secretary to take a job in the mill for the sake of her future. Elizabeth protested that she wanted to continue working with him for so long as he continued to write.

"But I want you to go now," Elliott said. "This work is petering out." Though Miss Mills did not know that Leroy had bribed Elliott by making him vice president and treasurer of the Fort Mill plant, she needed no further hint that the old man had proposed a truce, however temporary it might be. "I knew then," she recalled, "that he had given in to his father."

VIII / "The Unknown Writer"

Elliott's surrender came in June 1927 when he began work in his new job with Elizabeth Mills as his secretary. "He kept on writing stories for a while," Elizabeth recalled many years afterward. "He hid them in drawers and I worked on them with him. I often heard him chuckling as he wrote, and then he'd call me in and hand me a few sheets and say, 'See what you can do with this.' He enjoyed every minute of that, but not the mill work."

Elliott had told Leroy that he had four or five stories still unpublished and that he planned to complete those. Otherwise, he said, he would give his attention to the mills. He cancelled a trip to Hollywood to help supervise the filming of *Squadrons*, a play he had written, and halted negotiations to stage one of his stories on Broadway. These moves, as he pointed out to his father, entailed costly sacrifices.

Miss Mills saw that Elliott soon became unhappy in his new job. "He didn't work at first because he didn't have enough to do. He was fidgety. He would sit and file his nails or write letters." When she left stacks of mail on Elliott's desk, he simply laughed and handed the letters back to her. "You're always trying to make me work. You know more about these things than I do. Just answer them for me." He signed the letters as she had written them.

Elliott's father was a continuing irritation, and the Captain once became so exasperated by the old man's visits that he exchanged offices with his secretary.

"You don't want to do that," Miss Mills said. "Not with all this stuff stacked up in here."

"Yes, I do. When Father comes in and raises cain, there'll be no place for him to sit down."

But Elliott evidently intended to apply himself to the textile business. He wrote one of his New York agents, George Bye, "You are going to have to handle all my work from now on as I have gone to work. It's going to take all my energy to sell sheets. . . . But by handling [my work] I mean selling it, not reading it and sending it back to me. . . . Don't send it back with the information that it is rotten. I know that already. Any fool can sell a good story. . . . Get some big money out of it. . . . Give me a demonstration of the art of salesmanship in four figures."

Bye returned his stories, saying that none could be sold. He also complained that Elliott had sent him stories inferior to those already published. Thrown upon his own resources Elliott began badgering editors once more. Seven of his leftover stories were sent to "every editor in this country" and one was rejected six times by the same editor. Springs merely changed the title after each rejection and returned it to the editor, who bought it on the seventh submission. The worst of his stories, Elliott told friends, was one he had written in order to pay for a new plane, but that one was sold to the first editor he tried. "This is positively the worst story we have ever bought," the editor wrote. "Enclosed find check at our maximum rates."

One long story sold to a magazine at this time was cut by about one-third—and Elliott worked the rejected portions into three stories "and sold them for more than ten times the price of the original story." He later claimed that he had sold every line he had written.

His own success by mail and his failure to persuade George Bye to make submissions inspired Elliott to further efforts. He went to New York, bought a cane and a pair of spats, and sold half a dozen stories in ten days "at phenomenal prices." One publisher offered him a job selling advertisements.

He was so charming that he sold *College Humor* "Nurse in Vibe," a story which Bye had refused to submit, and still another oft-rejected story to *McClure's*. He then made two more memorable conquests at *Liberty*.

When the magazine's managing editor, Sheppard Butler, rejected "Fastest Lap in Lapland," a story in verse, Elliott besieged Patterson, who wanted to learn to fly. Springs took the publisher aloft at Mineola, Long Island: "I looped him and spun him and rolled him until I could have sold him the Brooklyn Bridge." *Liberty* took the story.

Soon afterward, a *Liberty* editor named Millar turned down a Springs story, and when Elliott offered to give it to him without cost, Millar tossed it into a wastebasket. "That's what it's worth in my opinion," he said. Springs retrieved his manuscript and took it to a party that evening, where he read the story to an enthusiastic audience. Captain Patterson, who was present, bought the story on the spot for $2,000. Elliott could not resist announcing that the story had been rejected by his editor that morning. Nor was this the last time he scored with the magazine.

One of Elliott's much-criticized stories was "The Non-stop Plight," a satire in verse on the epic 1927 transatlantic solo flight of Charles Lindbergh. The story dealt with the pilot's difficulties in performing normal body functions on the prolonged flight, and the editors of *Liberty* and other magazines rejected it for fear of offending the admirers of the folk hero Lindy.

When Lindbergh stopped in the nearby town of Spartanburg, South Carolina, on tour, Springs flew over to dine with him. After the meal, Elliott read aloud his burlesque. "He laughed until his tears soaked the tablecloth," Springs recalled. Moreover, Lindbergh advised *Liberty* "that they ought not to miss it"—and Elliott sold the "Plight" to the magazine for $2,000.

Elliott's secretary, who had married by now, noted that he enjoyed this phase of his literary career more than he had the lonely toil of writing at home. "He was very busy with books for a while. He had [a novel] *Leave Me with a Smile* bound in plaid cloth—they had a warehouse full of that." Elliott plunged into every phase of the production of his books and published some of them himself, under such names as the Elliott White Springs Publishing Company. He worked directly with illustrators, including Clayton Knight and James Montgomery Flagg, and did not hesitate to criticize and reject the work of these veteran artists until he was completely satisfied.

Elliott's publications continued to appear, belying his pronouncement that he had retired as an author and become a cotton manufacturer. In the four years after publication of *War Birds*, Springs published seven books. Four were collections of earlier short stories: *Nocturne Militaire* (1927), *Above the Bright Blue Sky* (1928), *In the Cool of the Evening* (1930), and *Pent up in a Penthouse* (1931) in a privately printed edition of three hundred copies.

Elliott made frequent trips to New York on literary matters, and these brought more clashes with his father. The two strong-willed, stubborn men, so similar in personality, now squabbled over Elliott's continuing publications—which poured from the presses during this period, leading Leroy to assume that his son had broken his word. In fact, the spate of repetitive works had been produced almost entirely during Elliott's year of seclusion. In addition to the short stories now appearing, there were also three novels, *Leave Me with a Smile* (1928), *Contact: A Romance of the Air* (1930), and *The Rise and Fall of Carol Banks* (1931)—the first previously published serially in *McClure's* as *Clipped Wings* and the second as *Above the*

Guns in *Blue Book. Rise and Fall* was actually a series of short stories, most of them also previously published. These all-too-similar novels illustrate Springs's penchant for overuse of his materials, a form of literary incest. *Leave Me*, the story of an army aviator who finds adjustment to civilian life difficult, was clearly autobiographical. If Elliott's claim is to be taken at face value, *Contact* was written in three weeks, to fulfill an agreement with a publisher—because Leroy objected so strenuously to the publication of *Leave Me*.

The old man was offended by all of these works and sent several of his employees to buy up copies of *McClure's Magazine* in which *Clipped Wings* (the original version of *Leave Me*) appeared in an attempt to prevent local residents from reading it. Of *Leave Me* he wrote his son, "I should not wish to have a copy of this book in my home. If you ever expect to engage in the cotton manufacturing business, I would strongly urge that you do not have this book published. . . . Your description of mill conditions, mill operatives and mill management will antagonize and be resented by all those in the mill business from operatives to executives." Leroy also warned that labor organizers would use the book as a text, an expose of cotton mill life by the son of a leading manufacturer. "Other mill owners," he said, "cannot understand why you would put your name to such rotten stuff."

Leroy persuaded Elliott to cancel *Leave Me*, which Doran was preparing. Elliott agreed, though he told Leroy that he would lose $50,000. It was only later, when Leroy, in a fit of anger, told Elliott that publication of the book was of no moment to him that *Leave Me* was scheduled for publication. Doran brought it out in 1928, but it was not a success. Elliott later conceded that his father's original judgment of the book was sound; it sold only five thousand copies when it was published.

The novels that appeared in the wake of *War Birds* had a common theme: an aviator, his true career ended by the Armistice, returns home to a difficult, humdrum existence—obviously an autobiographical tale. One critic commented that "the natural resiliency of Springs's mind" made it impossible for him to write such books convincingly: "He was far too intelligent and perceptive a man not to be aware of the effect of war upon its more sensitive survivors; but when he tried to make this the substance of his writing, it did not ring true. Cheerfulness kept breaking in. When for literary purposes he attempted to assume a point of view of failure or despair, he was not often able to do so effectively."

In the collected war stories that became the novel *The Rise and Fall of Carol Banks*, the hero is virtually indistinguishable from Springs himself.

During the war this flier also won a reputation as a bartender of genius: "*No* one ever asked for a drink that he couldn't and didn't mix. . . . He could make sump oil taste like Napoleon brandy. I have seen him make eggnog from henless egg powder, and I can swear he flavored julep in Bapaume with mint chewing gum." The return of Banks to an endless round of parties and drinking bouts in New York and New England is reminiscent of the work of Scott Fitzgerald—though Springs took his characters as they appeared to be—gay, casual, and one-dimensional; he did not probe into their psychological depths as Fitzgerald attempted to do. As the critic Clarke Olney wrote,

> This may seem to argue that Springs is superficial; but in one reader's opinion, his people carry more conviction than the tortured souls who grapple with obscure destinies in *The Beautiful and Damned* or, for that matter, [Ernest Hemingway's] *The Sun Also Rises* and [Michael Arlen's] *The Green Hat. . . .*
>
> At his best, Springs is preeminently a good story-teller. . . . His code is simple. . . . He is seldom sentimental. . . . [His] special talent lies in a racy, colloquial style, a wry humor, and an ironic twist in plotting. . . . Like many writers who are essentially amateurs, Springs is most effective when he sticks closely to things he has experienced or observed first-hand. In his stories of combat fliers, especially, and in representing the hard-bitten humor of intelligent fighting men, he has few equals.

The major weakness of Springs as a writer, Olney said, was his inability to judge his own work, "a deficiency by no means uncommon among artists great and small." But he added, "The proper way to evaluate Springs' literary accomplishment is to consider his best work, not his worst; and a collection of his best stories could make a sizeable volume. . . . Within a limited field, he could write with the best [of his contemporaries]."

Julian Starr, a journalist who worked for Elliott, was less favorably impressed by his writing. "I think most of Col. Springs' literary output was mostly just potboilers. He was a better salesman than he was a writer, and as a matter of fact I think he spent about as much time selling his stuff by trips to New York and talking with publishers as he did writing."

But Starr added, "He did make one contribution to American writing [of the day] . . . a new style . . . not with the happy ending or sweetness and light; it was a much more realistic style. He was a master of hyperbole . . .

something new, I think, to American magazine writing . . . in the period right after the war when people were tired of the heroics."

If Elliott yearned for critical acclaim, he did little to attract or encourage it. He once wrote to a college president who offered an honorary doctorate: "If the degree of Doctor of Letters were printed on Lastex it could not possibly be stretched to cover my subject matter. . . . My scribblings had no literary merit. I still have no illusions about that." Though he frequently feigned indifference to his status in the literary world in such fashion, he evidently bore secret wounds about his failure to win critical recognition. He claimed that Princeton was "slightly ashamed of the stuff I published."

Elliott never publicly clarified the extent of his authorship of *War Birds*, his most powerful work. Even in the 1980s the book is frequently catalogued as the work of John M. Grider, as edited by Springs. It was only in 1951 that Springs revealed, in the foreword of a new edition of *War Birds*, that the diarist was in fact Mac Grider, whose "spirit still lives on in the pages" of *War Birds*. Even then Elliott did not explain that he had used only a few pages of Grider's brief diary, which ended before the cadets landed in England.

This version, too, contained a misleading account of the book's origin. Elliott said that he had published the diary because Grider had "given me very definite ideas about how he would like it done in case I survived him." But he added, "Though *War Birds* is an individual story, intended only to refresh the mind of the writer in later years, it became the actual history of these 210 men. . . . Though it gives the opinions and prejudices of one individual, these . . . were shared by us all. . . . The ten men whose names appear in it most prominently read it and compared it with their own diaries and records. They gave their endorsement to it without asking for a single deletion or change." Springs made no further public explanation of the genesis of *War Birds*, and it was only in self-defense, against the claims of Grider's sisters, that he made a guarded confession of his methods. He never went so far as to claim authorship openly.

In his eagerness for immediate publication, Springs rushed other books and stories into print with little consideration of their literary merit—and in the process turned out much hack work and repeated himself almost endlessly. Elliott acknowledged that he had drawn heavily—almost exclusively—upon his war service for his stories and novels: "I wrote so much about my own experience that I do not believe that I could squeeze another drop out of it."

Still, though his work may be criticized as having been based almost exclusively on his few months at war, it is evident that he was much less effective when he strayed from this source. Particularly in collaboration with Gus Travis, a Charlotte, North Carolina, newspaper man, Elliott exhibited faulty judgment of his own writing and published much material of little interest or value.

Critics who passed over the work of Springs as unworthy of serious consideration may have been influenced by the rather bizarre pattern of his life, his sensational escapades, his myriad interests outside writing, and particularly by his deliberate abandonment of literature in favor of a career as a textile executive. A further barrier to an appreciation of Springs's work has been the inaccessibility of his voluminous papers, most of which remained closed until the preparation of this biography.

Helen Vassy Callison, a scholar who had limited access to some of the literary materials left by Springs, characterized him as "The Unknown Writer." One reason for the relative obscurity of such a popular author, she felt, was "the milieu in which Springs lived and wrote." Mrs. Callison quoted an observation of Henry James in his study of Hawthorne that anyone "who has written a book is in many circles the object of an admiration too indiscriminating to operate as an encouragement to good writing." James felt that the finest literature was usually produced by writers belonging to a group that furnished the "stimulus of suggestion, comparison, emulation." The solitary worker, James added, was "apt to make awkward experiments; he is . . . more or less of an empiric."

Though Springs knew a number of other writers, he saw them seldom and was on an intimate basis with none. Many of these literary friends were authors of war stories who wrote mostly for male audiences—Hervey Allen, James Warner Bellah, Clayton Knight, Charles MacArthur, Leonard Nason, Burton Rascoe, Monk Saunders, and John Thomasson. In later years he was friendly with writers who lived in his region: Elizabeth Boatwright Coker, Julia Peterkin, and Carl Sandburg.

Not only was Springs far removed from the influence of a literary group but he also lived in the midst of manufacturers and merchants who had no interest in letters—and for years he endured the scorn and displeasure of a stern, moralistic father, who not only perceived little value in a literary career but continually upbraided his son for what he considered a depraved interest in writing of aviators obsessed with gambling, liquor, and immoral women.

Though he did lack the informed criticism and intellectual stimuli he might have gained from a group of literary contemporaries, Springs exerted a strong influence on the popular literature of his time. The British writer and aviator Arch Whitehouse observed that there was little interest in the literature of World War I until *War Birds* appeared—and that the book inspired a flood of imitations, chiefly by pulp magazine writers. The influence of Springs on American films was also strong.

The popularity and dramatic appeal of *War Birds* seemed to augur well for a memorable Hollywood production. For at least eight years a succession of screen writers tried to produce an acceptable shooting script from *War Birds*, but all failed including William Faulkner, who had just begun his distinguished career as a novelist. Howard Hawks, already a celebrated director, felt that Faulkner could write the needed script. The Mississippian did not succeed, despite weeks of work and the voluntary inclusion of bits from his own war stories, "All the Dead Pilots" and "Ad Astra."

The script with which Faulkner and others began work had been produced by Elliott and Merlin Taylor, a New York playwright who collaborated on brief screen treatments, using some material from the book almost verbatim. Though hard work was needed, Taylor said, "a fine and thrilling play" could be made from *War Birds*—but "for the theatre this tale is too straightforward and uncomplicated." At Taylor's suggestion, "a Hun aviator," a British girl, and a love triangle were introduced. But, though it strongly influenced several popular war films of the period including *Wings, Dawn Patrol*, and *Body and Soul*, Elliott's *War Birds* was never filmed despite months of hard work by Taylor and others. Elliott did make several other film sales: the play *Squadrons* to Fox for $15,000; the short story "Aeneas Americanus" to First National Pictures for $5,000; and "Sky-High" and "One Who Was Clever" to Paramount for $4,000 each.

Protracted excitement was provided by the three-act play called *Squadrons*, based upon the adventures of the 148th Squadron in France. Elliott collaborated on this with A. E. Thomas of New York, who did most of the writing. Thomas leaned heavily on *War Birds* and made use of scenes in England, but the script wandered far from the text of *War Birds* in the end. Thomas worked on the play for some years, but though it was finally sold to Hollywood and it was praised by such theatrical stalwarts as George M. Cohan, Winthrop Ames and Jed Harris, *Squadrons* was never produced either as a film or a play.

Despite Elliott's fascination with literary life, his secretary noted a change in him during this time. "I could see his progress as he began dictating letters about the mill business. He was catching on. He was constantly thinking up new ideas. Anything different appealed to him—and once he had an idea he did something about it. No grass grew under his feet. He was interesting to work for because each morning he had some new scheme. He was always thinking of ways to improve the output as well as the working conditions of his employees—and later on to improve their living conditions. I never knew what to expect from day to day. He was so energetic."

The Captain, as Elliott was known, was popular with Springs employees from the start—but this was due to his reputation as a war hero and a celebrated author, for he had little contact with the workers in this period. "He was a loner and didn't mix with the general run of workers," Elizabeth said. "He once told me he would like to have a beer with my husband but couldn't do it because others would want to buy him one. He wouldn't do it—wouldn't try to be close with everyone."

As his attention turned upon problems of the family business, Elliott made an early attempt to modernize the company's dull, unimaginative advertising, which was then virtually nonexistent. To the old-fashioned letterheads of Fort Mill Manufacturing Company, whose design smacked of the 1890s, Elliott added the first of the double entendre slogans for which he was to become notorious: "You can't go wrong on Fort Mill sheets."

The effect upon the textile trade of 1927 went unrecorded, but Elliott was sufficiently encouraged to persist. When he saw an advertisement for the Simmons Bed Company depicting "Mrs. Vanderbilt's bedroom in Newport," the Fort Mill publicist was inspired to caricature. For his prospective ad he claimed acquaintance with a New York speakeasy hostess, by name Vanderbilt, a blonde temptress who was a "very very distant" relative of the Newport tribe. He first featured Miss Vanderbilt in an ad for Fort Mill sheets, as drawn by Elliott's old friend Clayton Knight—in the then-fashionable style of the illustrator John Held, Jr. Perhaps in order to avoid controversy, Elliott changed his heroine's name to Maizie Smith and devised an ad which presaged some of his future antics in the field.

The illustration for this projected ad of 1928 provided a treasure hunt for readers alert to salacious innuendo. Miss Smith's bedroom featured "Stop" and "Go" signs at the door, a bedside cash register (with "No Sale" rung up for the last transaction), a fire alarm gong, a taxi meter on the headboard, an oil can beside the bed. The sheets, turned down invitingly, were being toasted in champagne by a bejewelled Maizie. Elliott's maiden effort at advertising:

FORT MILL COLORED SHEETS
are chosen by
the popular little hostess
of Fifty-third Street
NO MATTER HOW SLOW THE PARTY
FORT MILL COLORED SHEETS
ARE ALWAYS FAST

This proved to be a false start, for the ad was apparently vetoed by Leroy, who was undoubtedly baffled by Elliott's elaborate joke. The whimsically appealing Maizie Smith had no immediate successors. The advertising campaign that was to jolt Madison Avenue and win national recognition for Elliott's sheets was still almost twenty-five years in the future.

The attention of the author-advertiser was now forcibly drawn to his father's affairs and to the future of the Springs enterprises. Elliott was by no means the only victim of Leroy's violent temper. The old man's altercations with his associates continued, and one of these almost cost him his life. For five years Leroy had hired Eldred Griffith of Charlotte, a prominent and experienced broker, to buy and sell cotton for him on a commission basis. Springs gambled constantly in cotton futures, and Griffith skillfully guided him through market fluctuations.

But in 1927 Leroy concluded that Griffith was "disloyal" and notified his seventy-six-year-old associate that their agreement would be cancelled. The books were audited, Griffith was paid $9,000, and the settlement was accepted, in writing, by both parties. But Griffith soon became convinced that he had been cheated out of about $100,000. He began to harass Leroy by telephone and halted him on the streets of Charlotte more than once, demanding a new accounting. Leroy replied that their business had been terminated and that he would not pay him more. He refused to discuss the matter thereafter and ignored warnings that the unstable and aggressive Griffith might cause trouble.

One morning in February 1928, Leroy was on his way to the office of a cotton broker in downtown Charlotte when Griffith hurried from a nearby building shouting, "I want to talk to you, Springs!" Leroy had a glimpse of the old man's angry expression and walked faster, but Griffith kept pace, warning him to halt. Leroy replied without a pause, "I don't want to talk to you about anything. Don't try it." A few seconds later, as Springs made his way through a crowd to the door of his broker's building, Griffith thrust a pistol barrel against his temple. Leroy felt a "dull shock." He did not hear the weapon's report, but the force of the bullet knocked him to his knees.

"He's killing me!" he cried to bystanders. "Don't let him shoot me again." He rose and staggered, half-blinded, into the street, still shouting, "He's killed me! Call Dr. Brenizer."

With blood flowing from his head he hurried across the street, followed by Griffith, who continued to snap the trigger. Springs heard the rapid clicking of the hammer as the antique weapon misfired (it was said to have been a relic of the Civil War). His vision still blurred by the blood, Leroy entered a crowded drugstore and locked the door behind him as Griffith approached.

"Don't let him in," Springs called, but someone in the frightened crowd opened the door and Griffith burst in. Springs turned back into the street, supposing that Griffith was still pursuing him. A young woman emerged from a restaurant, led Springs inside, and swabbed the blood from his face. Someone disarmed Griffith, and Leroy was rushed to a hospital in an automobile.

Dr. Addison Brenizer removed a bullet that had flattened against the skull. Leroy recovered rapidly and was released from the hospital three days later. Vowing vengeance against Griffith, he bolstered the state's prosecution of the case by retaining Clyde R. Hoey, a prominent trial lawyer who was soon to become governor of North Carolina. Griffith's trial, which opened two months later for an expected run of several weeks, ended within an hour. Leroy's anger had subsided, and he proposed a compromise under which the presiding judge placed Griffith under a peace bond of $25,000 to discourage further attacks.

Though there were no obvious aftereffects of Leroy's head wound, Elliott felt that his personality was permanently changed. In any event, his father seemed to lose interest in his mills; he devoted himself increasingly to playing the stock market, which was creating new excitement as it continued to rise to record levels. And once more, as he had six years earlier, Leroy agreed to sell the family textile plants. In March 1928, he negotiated with Edwin Greene to merge his business into a larger corporation. He and his partners were to be paid $14,500,000 in common and preferred stock, plus an unspecified amount of cash. But once more, after formal agreement had been reached, Leroy changed his mind and withdrew from the deal.

Leroy moved with Lena to New York, where they lived in the Ritz

Tower. He spent much of his time gambling in the stock market, caught up in the speculative frenzy of the time. Elliott appeared in New York, begging his father to withdraw from the market. He followed him during his visits to bucket shops and tried to persuade brokers to cancel orders placed by Leroy.

When he returned to Fort Mill, Elliott implored Leroy by mail, hoping to prevent the dissipation of his fortune:

"I beg and beseech you, please don't let those vultures in New York get you any further involved. . . . they'd be glad to see you busted tomorrow if it meant an extra nickel in their pockets." Elliott knew that his father was in the hands of two brothers of unsavory reputation. "When I see you under the influence of a pair of crooks like [these] boys, I can't believe my eyes and ears. They are notorious. . . . They get hold of some rich man and demoralize him by the use of likker and women. . . . Then they stick him by working off bad stock on him. The whole town knows. . . .

"I can't sleep for worrying over what these contemptible pimps are trying to do. . . . for God's sake, Father, stop before it is too late." He realized that his pleas were futile: "You will tell me where to go for writing you this and get very mad at me."

Leroy rejected this advice, even after the spectacular crash of 1929. Elliott continued to warn his father about the "crooks" who still plagued him to buy little-known stocks: "The stock market is not your business and you don't need the money. . . . Please stop now, Father. . . . You certainly don't want to risk the work of a lifetime on one turn of the wheel. You, who have ruled men all your life, are not going to end up as a pawn of the cheap brokers and tin-horn touts."

Father and son continued their squabbles on a variety of topics. A cryptic remark by Leroy about the death of Elliott's mother was a crushing blow to his son and prompted one of his most emotional challenges to his father. During one of their arguments Leroy said casually and apparently without further explanation, "Your mother died needlessly."

Elliott wrote Leroy a few days later, "Have you any idea what effect that had on me?" He continued with a rush of feeling: "Mother died when I was ten. Since then my love for her has increased from year to year. I never talk about her to anybody. I don't think I have mentioned her to you since she died. . . .

"Mother is just as real to me today as she was in 1906. I know she wants me to stick to you and do what I can to make your last years pleasant.

There is no hope for them to be happy . . . I know she is helping me to swallow your repeated insults, your false accusations. . . . Without that comfort I would have given up long ago."

He then tried once more to explain the conflicting emotions aroused in him by his father: "I will never be, nor do I want to be, anything but Leroy Springs's son. I have always tried to please you and have always hungered for a word of praise from you. The fact that I have never had one has been a great disappointment to me. . . .

"I thought once that if I had no business connection with you, we might get along. That did not work. . . . The fault is mine. I am your son and it is my duty to bow to your ideas, follow your direction. But I am nervous like you, and I am hot-tempered like you."

There was no indication of an improved relationship between father and son, but the old man was interrupted in his gambling spree by Lena's declining health. She had surgery in New York in 1930 and was soon taken to a mental institution in Baltimore, suffering from acute emotional problems.

In South Carolina, the Springs textile mills were faring poorly in Leroy's absence. He had delegated little authority to his subordinates, though the nominal leaders were W. C. Thomson, vice-president; Lee Skipper, general superintendent; and H. R. Rice, treasurer. Elliott, who also held the title of vice-president, found himself powerless. He complained to his father: "You told Lee not to pay any attention to me but to take orders only from you."

Elliott also made another rare confession to Leroy, which indicated that he was suffering one of his periods of depression: "I am blue, discouraged and despondent. The whole world seems headed for hell." He reported that the mills had been barely profitable in the final six months of 1929, with a net of $183,000. This was a devastating decline in profits. The mills earned about $1.5 million annually from 1922 through 1926, and in 1927 earned $2 million. He assured Leroy that the trouble was with salesmen in New York and not in the South Carolina management.

But he also confessed to his father that much of the blame was his own: "I have failed to be of any use to you. . . . As time progresses and I stand still, I naturally lose confidence in myself and mistrust my own judgment. Consequently I have been following your suggestions literally. . . .

"Somehow I have failed dismally. The best I can say for myself is that I did try. Now I am exhausted by my own effort. I no longer have the optimism to offer suggestions."

The Springs companies were fortunate to be in continued operation in these times. The Southern textile industry was wracked by labor strife in the midst of the economic stagnation that followed the stock market crash. In Gastonia, North Carolina, only a few miles distant, communist agitators had provoked a violent textile mill strike in which the local chief of police was killed, and the community's business life came to a virtual standstill.

Mill hands of the Springs empire—like others in the industry—were poorly paid in that era. Their incomes ranged from $10 to $12 per week for common labor (pickers and card hands) to $17 or $19 per week for the more skilled doffers and weavers. But though conditions seemed to invite labor agitation, the workers apparently felt an identity of interest with Leroy and his family, and there was little unrest. Elliott's children had begun to grow up as scions of the one wealthy family in an economically stricken area.

Elliott still had an eye for attractive women. He made occasional trips between the Lancaster and Fort Mill plants—more than were necessary— just to see two pretty girls who worked in his mills. Springs confided to a companion on one of these inspections, "See that one—she reminds me of the girl I had in New York the other night."

Elliott made occasional forays to New York, and there he was often accompanied on his tours of speakeasies and night clubs by his wartime friend, Jake Stanley. Jake's bride, Maxie, was not fond of Springs on first acquaintance. To her dismay he occasionally visited the Stanleys on Long Island. "He would arrive on our doorstep with a five-gallon jug of bourbon and a strange woman, often as not."

Maxie and Jake once forced Elliott to sleep on a couch, while his girlfriend of the moment slept in the guest room. Elliott complained to Jake, "I'd never do this to you," but Maxie was firm, and Springs was foiled. Maxie was determined to tolerate Elliott, however: "I had two little kids to bring up and he drank too much. But Jake said he had saved his life once in a dogfight and was his best friend."

In 1930, after eight years of marriage, Elliott made a rare—perhaps his only—attempt at formal apology to Frances. He wrote her a letter acknowledging his shame at having hurt her. He also pledged to control his heavy drinking. He added, perhaps in reference to his infidelity, "I've been selfish and inconsiderate and generally damn foolish. I'm surprised you've stood it as long as you have." He also apologized for the deep reserve that now marked his relationship with her. "Whether I give demonstrations or not I love you more than you think. Put up with me a little and I'll prove it."

Indeed, as several of his associates observed, Elliott was always circumspect when he was in Fort Mill. Friends might "pour him on board" his train in New York, but Springs was always sober when he reached home, and there were no reports of extramarital liaisons there.

Townspeople of Fort Mill probably gossiped about the pattern of domestic life in the White homestead in these years, and some must have noted that Elliott's family did not seem to be happy, for all the amenities it enjoyed. At Elliott's insistence, Sonny and Anne were reared much like wellborn British children of the era. The children lived in a wing on the opposite side of the house from their parents, under the care of an able, strong-willed nanny, Tony Dehler, and spent little time with Elliott and Frances. "I didn't know my parents well," Anne recalled later.

Tony, one of five or six servants in the household, was a young German who was usually patient and stolid, though authoritarian by nature. Tony entered the Springs home when she was in her thirties and was to remain with the family for fifty-three years, serving the second generation of children after Anne's marriage.

Anne reminisced much later, "I can't remember eating a meal with my parents until I was twelve years old, and I went away to school then." She also remembered that there was little warmth in family relationships. "No hugging or kissing, ever. And I never sat on my mother's lap." She recalled her mother as "elegant and proper" and both parents as undemonstrative almost to the point of indifference. "They never spanked us. Mother was not a disciplinarian. Tony did all that." The German woman was a health-conscious nutritionist; she fed the children only soaked rolled oats for supper for many years. And each morning before breakfast she led them on brisk walks of from one to five miles. Tony also saw to it that the children attended church regularly and lectured continually about sin and temptations. The governess also made them fluent in German, for they were obliged to speak only in her native tongue while they were in her presence.

Anne retained an almost dreamlike memory of the daily lives of her parents in the large, high-ceilinged rooms crowded with dark Victorian furniture, the walls hung with portraits of stern-faced ancestors and with more recent paintings of Elliott and Frances, scarcely less forbidding.

"Mother ordered the meals but never went into the kitchen," Anne said.

"Every night she bathed and put on a long gown—frequently velvet—and they dined at opposite ends of the long table. She must have been very lonely."

Anne recalled that there were almost no family vacation trips—and she remembered particularly that her parents never spent her birthday with her. "That usually conflicted with the Yale-Princeton game, and of course they went to that."

Elliott's daughter also remembered the all-night parties given by her parents during her youth, when she sometimes rose early in the morning to find people "still partying." In retrospect Anne realized that the lifestyle of her parents and the religious teachings of Tony Dehler created stress for her and Sonny. "We felt the conflict between the way Mother and Daddy entertained and the things Tony taught us. I felt it especially. Once Sonny said some of our guests were drunk and I remember hitting him and crying that it was not true."

Tony herself was so distressed by the behavior of house-party guests that she occasionally placed hand-lettered signs by the swimming pool: "Quiet is requested for the benefit of those who are sleeping." These scenes ended abruptly, Anne recalled: "It was just like the closing of a door when my grandfather died and Daddy went to work."

Leroy died in a Charlotte hospital April 7, 1931, after a brief illness, at the age of 69. At Elliott's direction he was buried beside his enormous plant in Lancaster.

Elliott made no final appraisal of the father he both loved and hated, respected and reviled—and had so signally failed to please—but he certainly realized that with the death of Leroy he had literally entered a new world. Though the most vital—if destructive—relationship of his life had come to an end, his father's enduring influence could be detected in Elliott's personality: an emotional instability manifested in occasional moods of depression and a strained, distant attitude toward his own children. More positively, Leroy had also passed to him an indomitable resolve to succeed and a shrewd and unconventional cast of mind which chafed at constraints.

The fortune left by the stern old man was to fuel the final phase of Elliott's career and help to make him one of the wealthiest Americans of his generation, but on the day of Leroy's death, the son was blissfully unaware of the pitfalls that awaited him before he could claim that fortune.

IX / "Stay at Home . . . and Work Like Hell"

Almost everyone who knew Elliott Springs—friends, employees, and competitors—expected the thirty-five-year-old maverick, now master of a princely fortune, to toss away his inheritance within a few years. As one historian noted, competitors were elated: " 'Here is this airplane-flying, book-writing playboy undertaking to be a textile executive. Our time has surely come.' "

These expectations were not unreasonable. Elliott's training had been brief and sporadic; his attitude was that of a rebellious dilettante who shunned regular work and publicly scorned the dull life of a textile magnate. His true loves were writing and the wild living his marriage seemed not to have cured. As the ever-convivial son of a hard-drinking father, so the gossips said, he would be incapable of coping with the textile empire left to him, even in the best of times. The added burden of the depression presaged certain failure.

And Elliott's task was to be infinitely more demanding than the most doleful of his critics supposed. Few people were aware of the realities behind the facade of the apparently flourishing Springs companies.

As he inherited them, the mill plants were valued at $7,250,000; annual sales were about $8,000,000, on a production of 36 million pounds of cloth. Leroy's net estate was valued at about $5,000,000, giving him an informal ranking as "the richest man in South Carolina."

Leroy may have deserved his reputation, but in the depression year 1931 this legacy to his son proved to be a mixed blessing. Elliott learned, to his dismay, that his father had left no will. Under South Carolina law he inherited two-thirds of the estate and Lena one-third. During a week's search for a will among his father's papers, Elliott discovered some unsettling facts.

The stocks in which Leroy had been gambling, 100,000 shares in a variety of corporations, were held in margin accounts by three New York brokerage houses—volatile securities so vulnerable to market changes that they might well be lost because of insufficient margin. Elliott turned to his former treasurer, W. R. Thomson, one of two surviving directors of Springs mills.

Thomson resisted Elliott's pleas that he sell some stocks in order to protect the portfolio on the ground that he lacked authority. Thomson also said firmly that he would surrender financial control of company assets only to the administrator of the estate. Courts were prevented from naming an administrator for thirty days and would then automatically select Lena, unless she declined to serve. Troubled by her mental and emotional condition and uncertain as to her ability to handle the estate, Leroy's widow agonized over the decision for more than two weeks before waiving her right to act as administrator. Elliott then assumed the post.

Still, Leroy's New York brokers would accept no orders from Elliott until he became president of the Springs textile enterprise. They also made it clear that they would not hesitate to liquidate Leroy's accounts if prices should fall and new margin were required. Though for several days the temporarily helpless Elliott feared that he might lose his inheritance before he could extricate himself from the dilemma, he finally found a solution in the bylaws of the company: the two directors could choose a third, and a successor to Leroy could then be elected president. Elliott persuaded Thomson and his fellow director to cooperate and thus assumed control of his father's affairs.

He immediately sold some shares of stock to make the accounts secure for the moment, then hurried to New York to dispose of the "cats and dogs" in the large portfolio. Since there was no public market for some issues, he was forced to negotiate privately with the owners of such corporations as Gude Windmills, Wolverine Petroleum, Rainbow Luminus, Fashion Park, and Louisiana Refinery. He realized little from such stocks, and others were found to be worthless, without a market of any kind.

Elliott also discovered a complex pattern of debt among his father's corporations that, if not promptly resolved, would impoverish him. The Springs textile operations had a debt of $5,777,000, secured by all the assets of Leroy's estate, including the margined securities.

Leroy had made a verbal agreement with Thomson to liquidate the Lancaster corporation as soon as possible—but Elliott insisted that this could not be done, nor would there be any dividends until all debts were paid. Elliott slashed his own salary as president of the Lancaster Cotton

Mills and drew no salaries from the other mills nor from his father's other companies, the Bank of Lancaster, Leroy Springs & Company, or the Columbia Compress Co. He also waived his fee as administrator.

Thus far, though he had acted promptly and resolutely, Elliott's moves had been made in private. He now began to deal with his apparently insurmountable business problems under public scrutiny and did so with astonishing assurance and skill—and with the same unflinching courage he had displayed in France. Within a few months the industry realized there was a new force at work in South Carolina, and his competitors saw that they had seriously underestimated young Elliott. But he was tested to the limit by the formidable obstacles he faced.

His father's neglect of the physical properties, particularly after he was wounded by Griffith, had left some plants in a state of ruin. Elliott was forced to scrap half the machinery in the mills and to make extensive repairs to the remainder. He shut down the Springsteen plant and ordered all of its machinery "thrown out of the window"—every spooler, warper, picker and roving frame in the huge building. He converted the plant into a cotton warehouse. This was merely the first step.

Three-fourths of the workrooms throughout the system required new heating, lighting, wiring, humidity controls, and major structural repairs. Elliott had no delusions about the cause of all this disarray. Leroy's mismanagement had brought the enterprise to the brink of disaster.

For the past ten years, Elliott conceded in an official report, his father operated without adequate mechanical repairs and had deliberately neglected his plants: "The roofs of all the buildings had been allowed to decay. No floors had been repaired since the war, and the large surplus which had accumulated was entirely at the expense of the physical property." In fact, Elliott felt, the plants were in such deplorable condition that the only ready assets left to him were a stock of "questionable cloth, a personal account of the deceased president and an open account with a bankrupt commission house in New York."

Kindred problems seemed to be even more serious. The mills so poorly maintained by Leroy were producing second grade goods, albeit at high cost. Finishing, which was done by outside plants, was unacceptable to many customers. Sales were in the hands of commission merchants who sometimes competed as manufacturers. Housing for mill workers was almost primitive. Villages were without sewage systems, and water supplies were unsanitary. Recreational facilities, insurance, health care, and retirement programs were nonexistent—as they were throughout the industry.

Elliott had a clear choice: he could convert his liquid assets, close the mills, and retire to a life of luxury—or he could attempt to revive a sickly enterprise in face of the most severe handicaps in modern economic history. He did not hesitate.

Few people realized how fully Elliott had committed himself to learning his new business or how hard he worked at the task. Resolved to familiarize himself with every technical detail of cotton operations, Elliott kept a loom in the basement of his house and worked at it by night for several years, testing innovations proposed by his workers or supervisors. He absorbed these lessons quickly, and the experience left a deep impression upon Springs. He began to view textile mills in a new light.

Elliott discovered that "for a man who loves machines, a cotton mill beats an airplane." He undertook a serious study of the mechanics of the complex process that began with a bale of cotton and produced fine cloth from huge "thumping, whirling and crashing machines" that combed out waste, spun millions of threads onto bobbins, and whacked the bobbins back and forth in a loom one hundred sixty times per minute. He was not content until he had learned the secrets of all the machines in the plants.

Such intense concentration upon the technical aspects of the business, reinforced by his phenomenal memory, made Springs an increasingly effective executive. "He had total recall," one of his plant managers said. "Even after years of mechanical changes had been made, he could tell you everything that had been done mechanically in the plants. And, like any good, experienced mill man, he could walk into a plant and tell by the sound whether things were running right."

Thus Elliott's daily visits to his plants were not casual reconnaissances but rigorous inspections, based upon firsthand knowledge of the machines. His employees became convinced that he knew the origin of each machine, its date of purchase, record of repairs, its life expectancy, and capabilities. Few of his workers were aware of the long, secret process by which he learned the fundamentals of the business.

Springs developed a management style that was unconventional in other respects. He saw no reason to assign others to tasks that he could perform. He served as his own officer of the day. On Saturdays, as one of his executives recalled, Springs visited the plants in Chester, after spending the week in Lancaster, Fort Mill, and Kershaw: "He never took it easy like most millionaires. Other textile owners depended on their subordinates, who were sometimes good and sometimes not so good. He knew his business and attended to it in every detail. He visited all the mills every week."

By the time Elliott took over the family mills the greatest depression of the modern era had devastated the nation's economy. One-fourth of all Americans—about thirty-four million people—belonged to a family without a full-time wage earner. An estimated two million men roamed the country in a vain search for jobs. Farm families had been driven off the land by the collapse of food prices. One-quarter of the land in the state of Mississippi was sold at auction in a single day. In many areas, like Harlan County, Kentucky, where the coal-mining industry had ceased to operate, rural people managed to survive by eating dandelion and pokeweed greens and blackberries gathered from the wild.

In Chicago fifty men staged a fistfight over a barrel of garbage. Banks failed, and some cities and counties, now without money, issued scrip to meet their debts. In more than one bankrupt city, animals in zoos were killed and their meat was given to the poorest families.

Scores of textile mills had closed, many of them permanently, and survivors were operating only a few days each month—just enough to fill the infrequent orders for cotton cloth. Other mills in South Carolina were retrenching, and none of them had bought new machinery since the onset of the Great Depression. Control of almost any mill could have been bought for a song in the open market.

Against this background and by sleight-of-hand financing that seemed a near-miracle in later years, Elliott began the revival of his mills. He placed orders for 150 carloads of used machinery from bankrupt New England plants. He announced in a news release to a startled industry that the real value of this old but reliable machinery was about $10 million. He did not reveal the actual cost, which one of his men said was "about five cents on the dollar."

He prospected widely for bargains. From Westinghouse he bought 150 new motors at only $15 each, using some old models in trade. Elliott bought twelve thousand used long-draft spindles from Pacific Mills for ten cents each. "I spent a dollar a spindle fixing it up," he said, and this provided "about the best spinning I have." Elliott also found fifty thousand old Casa Blanca spindles that had been junked as worthless by three mills in South Carolina and had them modernized at low cost in his machine shops.

The old machinery performed miracles. There was Lee Skipper to prod the working force, and, as one plant manager said, Elliott had "some of the best rebuilders of machinery in the world in his shops." Elliott took pride in the performance of his antique equipment, which he insisted was the oldest then in use. To a friendly competitor who had claimed to have older dobby looms than those at Springs, Elliott wrote: "I question that seriously. I have 250 dobby looms at the Gayle plant which I am sure are older than anything you possess." He traced their pedigree through American textile history: "Baldwin got them from Whitmire, Whitmire got them from Laurens, and Laurens got them from the skipper of the Mayflower."

He then announced an order for millions of dollars' worth of new machinery from the firm of Crompton and Knowles. As a Charlotte radio announcer recalled the transaction: "All of Elliott's competitors thought the world was coming to an end, and none of them had spent a dollar on new machinery since the crash. But when they heard this news from Springs over the radio, they told themselves, 'He must know something we don't,' and began to buy. Crompton and Knowles soon had the heaviest bookings in their history."

He financed these moves by postponing all possible debt payments, diverting most of the cash flow of the mills and converting liquid assets—including "the last $50,000" of his personal funds. Springs reduced his risks to a minimum by abandoning the cotton purchasing methods used by his father, who had tried to "buy cotton cheap and sell cloth dear." Leroy was usually successful but had frequently been penalized by market fluctuations. Elliott virtually eliminated such risks by hedging—when he accepted an order, he bought cotton futures to fix the cost of making the cloth. Fluctuations in the cotton market were thus minimized, and the company's earnings came from manufacturing rather than speculation.

Elliott's goals were to keep his stockholders satisfied during the trying times, "and to see that our plants can meet competition," but he also had his employees in mind: "I expect to be the last one to reduce wages." His volume and productivity increased, a contribution from employees who were grateful for regular jobs in a period of mass unemployment.

Springs also provided an example for the industry by signing an agreement to eliminate night work for women and children in the Kershaw and Lancaster mills. A year before the inauguration of Franklin D. Roosevelt, Secretary of Commerce Robert P. Lamont congratulated Elliott on taking the lead in this field.

Roosevelt took office in March 1933, declaring that "The only thing we have to fear is fear itself." In the following months the intrepid Springs continued to confound his competitors. In the fall, when others were still sunk in gloom, Elliott bought an old J. P. Stevens mill in Chester, junked or overhauled all its machinery and equipment, and spent $651,000 in renovation. By the end of that bleak year he announced that he had more than forty thousand spindles and eleven-hundred looms in the plant—and was running two full shifts daily, despite an operating loss. He had resolved to keep his workers busy as long as possible. When he was unable to sell the cotton cloth he produced, Elliott simply stored it in warehouses to await a better market and continued to operate on such resources as he had.

But Elliott now began to feel the sting of the new administration's economic policies. He was forced by government edict to curtail production by 25 percent in 1933—but was denied an increase in prices to help compensate for loss of volume. Springs bristled at the high-handed methods of Hugh ("Iron Pants") Johnson, the chief of FDR's new National Recovery Administration (NRA): "General Johnson signed the order compelling me to do this but informing me that it was voluntary. . . . That leaves me halfway up a tree and I don't know whether I'm on my way up or down." The NRA imposed rigid controls over wages, hours, and working conditions.

Johnson's restrictive policies against industry, in fact, blocked an even bolder move Elliott had hoped to make. In the darkest months of the depression he made plans to revolutionize the family business by building a bleachery to finish his own goods. He hoped to manufacture sheets for the world market. Planning for this move had been under way for months when the NRA was created. Elliott felt that he could not launch the new enterprise under Johnson's regulations and gave up the idea. He was to revive it only ten years afterward.

If he found these years of desperate effort to save his mills distasteful, Springs made no complaint, but looking back years later, he distilled the essence of the experience into a simple formula. He told an employee, "The way to make money is to get into something you don't like, study it for five years and then go to work." And for continued success, he advised, "Stay at home, do it yourself and work like hell."

Elliott claimed that he had launched his career with no help whatsoever from even the most friendly of his competitors. Since he had no previous management experience and had never "sold a yard of goods . . . I was forced to look to my father's friends for counsel and advice. I got entirely different opinions from each source and, since no two could agree on any course of action for me, I was forced to fall back on the policies which had built up these corporations."

Elliott made other prescient moves that had little resemblance to his father's methods. By the summer of 1933 he had merged his refurbished plants into a single corporation, The Springs Cotton Mills, thus creating the nation's fourth- or fifth-largest textile firm. This consolidation ended Leroy's archaic system under which each mill operated independently, a tiny fief ruled by its plant manager. For the first time the Springs mills were to become unified with central departments for purchasing, personnel, law, engineering, and accounting. Wages and work loads were standardized, and each plant was assigned a specific production role.

Though there was scant hope of adequate profits in the next few years, these moves had an immediate effect on production and costs that was impressive to those familiar with the mills. Waddy Thomson, who had left the firm to open a plant in Greenville, praised Elliott: "I believe the investment you are making will prove profitable. I congratulate you on the good judgment you have shown in putting all the mills on a highly efficient operating basis. I think you have done a splendid job and have done it in a practical and conservative way."

Though there was no room for it in his plants at the time, Elliott continued to order new machinery with options to buy more as a protection against anticipated price increases. In the five years following 1933, when competitors were still retrenching, Elliott spent more than $95 million to modernize his plants, an almost incredible record. This investment required most of the firm's cash flow for years and strained its resources to the limit.

Springs had only begun his struggle to make the mills profitable when he was threatened by labor strife. Militant textile unions, with the blessing of the New Deal, moved into the South and attempted to close nonunion mills by sending caravans of unemployed or striking workers throughout the region. These flying squadrons, as they were called, forced many mill owners to close their doors.

Like his father before him Elliott was implacably antiunion and believed that his workers fared better under his paternalistic leadership than they would under the influence of the "radicals" who had invaded the South in hope of organizing the industry. Unlike Leroy, Elliott respected his own workers and felt an obligation to provide them steady employment and to improve their lot, in his own way.

Not only was Elliott one of the most defiant mill owners in the industry, he was fully prepared for a violent struggle and planned his defense against the unions in military fashion. His plane gave him an advantage over competitors who were also besieged by the flying squadrons. Rather than wait behind barricades he sent the company pilot Cecil Neal and one or two other employees to spy on the enemy in other towns in the Carolinas. "We flew to struck plants and mingled with the crowds, just listening," Neal recalled. "He wanted to keep up with things and know the sentiments of the workers."

At Elliott's request the sheriffs of nearby counties swore in special deputies to protect the mills, but he was determined to help fight his own battles. A *Time* magazine photographer posed him behind a machine gun mounted on a truck, ready to meet an attack from the flying squadrons, and a national audience envisioned the labor struggle in the South as civil war of sorts.

When an invasion threatened, Springs himself flew patrols over nearby roads, scouting for convoys of the enemy. He seldom found them—and in September 1934, in fact, he was taken by surprise when a flying squadron reached the town of Chester. Quite by coincidence Elliott was visiting one of his plants there when strikers from other textile towns gathered in front of the building and began hooting at workers inside the mill. Elliott went out to confront them.

"Who's the leader of this mob?" he asked.

Three men came forward and gave their names, "O'Shields, Head, and Tucker." O'Shields, a dark, burly, bald man from Union, South Carolina, was the spokesman.

"You'd better shut this damn mill down," he said. "If you don't, we'll close it for you."

The men denied that they would resort to violence themselves but said that not even the National Guard could halt the mob if Springs refused their demands for an election.

"We're going to keep going, too, until every mill in South Carolina is shut down," O'Shields said.

Elliott agreed to close the mill for a few hours while the strikers held a meeting across the street on the lawn of the National Guard Armory, but he refused to make further concessions. The mob now numbered several hundred, but no workers emerged from the Springs mill to join the intruders. For an hour or more union organizers harangued the crowd, but the strikers then dispersed.

O'Shields reappeared without his mob the following day and, in the absence of Springs, had a heated argument with A. H. Robbins, the general manager. Bystanders interfered to halt a threatened fistfight between the two.

When the raiders had left the neighborhood Elliott ordered four plants closed temporarily to avoid violence—but his Chester workers took matters into their own hands soon afterward. A band of men from Chester (many of whom were not Springs employees) armed themselves with ax handles and drove into the country where they overturned the cars of a flying squadron caravan and repulsed the invaders after a brief, furious encounter.

After conferring with many of his workers Elliott ordered production resumed. "They assured me that they were ready to defend themselves against further raids," he said, "and expressed great indignation at the affront to their own dignity. I begged them to avoid all violence and leave the matter to the constituted authorities of the state."

The Springs mills, meanwhile, operated on a full schedule, and, as Elliott said, "hundreds of extra workers" from struck mills applied to him for jobs. Other textile operators in the region succumbed to pressure by the squadrons, but the militant Springs refused to budge. After receiving threats against his family he merely sent Sonny and Anne to safety in Charlotte and continued his resistance.

Soon afterward, Elliott condemned the flying squadrons and the pro-union roles played by New Deal officials in a defiantly partisan outburst prepared as a radio address, in hope that it might become a rallying cry for Southern mill owners. For some reason Elliott's speech was never broadcast, but it circulated among his friends, who accepted it as a kind of credo of their own.

Elliott explained his resistance to the flying squadrons and his determination to continue operation:

What was I to do? Would anyone want me to desert my workers and leave them to charity while I went elsewhere? . . .

Whatever happens, I must keep my place beside my workers . . . a silver-tongued orator may, like the Pied Piper of Hamelin, persuade them to surrender their birthrights. . . . They may choose a leader in my place. But let this be known to all. I will never let anyone drag me into a fight with my own people. . . .

I agree with Mr. Roosevelt that the rights of humanity come before the rights of property but anyone who cripples my management and prevents the efficient operation of my plants throws a boomerang which in the end hits my workers.

I must have credit to buy my cotton. I must have customers to pay for my goods. I must have cash each week for my payroll. If there is strife between me and my workers there will be neither credit nor customers nor money, but, most important of all, there will be no work for the people. . . . To finish my present program of improvement I shall have to spend a great deal of money for machinery. Where is the bank to lend this to me if my organization is torn by strife? There must be confidence both in my management and in my workers before the money will be forthcoming. A wedge of bad feeling between us will ruin not only me but them.

These mills were built by my father and my grandfather. They were manned by the fathers and grandfathers of the present workers.

Then, overlooking the strike put down so firmly by the grim Leroy in 1921, he declared, "For three generations there has never been a serious dispute between us. There is no dispute between us today and the flying squadrons of terrorism have left our workers standing like a stone wall behind their looms—not for me and the company, but for their rights as American citizens to determine their own destiny."

Though the public was not to hear the speech, one of Elliott's friends from New York wrote of Franklin Roosevelt's reaction: "I gave a copy of your radio address to Walter Chrysler and he showed a portion of it to the President when he was with him last Friday. It made a profound impression on the President, who was amazed that such things could have been."

Elliott found an opportunity to address his employees with more positive results. He permitted the Textile Workers Union to hold a rally for his workers at the Springs baseball park in Chester and closed his plants for a time to permit employees to attend the rally if they wished. The meeting drew a large crowd for a free picnic and entertainment. Elliott listened from a seat in the rear as union leaders harangued the audience from a podium. After the unionists had denounced mill management, reminding his workers they were poorly paid, Springs mounted the platform and faced his employees with a calm, confident manner. He made no defense of his stewardship, but said,

"I've heard all the speeches. Since I own the company, it was interesting to hear what they said." He pulled a key ring from his pocket. "If you do strike as they want you to, I'm going to use these keys to all the plants.

"The day you walk out, I'll take my family and go to Europe. I have all the money I need. I don't have to stay here and struggle to keep the mills open and risk losing money.

"I'll also sell this park. I hope you will find other places to take your kids."

Elliott made his way silently through the crowd and disappeared. His vivid, forceful presence had an obvious effect.

"The son of a bitch means it," said a man in the crowd.

The subsequent vote on representation of the workers was virtually unanimous against the union.

The attitudes of his labor force toward unions were all that Elliott could have wished. They were poorly paid and lived and worked under harsh conditions, but like other Southeastern mill workers, they were the proud, independent descendants of early settlers, largely of English and Scotch-Irish ancestry. They identified their interests with those of Springs and his family and were easily inspired to resist outside influence by labor leaders. Many were members of fundamentalist sects whose teachings were anti-union. There were also traditions of violence and blind partisanship among these low-income white Anglo-Saxons whose lives were spent under the most parochial of circumstances.

Springs was well aware of the importance of this heritage in his struggle against the unions. He once sent a list of children in the Fort Mill school to a correspondent: "Please note the names on the class roll. The majority of these children come from families who work in the mill. I doubt if you would find such names in a New England mill community. That is why I think Mr. [John L.] Lewis and Mr. [Sidney] Hillman are going to have a tough time down here."

But government as well as organized labor continued the effort to unionize the Southern textile industry. In the wake of Elliott's victory over the flying squadrons, Secretary of Labor Frances Perkins sent investigators to Lancaster to probe his alleged discrimination against strikers. Elliott telegraphed his old friend Tommy Hitchcock, a New York investment banker with Lehman Brothers, "Department has advised me that investigation will be conducted by William Gaston now with Lehman Brothers. Is this correct and if so can you use your influence to see that I am sent to Atlanta [Federal prison] and not to Leavenworth?" Elliott reported that the agents sent to South Carolina by Miss Perkins were "pretty tough customers," some of whom were recalled "for preaching communism and starting revolutions."

But nothing came of this government investigation, and though labor unrest continued in the region, the Springs mills were never in actual danger of organization. The flying squadrons had threatened violence only in Chester. Elliott accurately forecast that a government probe of his mills would be "a mere formality," since union leaders had simply included all mill owners of the region in a blanket charge of discrimination against union members. "The man who made the charges against me deserted his wife and three children and disappeared some time ago," Springs wrote. "The wife is still working for me and consequently that will end any charge of discrimination."

By the end of 1934 Elliott had become so exasperated by government interference in his business that he was ready to join a third-party political movement. "The conservative Democrats now have their backs to the wall," he said, "and the wall is being undermined." The New Deal, he felt, had alienated most Southern business leaders: "I have been to three conventions in the last month attended only by staunch Southern Democrats, every one of whom voted for Mr. Roosevelt. There was not one of them . . . who would ever do so again." He despaired of the Democrats, but Elliott also rejected the Republicans, whose "stupidity" had discouraged even conservative Southerners from joining that party.

Despite his increasing irritation over Roosevelt's policies, Springs made occasional efforts to placate the New Dealers. In response to the president's charge that Southern textile workers were forced to live in mill houses and were "reduced to peonage," Elliott built fifty new houses on farm acreage near his Lancaster plant and offered them to workers on easy terms, for lease or sale. He reported the demise of the experiment a year later: "Not a one has been sold so far. Our workers prefer to live in the village and with rents so cheap as they are no one seems to want to assume the burden of taxes, upkeep and interest. . . . Since the mill has been running steady and paying good wages, there is no incentive to farm, though I believe truck farming on a small scale in this community would be very practical."

Though he realized that the textile industry, like the nation at large, could not emerge from the Great Depression for several years, Elliott had the courage and foresight to make handsome profits from purchases of stock. His investment acumen owed much to his close observation of conditions—and to his cynical view of the behavior of his competitors. In the unpromising atmosphere of 1933, he bought large blocks of textile stock, "in any mills represented by an officer of the Cotton Textile Code Authority, as I figured they were in a position to protect their own interests."

He also observed that some mill stocks were active only about the time the annual statement appeared, when they rose in anticipation of increased dividends or other good news—and then sagged for another year. He bought these when they were out of season and sold them just before the annual meetings. He also studied the activities of his competitors in the cotton market and bought their stocks when he noted that they accumulated inventories of low-priced cotton and were poised for a period of profitable operations.

Elliott's domestic routine, which had altered so drastically with the death of his father, remained remarkably subdued. The wild parties were a thing of the past. He sold his planes and gave up flying for several years. There was virtually no social life of any kind. Preoccupied by his work at the mills, Springs spent little time with his family. However, he developed the habit of taking his daily problems to his wife, pacing the floor, and reviewing the day's events as she listened quietly.

"Mother was a great listener," their daughter recalled. "She learned a great deal about the business. She didn't do much except make Daddy comfortable. Her role in life was to please him. He was always right. He was her project, her center of attention—she had been conditioned to that by her upbringing."

Though she devoted most of her time to her husband, Frances Springs had other interests. She raised orchids with such success that a South Carolina breeder named a variety for her. She frequently played gin rummy with Elliott's old friend Rhetta Blakeney. She made weekly trips to Charlotte, where she visited her hairdresser and sent her chauffeur into a favorite store for grocery shopping—and then spent the rest of the day playing cards with friends. On her frequent trips to a fashionable dress shop in the city she always carried sherry and biscuit and staged a party in a fitting room with her fitter and saleswoman.

One younger woman in Fort Mill whose husband worked for Springs recalled that Frances made several visits to her small house in an unfashionable neighborhood, keeping her chauffeured Rolls-Royce waiting while she enjoyed a meal of hotdogs. "I think she was embarrassed to order them prepared at home," her hostess said. In later years, as her poor vision worsened and she could no longer read, Frances watched soap operas on television, a recreation she concealed from all but her intimate friends. One friend felt that Mrs. Springs's reputation for aloofness in Fort Mill stemmed from her poor eyesight, because she literally could not recognize people even at close quarters—and was made nervous by the press of crowded parties.

Elliott's attention was drawn to his children's school activities on occasion—usually those involving Sonny. The boy began playing football in the sixth grade under the tutelage of his public school principal, Miss Righton Richards, a lively, plump young woman who was the daughter of a former South Carolina governor. Miss Richards, who played many roles at her school, coached football with a fine disregard for the rules of the sport that amused Elliott. Before each game she admonished her small charges: "Now don't forget—hold 'em. Hold 'em by anything you can get your hands on." Miss Richards explained her training for such a post: "I was brought up with six brothers—so it was fight or die. I fought."

Springs watched many of the games in which Sonny played and embraced him joyfully when he scored a touchdown—undoubtedly reliving the days when he had played so ferociously as a youngster at Asheville School. Miss Richards remembered Springs as an interested, even occasionally affectionate, father, but added: "I never saw Mrs. Springs hug her children. In fact, I saw Anne in her lap only once, as long as I knew them." Anne emerged from her childhood with the feeling that though her parents loved her, they had neglected her in some ways.

A reminder of his father's death was forced upon Elliott in the midst of his struggles. Eldred Griffith, the old man who had gunned down Leroy on the streets of Charlotte, called to demand payment of the $100,000 that he still claimed Leroy owed him. Elliott refused bluntly. Though he was warned that Griffith was having him followed continually, Elliott made light of the danger, because he went to Charlotte only occasionally and, as he said with an air of pride, drove "the fastest cars in Carolina, a Lincoln 12, a Master Stutz and an Auburn 12."

Still, Elliott hired an Atlanta detective agency to keep watch on Griffith and received reports on the troublemaker, who often appeared at the Charlotte barber shop where Springs had his hair cut. Griffith had tried to bribe a barber to call him when Elliott appeared.

A detective reported threats by Griffith: "I'm seventy-nine years old and I've got to look after myself ... I got beat out of more than $100,000—and I'm trying to get something out of some heirs now. It don't look like I'll get anything by going to court—but if I don't get my money I'll see to it that they don't get no good from it."

This menace came to naught, due either to Griffith's growing senility or Springs's evasive tactics. Elliott continued to make his infrequent trips to Charlotte without incident.

August 1934 brought a new crisis to the Springs empire when the only bank in Fort Mill closed its doors and left the town of two thousand literally without money. The only currency in circulation until deposits could be freed would be the payroll of the two local plants of the Springs Cotton Mills. Merchants were unable to offer credit, and the economic life of the community was at a standstill.

At the prompting of the National Recovery Administration, Elliott had agreed to curtail production by 25 percent by closing the plants for one week in late August. "This would be a calamity for the community," he wrote to the Code Authority in New York. He asked permission to remain open for the week and make up his assigned schedule later. "The mill is operating at a loss and I can assure you I have no desire to operate it except for the benefit of the help and of the community."

His request was eventually granted.

Elliott was increasingly perturbed by the "socialistic tendencies" of the New Deal. After President Roosevelt sent his "Soak the Rich" tax message to Congress in 1935, Springs wrote his New York banker, "I have suddenly lost my taste for business. . . . The tax rate is already pretty steep but I know President Roosevelt is going to increase this because he says, 'Wealth in the modern world does not come from individual effort . . . the people in the mass have inevitably helped to make large fortunes possible.'"

Elliott said that he had not counted on the government for help, because it was "a fair weather friend and the partnership ceases when I guess wrong. . . . the very eagle on the dollar screams at me in derision."

He warned that inflation would inevitably result from New Deal policies, especially from its welfare programs. "No man and no government has ever been able to distribute wealth. It is only poverty that is distributed. . . . The Roman Senate, caught between the power and popularity of the Caesars on one side and the rabble on the other, passed laws to feed, at the expense of the state, all who were born Roman citizens. Our Senate has . . . improved on the old Roman deal and now everyone who can vote will soon receive manna from The Great White Father, no matter where he was born."

The most trenchant summary of Elliott's anti–New Deal philosophy accompanied an invitation sent to another textile executive for the opening of the Marion Sims Hospital in Lancaster in 1940. "Our maternity ward will be [fully equipped] and, while it might be unusual to have a cotton shipper admitted to this department, we know that the government has already done everything to you but make you a mother and, now that they are going through the motions, we must be prepared for any emergency."

He became more secretive than ever in the conduct of his business.

"This organization has always been firmly opposed to publishing statistics of any sort," he told a competitor. "It has seemed to us that in advertising to our customers our production and stock of goods that we were sitting in a poker game where our opponents could see our hand and we could not see theirs."

A few days later Elliott confided to another manufacturer that he was expanding his plants, adding 1,350 conventional and 350 wide looms. His expansion at Fort Mill alone would add twelve thousand spindles. He also expanded the huge Lancaster plant and unceremoniously built the addition over his father's grave. "It's what he would have wanted," Springs told his engineer and refused to have the body moved. Springs told friends that he had moved his mother's casket from Charlotte to Fort Mill and that he had sworn he would not endure such anguish again. Though he was assured that the new section could be built around the grave, Elliott vetoed the suggestion—and Leroy's nearby resting place under the plant was marked only by a plaque.

X / "My Ragged Individualism"

Elliott's Christmas card for the year 1935 was a jocular promotion piece in disguise which, to his delight, distressed literal-minded recipients. A Wisconsin cotton manufacturer, Sam Schwartz, protested the "pathetic" picture of the barefooted boy and girl in the Springs mills: "Is it possible that your booklet would convey a holiday spirit with such conditions existing in industry? No doubt these conditions do not now exist in your mill since the Child Labor Act was enacted."

Elliott responded,

> The children shown in the picture are my own. I realize I should have either restricted the cards to my personal friends . . . or else put in an explanation. . . . No children under sixteen years of age have been permitted to work in the South Carolina cotton mills since 1911 and I thought this fact was so well known that an explanation would be superfluous. However, with all the vicious propaganda that has come out of New England and Washington, I am not surprised that some of my midwestern friends should misinterpret the card and I hereby apologize for misleading them.
>
> P.S. Also the workman in front of the picker happens to be me and the weaver behind the loom is my wife.

Few readers could appreciate the subtle impact of Elliott's little hoax. In fact, he had been influential in halting illegal practices of hiring young children and permitting women to work under intolerable conditions—practices which he never tolerated in his own mills.

Elliott received little credit for his role in this reform, but Robert Stevens, of the giant J. P. Stevens Mills, acclaimed him privately, "You alone are responsible for the recent success in securing 80 per cent [compliance] on the women and minors recommendation. . . . You have made a contribution to the industry for which all of us are indebted to you."

Mr. Schwartz, however, was not alone in his reaction to the Christmas card depicting the Springs family group posed in the mill clad in overalls.

Perhaps because of the local comment inspired by the card, Frances and the children came to resent Elliott's wry joke, and Sonny and Anne were particularly indignant because their father had exposed them to the ridicule of their schoolmates.

The National Industrial Recovery Act was declared unconstitutional by the U.S. Supreme Court in 1935, a body blow to the New Deal's program for reviving the U.S. economy. But not only did Franklin Roosevelt's popularity remain undiminished—many conservative industrialists sought to carry out his goals in other ways. Some textile mill owners, led by Walter Montgomery of Spartanburg, South Carolina, formed a Print Cloth Group to regulate wages and prices by voluntary action.

It was then that Elliott emerged as the leading nonconformist in the industry. He pointed out that this action would permit most textile mills to gain an advantage by operating without restrictions, and he declined to join the group: "I do not seem to be in agreement with your ideas. I have absolutely no confidence in the New York branch of our committee. I have never believed that any one group in the industry could lift itself by its bootstraps if competing fabrics . . . were left to seek their own level."

Thus far, Elliott said, he had adhered conscientiously to the NRA code and had gone further than required by raising "sub-standard workers up to [a total of] $12 a week."

His operating schedule in the absence of the NRA, he confessed, was so unsatisfactory that his instincts for survival must soon be tested to the utmost: "I am shutting down everything next week at all of our plants and my present policy will be to run just enough to feed our help. This is bad for the help and bad for the stockholders and I presume I will have to work out some other plan of action . . . at the moment I have not the faintest idea what it will be, but, if I expect to remain President of these mills, I will be forced to keep them on a competitive basis."

Elliott made further concessions to the curtailment program by closing most of his plants for three weeks at monthly intervals during the summer—but he adjusted his schedule to market conditions and continued to run without interruption at the Fort Mill plant, which had completed its assigned part in the program for the year. He refused to announce any of these moves until one week in advance of closing, but he was careful to keep his selling agents fully informed.

Though he expected his problems to continue for years, Springs felt that the textile industry would ultimately flourish as it never had in the past—and that the South was to be the scene of its renaissance. He was confident that the southward migration of New England mills would continue. Elliott rejected the charge that cheap labor was the major motive for this movement. Most New England textile workers, he said, "never see the real owners and managers and have a very hostile attitude towards their own jobs." By contrast, he said, "Southern mill workers are . . . cousins of the stockholders and managers of the mills. They have an affection for their jobs seldom seen in industry."

The Northeast, Elliott said, had lost its advantages—superior management and equipment—through "bad political conditions" that raised property taxes to an unbearable level. He claimed that the mild climate was an added advantage to the South, where living costs were lower, and cotton, the raw material, was also near at hand.

The scorn that he had been heaping upon the New Dealers Elliott now turned upon organized textile groups such as the American Cotton Manufacturers Association and The Cotton Textile Institute (which he called The Cotton Textile Prostitute). He regarded these organizations as enemies and, though he occasionally joined them, he as frequently resigned.

Most irritating to Springs was the insistence by leaders of these groups upon publishing industry statistics. He felt that revelation of production volume during slow markets placed manufacturers at the mercy of customers—who would know precisely when the overstocked mills were vulnerable to demands for reduced prices. Elliott went so far as to seek a court injunction against the institute to prevent publication of damaging figures, which he claimed were bringing ruin to the industry:

> Neither Japanese competition nor the processing tax nor the rivet in grandfather's neck are responsible [for the slowdown] . . . it will continue as long as our customers are informed by you that there is a surplus in our warehouses.
>
> My ten-year-old son knows enough about merchandising to realize that when he gets duplicates at Christmas he must swap them off one at a time without letting his victims know he has more than he needs . . . I regret that I should be a disturbing factor in this industry, but I still claim the privilege of cutting my own throat.
>
> I was raised to be a good Christian and always turn the other cheek but not even the Bible requires that I pay the traveling expenses of the gentleman who does the smiting.

He also suggested a means of muzzling pessimistic Southern textile barons when they gathered in New York for meetings: "Have [them] met at Pennsylvania Station by a brigade of bathing beauties bearing tubs of champagne, so as to put them into a good humor. Then they . . . won't walk up and down Worth Street telling all the customers that mills are over-producing, running too long, and are going to cut prices. . . .

"However, I realize that the majority of the industry is against me and feel that it is necessary to act as guardian for our customers and keep them posted as to when to buy cheap goods."

Elliott was hardly less irritated with policies of the American Cotton Manufacturers Association, whose "associate members" preyed upon mill men:

> I attended my first ACMA convention in 1906 in Asheville. It was a very pleasant and profitable affair. My next one was at Pinehurst in 1932 and it was a disgrace. The Bankers, Brokers and Bastards, disguised as associate members, took over the convention. . . . The minute any cotton mill man stuck his head out of his room, he was pounced upon by the waiting customers' men, salesmen and peddlers to be dragged off willy-nilly. I had never been so enthusiastically greeted since I landed in Paris in 1918, and for the same purpose . . . I ended up with four salesmen at my home for the week-end.
>
> I made the mistake of attending the convention last year at Palm Beach and am still nauseated. . . . The smell was so bad that a committee was appointed . . . to stop this hijacking.

This convention, he said, was dominated by a New York banker who had led the fight in Congress to abolish the United States tariff on textiles—a financial statesman who offended Springs with his proclamation: "I am interested only in International Business and not in Southern Slavery."

Elliott proposed an end to associate memberships, but, aware that his protests were in vain, he merely forbade his subordinates to attend conventions and withdrew the company from the association. No cajolery was sufficient to budge him.

Even during this cheerless time, Elliott's irrepressible sense of humor colored his conduct of the business—as, in his uninhibited fashion he conducted warfare against textile machinery manufacturers. Elliott was seldom bested in these encounters. He once invited Clare Draper to Fort Mill to witness the performance of fifty-two new Draper Machinery Corporation looms. The two men entered a plant that was shuddering under the vibration of the powerful machines.

"They'll shake down the building," Elliott said. "I want you to convert half of them to left-handed action to neutralize the effect."

"Impossible," Draper said. "It can't be done. It's never been done."

When the manufacturer left, Springs directed his shop foreman to make the conversions. The shop fabricated a few new parts, and the problem was solved with a minimum of trouble and expense. Elliott then asked Draper to return and observe the results.

"This was all we had to do," Elliott explained.

"Well," said Draper, "next time I'll know better than to tell you it can't be done."

To the president of another machinery firm Springs wrote: "I can assure you again that we are even more anxious than you to get our roving running properly. I was advised in October, 1937, that you were coming down to settle our dispute, but you did not arrive until January, 1938. While here you promised Mr. Rowe would be sent down as soon as possible to furnish the technical data . . . Mr. Rowe arrived in November, returned to the shops in December and advised us to hold everything in abeyance. He came back in February and left again in April to prepare a report. The only report we have received from him since was a picture postcard from Sweden."

At another point he wrote: "I have not acknowledged your letter . . . because my temper has been so bad I would have had to use asbestos stationery. . . .

"My organization is completely demoralized, my reputation is ruined, and my soul is seared with disgust. . . .

"It looks as if Saco-Lowell has now accomplished what the Institute and the Print Cloth Group have been unable to do, namely to curtail the production of The Springs Cotton Mills."

Elliott complained that his opportunity to produce fine broadcloth had been lost. From a production rate of only 15 percent seconds (defective cloth), weavers now produced more than 30 percent seconds—despite the use of better cotton and improvements to other machinery. He wrote: "I would like to say in all fairness to your organization that they have pro-duced some of the finest alibis that the textile industry has ever seen. . . . Your men have four times set the rolls wrong on your attachments and left the mill in hopeless condition. Their explanation . . . was always that the floor was dirty or the door knobs loose. . . . Your service has been criminally negligent."

Elliott reluctantly declined orders for broadcloth and told his customers that he could not produce it.

In the midst of these controversies a trade council promoter wrote

Elliott from New York, asking him to recommend a manufacturer of textile machinery with a reputation for honesty, quality, strength, and reliable service. Elliott responded:

"It is with deep regret that I inform you there is no such manufacturer in the United States. We have had experience with such manufacturers since 1889 and the only effort they have made was to take the gold out of our teeth. . . . We have never bought a loom that we did not have to rebuild within five years. . . . As for service, practically all the cotton mills in the South have been forced to equip shops to manufacture their own parts."

Elliott's impatience with his selling agents and suppliers became part of the folklore of the industry. His associates were seldom left in doubt as to Springs's opinions. He once wrote an agent who threatened suit over a sales contract, "As long as you can handle [sales] better than any other commission house, I will stay with you, but . . . the very day you cease to satisfy me you are getting a better price than I can get elsewhere, that very day I will notify you of a change in account." As to the suit, "it is too ridiculous to do anything more than treat it as the blackmail it is."

To a Charlotte cotton broker who was a longtime friend, Elliott wrote pointedly, "I notice you offer me cotton at one price and then when I do not buy you come back and offer it to me at a lower price, which makes me think I am a sucker to buy any cotton at all from you. If you expect a preference on my cotton purchases, then I have a right to expect your lowest price the first time."

In 1936, when Congress enacted a "processing tax" to be applied to the finishing of textile goods, a North Carolina bleachery advised Elliott that it would add a 1½ percent charge to its invoices. Elliott rejected this indignantly: "Of course I do not like the idea of the finishers getting together and going into an agreement to boost prices 1½ per cent. It is quite obvious that if they can get away with this, it is only a question of weeks before they get together again and boost prices.

"For that reason I am considering building my own bleachery."

One secret of Elliott's profitable operations in these depressed times was his astute judgment of the market in raw cotton. He bought twelve thousand bales in the futures market one spring, and by autumn, when prices had risen sharply and he might have turned a profit by selling his contract, he used the cotton to produce goods instead. The timely purchase of raw material at low prices enabled him to profit while competitors were struggling. As he pointed out to a friend, these profits could not have been made had he waited several months to buy cotton—a position in which many other mill owners found themselves.

Such intuitive moves—and his inability to delegate real authority—gave his friends pause. Waddy Thomson, the former treasurer who was still a director, told Elliott, "We'd never find anybody else to run this company if something happens to you."

"Nothing's going to happen to me," Elliott said brusquely.

Though his protests had little effect, Elliott was among the first Americans to campaign against the free import of Japanese textiles. He wrote to a newspaper editor, "For every yard of cloth shipped into this country by the Japanese, an American workman goes without as much wages." He predicted that Southern mills would be running half-time within two months and one-fourth time within a quarter. "By August the workers will be starving . . . the government has to have taxes to pay the WPA workers and if the cotton mills are shut down they cannot pay taxes and the mills . . . cannot buy equipment from the heavy goods or steel industries and other workers will be thrown out of employment." Japanese textile workers, he said, were paid five cents per hour, as against about forty cents per hour for workers in the Carolina mills.

Washington's New Dealers were hostile and indifferent toward cotton mill owners, Springs claimed, and had rejected all pleas to limit Japanese imports. Springs placed much of the blame for the import problem upon Southern congressmen who, "though elected to represent the Southern textile workers, sit idly by while the cotton mills in their own home towns are closed down in order that the Japanese might prosper. . . . The New Deal promised an abundant life for the working man, and it has certainly brought it to the Japanese working man."

Elliott was particularly incensed over the attitude of Frances Perkins, the secretary of labor, who was at that time holding hearings in Columbia on the plight of Southern textile workers. "She is freely discussing Social Security, minimum wages, maximum hours, unionization and other pet theories of the New Deal. Whether or not she is concerned with Japanese competition which is ruining the Southern textile industry is a matter which is locked within her own bosom."

Five years of concentrated attention to detail and battling government regulations, strikers, competitors, and suppliers had taken their toll on Elliott, so he claimed. In 1936 when he surrendered some of his more onerous duties to others and gave up the purchase of machinery, he explained to a salesman:

> Due to weather, my liver, the NRA, the AAA, the Wagner Bill, the rubber dollar, the gold bloc, the silver bloc . . . Japanese rags, Ger-

man bearings, The American Federation of Cotton Manufacturers, The Cotton Textile Prostitute, long draft, short traverse, high speed, slow rolls, big package . . . the Broadway uplift movement and the Park Avenue Callipygian movement, I find that my temper is getting the better of me.

When I reach home at night . . . my children dash frantically out of the house to hide in the barn. My wife has . . . been taking lessons in knife-throwing. . . . Illegitimacy is usually congenital, but I have achieved it through my own efforts and have become known throughout the trade as a self-made bastard.

Consequently . . . I am turning over the task of purchasing and rejecting new equipment to our Treasurer . . . I am going to take my family to the seashore for the summer. . . .

Each day I will go out on the beach and sit my ragged individualism down on the Constitution of the United States, the Sherman Antitrust Law, and the Clayton Act. . . . Sooooo, from now on, see the Treasurer.

Springs had lightened his duties at a time when it appeared that the clouds of the Great Depression might be lifting. Though it was to be a passing phenomenon, a mild business recovery began in 1936, and Elliott profited despite the low price scale then in effect. His associates noted his new spirit of optimism. During 1936 the mills declared their first dividends since the death of Leroy Springs—and Elliott made substantial loans from his own funds to settle intercompany debts. He also raised wages slightly and confided to a friend that he had booked "some nice orders" and bought cotton with which to fill them. "Business in general is good," he said but observed that his friends in the industry were publicly airing their problems with the government and the market: "They are trying to make cloth in the newspapers instead of the weave room."

His bold gamble of his family fortune to finance machinery purchases and plant expansions and to maintain full production schedules of previous years was paying dividends.

In the summer of 1936 Elliott took the first extended vacation of his managerial career and went with his family to Europe. The children spent several weeks in a Swiss household while Frances and her younger brother attended the Olympics in Berlin and travelled elsewhere. Elliott went off on his own to revisit scenes of his wartime exploits in France and then returned home.

To a reporter who asked if he saw any of his old battlefields, Elliott replied, "Yes, indeed. I went back to a cafe and found the same girl sitting at the same table, though the chair had been reinforced."

"Did she remember you as a friend during the war?"

"Yes, but she wasn't sure which war."

He crossed the Atlantic on the new zeppelin *Hindenburg,* which he hailed as a miracle of safe, quiet transportation: "It was a positively pain-less crossing. We went aloft at Frankfurt and two days and three nights later they closed the bar and we were ready for breakfast in New York. The ship is free of noise, vibration, rolling and pitching." He was especially impressed by the angled windows that provided glare-free views of the ocean from the passenger quarters.

En route home, Elliott befriended the urbane British author Alec Waugh, whom he entertained at his beach club near New York. He also met a German who had flown with von Richthofen's Flying Circus during the war. The whimsical Springs told a newspaper reporter that though the old aviators enjoyed the encounter, they fell into a violent argument and ended by choking their interpreter.

At Elliott's urging Frances and the children also returned on the *Hin-denburg* on one of its last flights, for it burned the following spring after a westward flight to the United States. The twelve-year-old Sonny was captivated by the experience and insisted thereafter that he was going to become an aviator.

Elliott's children were now growing up, but his relationship with them still lacked warmth and intimacy. Sonny and Anne attended public schools in Fort Mill and walked to and from school, always accompanied by Tony, whose presence was particularly resented by Anne. Even more embarrass-ing to the children were Tony's weekly visits to their schoolrooms—each Friday, on Elliott's orders, she sat in the back of the room to observe the manner in which they were being taught. Sonny and Anne usually wore overalls like most other schoolchildren of the town. "Elliott didn't want the kids to look 'big,' " one family friend said. Not only did he fear a kidnap-ping attempt; he was also resolved that his family's wealth should not be exhibited before townspeople—at least in such matters as clothing. Auto-mobiles and planes seemed to be exceptions.

Elliott occasionally schooled his children in sports. He taught Sonny to shoot and gave both of them elementary tennis lessons. He sometimes swam with them, though, as Anne recalled ruefully, "He had equipped the pool with those overhead trapezes in 1921, but when we were old enough

to enjoy them he took them down because, he said, they were too dangerous."

Elliott spent more time with Sonny than with Anne in an attempt to
establish rapport with his son. Elliott took him quail hunting when he had
reached the age of ten and two years later reported proudly that Sonny had
bagged a gobbler during one of their turkey hunts. The boy was also given
a motorcycle at the age of ten—both he and his father fell off, but Elliott
reported that it had been fun, in any event.

During these years Sonny usually ate breakfast with the family of W. M.
Epps, the town's chief of police, who lived a few blocks away. On his first
early-morning visit he explained, "Nobody's up at home," and was welcomed without question thereafter. Sonny's best friend was Steve Epps,
who was about his own age. The inseparable boy companions played in
the Epps home or elsewhere in town, but infrequently in the White
homestead. Sonny became more intractable as he grew older. He ran away
from home at least twice in his boyhood and was found each time at
Myrtle Beach.

On the rare occasions when Elliott took the children on trips, Frances
did not accompany them. Tony Dehler went along in her place and, as an
observer noted, "was like a mother to them—especially so to Anne."

Though his children may not have sensed it, Elliott took pride in their
accomplishments. He once wrote to his father-in-law, "Your grandson
graduated from Grammar School last night and, though his average was
97, he did not get first prize. Anne's average was 98 but she got no cigar
either. You have to be bright to get a prize down here."

Anne felt that she was neglected by her father, who seemed to favor
Sonny, but, as Elliott wrote to a relative, she outperformed her brother in
the Fort Mill schools. "Anne won the amateur night contest, playing an
accordion. Leroy [Sonny] has displayed no talent so far for anything but
falling off a horse, which he does with great regularity." Later he explained
that though Anne was younger, she was "larger, more active, more talented."

When Sonny was sent to Lawrenceville Prep in New Jersey in 1938,
Elliott gave the school a candid estimate of his son, a litany of parental
neglect and overindulgence: "School and life have been too easy for him
and he needs some incentive to ambition. He means well but has been
handicapped by a silver spoon. . . . Has had more toys, athletic equipment,
money, etc. than any other child in the county." Sonny, he added, had been

"somewhat spoiled" by a private swimming pool, tennis and squash courts, the private airport, and his own horse and motorcycle.

"He was always at the head of his class in public school but is no scholar and has never been taught the proper application and concentration. Quick to learn, but if he does not learn it the first time is easily discouraged and wants to try something else."

His goal for Sonny was a major in engineering at Princeton and graduate work in textiles elsewhere, "As he may some day own a cotton mill."

Two months later, responding to a complaint from Lawrenceville that Sonny talked too much, Elliott confessed that he could suggest no remedy. "His father and his grandfather before him both held the Junior World's Championship for free-style standing and running conversation with no holds barred . . . I am afraid it is a hopeless undertaking to curb this. . . .

"I note that he is impressed with his own importance, and that is one of the reasons I sent him to you this year. I sincerely hope that the masters will show no leniency in combatting this . . . I have forgotten the cure used on me but I recall that it was fairly painful."

Sonny made little progress at Lawrenceville, for which Elliott blamed the Fort Mill public schools, "where the teacher had classes too large for personal attention, and where he was able to lead his class without much effort."

Elliott punished the boy by sending him to summer school at Culver Military Academy in the hope that "they will keep him in irons until his behavior improves," but even the sterner regimen of the academy failed to reform Sonny to his father's satisfaction. He wrote to his son, "I wish you would not write unpleasant letters to your mother. I know you are required to write a weekly letter home, but you can take a piece of paper and write on it, 'I am well.' . . . There is no excuse for writing us two pages to complain about having to do it when you do not." Springs evidently did not sense the irony of this remonstrance, in light of the letters he had written home from France in his twenty-second year. Despite his complaints, Elliott enrolled Sonny for the term of 1939–40 at Culver.

Sonny's disposition and grades improved markedly during his stay at Culver, but near the end of it he wrote his father that he had decided not to attend Princeton as the family had expected. Elliott berated Culver officials as if they were responsible: "I have no intention of forcing Leroy to go to Princeton against his wishes . . . but neither do I wish anyone else influencing him to go elsewhere . . . I do want him to go to a first-class college and get a good education and not some state institution where he can loaf through."

In 1938 Elliott summarized progress during the eight years since he had merged his plants: Farmers had been paid $45 million for cotton, 780,000 miles of cloth had been delivered to customers, company salaries and wages had reached $31 million, federal and local taxes of $8 million had been paid, $4 million in dividends had been declared. All this, he added, had been achieved under certain handicaps: "Management has had its policies distorted and its prerogatives jeopardized by: The Depression, The Agricultural Adjustment Act, The National Industrial Relations Act, The Walsh-Healy Act, The Fair Labor Standards Act, The Excess Profits Tax."

Springs declined to close his mills "for the good of the industry" after the heyday of the New Deal. When he was asked to cease production for a month in the spring of 1938, he thought first of his employees: "a shutdown would be pretty hard on the help . . . I operate in small towns and the whole community is directly dependent on our payroll." In the end, he said, his policies had been the salvation of the mills.

His looms had increased from 6,500 to 13,000 and operated continuously on two shifts. He attributed this progress to the support of stockholders, workers, and other residents of the mill towns, "and the discriminating preference of customers all over the world."

He said that because his father had operated full time to guarantee continual employment, he had adhered to the policy. "This has cost me a great deal of money and all my textile friends, but it is too late to change it." Elliott was running his mills as long as he could to the limit of his resources, giving his employees maximum time at work, and was still simply storing cloth he was unable to sell at the time. Company trucks carried these unsold goods to warehouses as far distant as Charlotte. In fact, company warehouses were so full of cloth for so many years that Elliott formed a "mildew squad" to check the goods. A plant manager recalled, "We found whole sections eaten up by bugs and had to destroy them. We treated all the rest of the cloth that could be saved—and when World War II came along the mills made a fortune. That saved the Colonel."

By the end of 1939, with the war in Europe gathering fury, the Great Depression had ended for Elliott and his mills. His own salary for the year—a princely one for the day—was more than $141,000 and he also earned $106,000 in dividends, chiefly from his company's stock. According to his stringently conservative balance sheet, The Springs Cotton Mills earned almost $500,000 for the year and paid $193,000 in dividends. But Elliott now thought less of the profits for which he had struggled so long and more of the war of his youth.

Elliott had been desperately busy during these years, by day and night, on weekends and holidays, so that he virtually had no time of his own. His writing, which had once seemed so essential to his happiness, had been put behind him with apparently little effort. In 1938, in fact, when the editor of *Popular Aviation* asked him for articles, Springs replied, "I am trying to run a cotton mill, a railroad, a bank, a compress, and fly a plane and sail a boat in my spare time. Consequently, I am a little bit behind with my writing. I would be glad to oblige you, but I have lost my typewriter license."

Elliott's policies were not always appreciated by the residents of the small towns of his empire. Some businessmen complained that other industries were kept out because of Springs's domination of the area, at the expense of "progress." Elliott's associates conceded the truth of the charge but insisted that he had brought prosperity and stability to the region, asserting "we had no poverty and virtually no crime. He really cared about his employees and always did his best for them."

Springs was quick to resent other indications of ingratitude by residents of his empire. A $7,000 tax bill from the City of Chester for his Springsteen plant so irritated him that he forced a referendum on the matter. The people of the town, heavily dependent upon the plant's payroll, voted overwhelmingly to exclude the mill from its limits, thus creating the nation's only doughnut-shaped city.

Elliott was invariably prompt in arriving at his office—"like clockwork," as a telephone operator recalled, but he found time for what she assumed to be diversions. In an adjoining room he installed a model train, complete with a village landscape, and began most working days there with an inspection of the miniature railroad. The watchful operator said, "He'd start fooling with the train and ask me to call in Mr. Rippy, the maintenance man, and they'd talk and carry on over that train for quite a while."

His employees failed to realize that Elliott's rapt attention as he played with his toy train was related to his development of the increasingly profitable Lancaster & Chester Railway, which was now beginning to prosper with the reviving national economy on the eve of the Second

World War. In 1939 he gained wide publicity for the L & C with the purchase of the palatial car *Loretto*, which had been built for Charles M. Schwab, a former president of U.S. Steel. Elliott confessed that he bought the forty-year-old car for "a song and two whistles, just in time to cheat the scrap iron dealers." He carefully retained the splendor of the car's Victorian decor—Cuban mahogany paneling, gilt ceiling with carved cupids, crystal chandelier, velvet draperies, tufted leather upholstery, stained glass transoms, marble bath, and gold-plated beds. He had the *Loretto* remodeled for office use and parked it on a siding very near the White homestead. The car was complete with an office, pantry, kitchen, and two bedrooms, and Elliott added heat and air-conditioning as well as utility lines.

Acquisition of the *Loretto* inspired Elliott to further promotion of the railroad. Over the years he named twenty-nine vice presidents, "one for each mile of the track," including such celebrities as Lowell Thomas, Admiral W. F. Halsey, the golfer Bobby Jones, cartoonist Ham Fisher (creator of "Bringing up Father"), the writers Lucius Beebe, Samuel Hopkins Adams, James Warner Bellah, and Charles MacArthur (husband of Helen Hayes), his wartime friends Billy Bishop and Clayton Knight, the illustrator James Montgomery Flagg, the industrialist R. J. Reynolds, and later, Gypsy Rose Lee, the celebrated striptease artist.

The abbreviated rail line was much more than a toy because of its connections with the Southern and the Seaboard, and he took seriously his career as a railroader. When his requests for passes on other eastern railroads were refused, he responded huffily. To the New York, New Haven and Hartford, which replied that passes could be granted only to lines generating traffic for its own route, Elliott wrote: "[I note] that the New Haven does not consider the L & C Railway of sufficient importance to honor its officials with an annual pass. I have personally routed some 200 carloads over the New Haven in the past three or four months but you may rest assured that I will do my best to route this otherwise in the future."

Now, after a hiatus of about ten years, Elliott took up flying once more, perhaps because he felt that the threat of war hanging over Europe might bring him a second career in combat. He took a few lessons in Charlotte, flying a Cub trainer with Walt Mallonee, a youthful but experienced pilot. Mallonee found Springs to be "a very attentive" student who made takeoffs and landings without difficulty. In his second lesson Elliott flew almost flawlessly, winging over the countryside for two and a half hours.

Elliott continued his flying with the purchase of a Beechcraft, a stagger-wing biplane with a retractable landing gear that was a popular model of the day. He was not so much at home in the heavier plane, which had a cruising speed of about 200 miles per hour, but Mallonee schooled him thoroughly and sent him up for a solo flight. He gave Springs a final reminder: "Now don't forget your wheels. You'll have plenty of warning. If you forget to let 'em down the throttle will cut out, and the klaxon will sound, too—just be sure you remember."

Mallonee watched from a runway as his student performed perfectly in the air before descending for a landing. He saw that Springs had forgotten the landing gear. He shouted at the top of his voice, in vain, and could only watch as Springs landed the plane on its belly and finally lurched to a halt. "He just got to thinking about some big deal, I guess," Mallonee said. "He paid no attention to his throttle, nor to the klaxon either—but luckily he did very little damage to his airplane."

The new plane gave Springs an unaccustomed freedom which he relished. He made a four-thousand-mile flight through the Midwest and New England in the late summer of 1939 and felt "very much improved in body and soul. A cotton mill looks awfully small from 10,000 feet." Though he boasted that he might some day learn navigation in modern planes, he made certain errors: "I was unable to find Niagara Falls . . . and I picked up the Welland Canal in mistake for a river." Worse was to come when he flew into New York, for he parked his plane near the site of the World's Fair on Long Island without troubling to learn the location. He was unable to find it on his return. "Not even the New York telephone operator could locate it for me." It was apparently days later when the plane was found.

Walt Mallonee also discovered that Springs was a dangerously stubborn pupil at times. About a year after he had returned to flying, Springs bought a Waco that was powered by a 450 horsepower Pratt & Whitney engine. "Such a bad plane," Mallonee said, "that Springs acquired me with it." The pilot warned Elliott before his first flight: "Now, Captain, this one's different. You can't see over the nose, so you'll have a blind spot there. You have to use peripheral vision to see anything at all that's coming up ahead."

Mallonee found that the "dogmatic" Springs could not break his habits. Each time he came in for a landing, Elliott turned the plane's nose aside in an attempt to see the ground, and the plane would begin to spin. "Very dangerous," Mallonee said. "Young Sonny, who sometimes flew with him, would cover his head and yell."

Elliott eventually learned, but he did so without Mallonee's further aid.

Hitler's columns burst across the Polish border in September 1939, and World War II had begun. The young pilot joined the rush into the service.

Despite his animosity toward the New Deal, Elliott and Frances attended the Kentucky Derby in 1937 with a party from Washington that included Postmaster General James Farley, the political genius of the Roosevelt administration. The trip from the capital by private car was made more pleasant for Elliott by the presence of his friend Chip Robert of Atlanta, the secretary of the National Democratic Committee, who arranged the outing.

Elliott faced a renewed threat of labor strife in the spring of 1937, but it passed quickly. CIO organizers appeared in Lancaster, where they talked with workers who had belonged to unions at other plants before joining Springs. The organizers offered money to these men to help in a drive to unionize Elliott's plants. "As far as I can find out," Springs reported, "all of the employees contacted refused flatly to have anything to do with the matter and voluntarily gave us full details." At that time, he said, the average work week for employees in the plants was only thirty-five hours, and the union had scant appeal for his workers.

At first Elliott cooperated fully with other textile manufacturers in an effort to improve conditions that had crippled the industry in the early phases of the Great Depression. Though his instincts told him that he could succeed only through his own efforts, Springs became the industry leader in persuading other mill owners to limit output as a remedy for low prices caused by overproduction.

The leader of one such organization wrote Elliott, "I have worn out three pair of Springmaid sheets in the last few weeks from tossing and turning. I can't go to sleep because of wondering why Springs has not joined the American Institute of Men's and Boys' Wear, Inc."

Springs replied, "Some people are natural joiners and some people are not. Due to our connections with the cotton business, the peach orchard business, the cotton weaving business, the bleaching business, the dyeing business, the printing business, the banking business, the airplane business, I find we are eligible to join some 3800 associations. Each of these . . . writes us once a year and solicit our membership.

"Naturally, we can't afford to join all of them. . . . I hope this answers your question."

XI / "I've Run As Far As I Can Go"

Despite his poor physical condition, Elliott was determined to get into the war in some capacity. The Nazi blitzkrieg had hardly begun to roll when he applied for a passport as a journalist, hoping to make his way to the fighting front, but was refused by the State Department because of the hazards involved. By the summer of 1940, "so depressed" by German triumphs in Europe that other matters seemed to be of little importance, Elliott wrote to an old friend, "I will be forty-four in a couple of weeks, and nobody seems to want a combat pilot at that age, so I don't know what I will do about my reserve commission."

Though in fact he felt keenly his loss of vigor, he concealed his anxieties in a jocular report to another correspondent:

> For the past eight years I have been leaping from a bed of pain each morning, grabbing a cup of coffee on the run, and dashing thirty miles to an office to sit at the telephone until sundown, and then inspect ailing departments of seven cotton mills on the way home.
>
> I have a sandwich and a glass of milk at my desk for lunch and I carry an electric razor in the car to shave while waiting for the red lights to change.
>
> I long ago lost my appetite, have no opportunity or inclination to indulge my thirst, and when I see a wistful blonde with a green light in her eyes, my only interest is in finding out how much she paid for her dress, how many yards of cloth it contains, and how I can persuade her to use more yards in the next one.
>
> If she invites me to her bedroom, I would only try to sell her some Springmaid sheets.

Larry Callahan, who had been using his influence with younger Air Corps officers in an effort to get the aging War Birds into the fight, told Elliott that both England and Canada were rejecting American fliers but that he felt that "the informal, skeleton" aviation corps being organized in Washington would accept both of them

To his old companion of the French front, "Nigger" Horn, who was now an R.A.F. wing commander, Elliott wrote, "I hate to think that I am going to be useless in this coming fracas, and somehow I do not believe the British can win a war without me. I have a son fifteen . . . clamoring to learn to fly. I hate to think of doing my fighting by proxy."

His old friend of World War I, Dora, now married, wrote from London: "I do hope that you won't get into this horrible business. You did a big job last time, and you have a family now to consider." Springs confessed to her that he was not fit for flying service and had otherwise deteriorated, "I might dye my hair, but I . . . would probably give away my age the first night at the Savoy."

In September 1940, Elliott notified the War Department that he was available for active duty, but had no response for six months. Many of his key managers, most of them Clemson College men with ROTC training, entered the army, and Elliott grew more restless. He sought the post of air attaché in London but lost it to another retread. But when he finally went to Washington in the spring of 1941 begging for active duty, he was taken aback by the prompt official acceptance of his service. "They wanted to put me to work that afternoon," he wrote Callahan. "I begged off a little while to see what I could do here to get ready . . . if they really need me I want to go and to hell with the mills."

To the chief of air corps personnel Elliott explained, "I am operating seven cotton mills which have 8000 employees and produce five million yards of cloth weekly. Five of them are now supplying cloth for the Quartermaster Corps. . . . I am also president of a railroad, a bank, and a hospital. . . . If you could avoid calling me to active duty until fall, it would enable me to try and train my organization to function without me." Elliott realized that he could not compete with young pilots then in training and that he could not hope to fly modern fighters—but he resisted the prospect of sedentary service. "I am not particularly interested in swapping one desk job for another," he wrote.

But in June 1941, he did just that. He accepted the post of executive officer at Morris Field, the new air corps base at Charlotte, North Carolina.

Elliott was bored by the endless paper work at the field and felt that he was wasting time in this backwater while the nation was preparing to enter the global war. He also lived at a hectic pace because he commuted from Fort Mill to the base daily, arriving in time for 7:30 drill each morning.

His attempt to make a clean break with the mills was undoubtedly traumatic. He telegraphed M. Lowenstein & Sons, a major customer, "I have been in the army since June 1 and am out of touch with the mills or the market. Don't expect to be back in my office until Hitler is out of his. Suggest you talk to Mr. Curtis, who has full authority." But mill executives besieged him each time he returned home, and Elliott found himself harassed by business problems that he thought he had put behind him for the duration of the war. The chief disruption arose from the inability of his managers to cope with numerous government agencies. "I do not know what I am going to do about my business," he wrote. "The Office of Price Administration has my sales and purchasing policies tied in a hard knot, and I still have no machinery for my new mill. . . . It looks like I am going to have to reorganize my management before I can completely divorce myself from it. I may even have to go back to it for a while."

He was still proud of his business, and his command of its details sometimes amazed his employees. One day Elliott took an army major for a tour of the Lancaster plant and paused to explain the operation of a carding machine. For ten minutes he described the construction and function of the machine so thoroughly that when he moved on, the operator said to a fellow worker, "I've been working on this card for fifteen years and that's more than I've ever learned about this thing in all those years."

At the air base Springs felt increasing stress from the demands of his superior, General C. W. ("Jan") Howard, an autocratic regular who made his life miserable. General Howard, in fact, reminded Elliott of his father—insatiable in his demands and quick to find fault. For the first time since his childhood Springs found himself in a vulnerable position. Abruptly shorn of the baronial powers he had enjoyed in civilian life, unable to resist his superior, and frustrated by army red tape, he began to succumb to the pressure. Once more he felt that he was in declining health, but army doctors could detect no physical ailments from the rather vague symptoms he described.

Elliott revealed none of his frustration to his staff on the base, which admired him for his energy and unselfishness. He took his turn as officer of the day just as his subordinates did, though he was exempt from this extra twenty-four-hour duty. His secretary recalled, "I learned first hand what a wonderful person he was, always doing for others. . . . The officers under Colonel Springs's command really loved him." (This rank had not yet been conferred. Elliott remained a captain, though his post rated a lieutenant colonelcy.)

Elliott habitually went beyond the call of duty to log air time and soon found that his fears of obsolescence as a combat pilot were justified. An evaluation board permitted him to fly single-engine planes as pilot and multi-engine bombers as co-pilot, but, as he wrote to Jake Stanley, "I cannot get promoted until I have finished my correspondence courses, so it looks as if I will finish this war as a Captain. That is if I finish it." He reported that he was "trying to learn to fly" bombers and hot new fighters on instruments but was finding this difficult.

"My nose has been at the grindstone recently," he added. "We are right in the midst of maneuvers, which means we are up to our waist in generals." Elliott took an active part in large-scale army maneuvers in the Carolinas that fall of 1941 and was proud of the field's "usual standard of high efficiency." He was on duty in Charlotte when the Japanese struck at Pearl Harbor in December 1941, but his wartime duty was virtually over.

Abruptly, only a few weeks later, after seven months of service, Springs was stricken with severe abdominal pains, hospitalized locally, and then sent to the army's Lawson General Hospital in Atlanta. Doctors there could not diagnose his recurring intestinal complaints but warned him of developing cardiac problems. Impatient with his treatment, Elliott "blew up" and left in less than a week. Since he refused to resign his commission, he was placed on inactive reserve and declared ineligible for active duty.

He tried to return to full-time work at the mills but the constant activity of conversion to war production took its toll. Elliott became so morose and depressed that Frances was concerned for his mental stability. Still, he made the changeover promptly.

A few days after Pearl Harbor Springs offered his entire production to the military. In the first months of 1942 every loom was switched to government specifications, and record production of special fabrics poured out to be made into clothing and equipment for American servicemen and servicewomen around the world: khakis, coveralls, fatigues, windbreakers, raincoats, sheets, mattress covers, tents, sleeping bags, bandoliers, gas masks, gun covers, decontamination cloth, and adhesive tape. All of the Springs plants won Army-Navy "E" awards for superior production.

Doctors advised Elliott to spend six weeks in bed, but he resisted; "to give up work and worry is difficult." He claimed that he had consulted five stomach specialists—"every one available on the Atlantic coast," two of whom advised operating on his ulcer and three of whom prescribed "a quiet life, diet, and grin-and-bear-it."

To Callahan, who was now an air corps intelligence officer and was trying to make his way to England where American officers were already gathering, Springs wrote, "The only reason for an early demise will be that I am bored to death, or shall collapse from sheer envy that you will be on active duty before I can get repaired."

He added a plea, "If you can fix anything count me in and I will drink enough hot solder to pass the physical examination."

A former colleague at Morris Field urged Elliott to forget a second service career. "I cannot understand why you insist on being in the thick of the Army . . . and feel that life isn't worth while if you aren't there. . . . It seems to me so foolish for you to yearn to get back at the expense of your health and your life perhaps. . . . You are doing a man's size job with the burdens that you have."

Elliott was forced to accept this advice. He dosed himself with antibiotics and gave the mills his undivided attention. At full war production they were turning out six million yards of cloth weekly. The enormous stock of cloth he had accumulated over the years was dwindling rapidly and profits began to rise. Springs Mills earned a net of almost $400,000 in 1941, and the combined incomes of Elliott and Frances almost matched that figure. Washington bureaucrats summoned Elliott from his work to take over the textile division of the Office of Price Administration, but he resisted so vigorously that he escaped the duty. In the spring of 1942 Elliott learned that Jake Stanley had become a major and was to join Larry Callahan in England. Springs told an air corps colonel who was bound for overseas, "It breaks my heart that I can't go with you, but my stomach is still unavailable."

Lena died in May, leaving "a tremendous tax liability" that was to concern Elliott for several years and add to his burdens. Even now as he became increasingly tense and irritable, it was only his wife who seemed to realize that he was seriously ill and in need of immediate help.

In the fall of 1942, suffering from a "nervous breakdown," Elliott gave in to the pleas of Frances—and to his persistent depression. Now, for the first time in his life, he dropped his pretensions of supreme self-confidence and prepared to face emotional problems he had repressed since childhood. "I've run as far as I can go," he told Frances. "Too much worry over too many years. . . . The immediate cause of my trouble is the war and the universal ruin that I saw coming. The gradual breakup of my business, my family and my associations kept pounding on my brain." He agreed to go to the Riggs Clinic, a well-known psychiatric hospital near Stockbridge, Massachusetts, where he was subjected to shock treatments.

"I had the first treatment this morning and it wasn't bad," he wrote to Frances. "They're . . . a little strange I'll admit but no pain and no after effects." A few days later he conceded that the shocks were "a little strenuous but you feel all right by lunch time. . . . They only last a couple of minutes."

Otherwise, his life in the hospital was pleasant, if dull. He played bridge and rummy with nurses and other patients, went for long walks in the countryside, played pool and tennis and read for hours each day. In a handicraft therapy class with other patients Elliott made a coffee table and a toilet case. "Sounds ghastly, I know," he wrote Frances, "but I can take anything to get well . . . and I will not let myself get depressed."

He improved rapidly during the first few days: "I've stopped pacing the floor . . . and of my own accord have left off the sedatives." Soon, he predicted, he would be able to "concentrate even in the mornings." He urged her to cease worrying about him. "It's just a question of time and whether I have the courage to face it, and you give me the courage I might lack. The desire to get back to you will hold me together. . . . You don't know how much I love you and how much I miss you. But be patient and you'll soon have a husband as good as new."

He offered an oblique apology for his past behavior, "Remember I love you in spite of all the queer things I've done."

Although he confessed to her, "this is by far the hardest thing to do I've ever faced," he unburdened himself to his doctors and cooperated fully. One psychiatrist reported to Frances that Elliott's troubles were much older and more basic than those he had encountered at Morris Field: "The origin of his trouble dates back to the almost impossible environment to which he was subjected as a growing boy. It is remarkable to me that the unhealthy effect of his father was not greater than it was, and it speaks very strongly for the mental toughness of Col. Springs."

Elliott wrote his own version of this analysis:

> The doctor says I have been behind the eight ball all my life and this is the first chance I've had to shake off my nervousness. . . . [He] predicts great things when I absorb his teachings in mental hygiene . . . he told me that it was time I quit trying to cure myself and let him

cure me. He says I had a genuine war neurosis after 1918 and that I apparently cured myself by writing it out, but that I didn't have the concrete foundation under me to prevent its return, or rather the development of a new one under the pressure of business and the strain of the air base. . . . My troubles are rooted in 1918 and in Father. The doctor has discovered nothing that I don't know already.

The diagnosis, he explained, was that he was suffering from

acute anxiety developed from a chronic state of worry. When things go wrong I worry and that makes me less able to cope with problems and that causes more worry. . . . The outward manifestation is rest-lessness and the insomnia is the reaction.

The doctor is as confident I will recover as if I had the measles. He assures me that I will be better than I have ever been. . . . Just a nervous system that has been pushed too far and rebelled. I guess this is what I should have [done] in 1919 instead of the treatment I gave myself by always outrunning it and looking for excitement and drink-ing companions.

He also insisted that General Howard and Morris Field were not the root causes of his troubles: "War or no war, Jan or no Jan, I would have had to come here sooner or later."

Frances, at home in Fort Mill, also seemed to be in a depressed mental state, and Elliott was so alarmed that he assured her his doctor would accept her as a patient once he was on the road to recovery. He also dismissed her theory that she might have been a cause of his breakdown: "You have nothing to do with my condition, so banish the thought."

He added, "You are having a rotten time, I know, for which I am so sorry, but you can console yourself with the assurance that this is the first sensible thing I've done in years and it will do some permanent good."

He continued his assurances to her as the weeks passed. His doctor, he said, "doesn't consider me very bad off and assures me that I won't get any worse. . . . All I needed was to relax and that took time." But the doctor himself wrote to Frances: "He is still uncomfortable emotionally, particu-larly in the forenoon when his downswing mood is more evident."

After six weeks of treatment, Elliott warned Frances, "Don't expect any miracles. While I'm better, I could slip back fast." But two weeks later he reported that his doctor had read some of his books, especially *Leave Me with a Smile*, which included a fictional version of his relationship with

Leroy. That book, the doctor declared, was "a great work of psychiatry" that he used in treating Springs. It was perhaps this incident which prompted Elliott to write of his relationship with the doctor, "I don't know whether he is treating me or I am treating him now," but this was a passing phase, for he reported soon afterward: "I'll be better off if I give this doctor a chance. He knows what he's doing, which is more than I can say for all the others I've been consulting for years."

But Springs failed to achieve a complete cure at Stockbridge, and when he was released after a stay of more than two months, he spent a brief time in another institution at nearby Valleyhead—and later entered Silver Hill in Connecticut, a private hospital known for its effectiveness in treating alcoholism. Frances joined him there for a few days, and they then returned to South Carolina. (It is unclear whether she also received treatment there for the drinking problem she had developed.) Elliott's travail was nearing an end. He spent several weeks in a Philadelphia mental institution early in 1943, but when he returned home it was apparently to a normal life. As he had promised Frances, he returned to her "better than ever."

To intimate friends, Elliott reported only that he had introduced a new kind of martini to inmates and staff at Silver Hill. Though he continued to fret because he was missing the action of the war, he found his business running smoothly and at near peak capacity under the direction of Lee Skipper, whom he had named general manager upon leaving for Silver Hill. But there were problems.

Elliott's intestinal ailments returned, and he had "a terrible time" throughout 1942 and in early 1943. "In fact," he said, "I was surprised each day that I was able to get to the office." By the summer of 1943, Elliott had accepted the inevitable: he could not hope to pass the army physical despite his influential friends within the service. To Larry Callahan in London, who was "pulling wires" to have Springs brought over, he wrote dolefully, "I cannot hope to get a waiver on my artificial duodenum."

He remained in South Carolina directing the mills, which were busy around the clock until July, when a shortage of workers forced him to give up the third shift. Ninety percent of his output went into military orders, and he maintained production despite chronic shortages of coal, starch, and many other items.

Springs complained that the business was growing "increasingly complicated and unpleasant," largely due to government interference. His contracts were under continual renegotiation, a tedious, protracted process that diverted his managers from their duties. Shortages grew worse. "We are short of manpower, as well as everything else," Elliott wrote in 1944, "and unless we can get some coal by Friday, we are going to have plants shut down."

Manpower raids became common. Elliott's friend, Walter Montgomery of Spartanburg, was a particularly vigorous competitor. Elliott complained that five Springs-trained superintendents in Montgomery's plants were "continually upsetting our overseers" with offers of jobs.

Most other mills ran three shifts of forty-five hours each, but Springs ran two fifty-hour shifts in his weave room and "as much as we can in drafting and spinning, letting the second and third shifts alternate off on Saturday afternoons." For about a year one of his plants operated on Sundays in an effort to keep pace with government orders. Mills now paid time and a half for overtime, and Springs wages rose from a minimum of forty cents in 1941 to sixty-five cents an hour in 1945, with five cents an hour additional for workers on third shifts. Springs workers seemed to be content, for though three or four other mills in the area were closed by strikes, there was no union activity in Elliott's plants.

Even now, Elliott planned shrewdly for the future. He told one of his plant managers, "We're wearing out our machinery on this seven-day schedule. We'll be ruined at the end of the war if we have to replace or repair all of it at once. I want you to buy a million dollars' worth of parts right away. Just store 'em in a warehouse—every kind of part you think we'll need—and we'll put everything back into good shape when the war's over." For about two years the manager bought all available machine parts and filled three warehouses—but was able to spend only $900,000 in the process. Elliott's foresight staved off a crisis in 1945, when the mills returned to normal operations.

Inexplicably, Elliott's health was restored in the last days of 1943, and he was able to go hunting. He announced that his ulcer had healed, and he was optimistic about his recovery to normal health. "I know I am a damn fool," he wrote to an air corps friend, "but if I continue to improve . . . I am going to try to get back on active duty. . . . I ought to have sense enough to be satisfied to run these mills, but I cannot do it. The textile business never seemed more unimportant to me, and, while I suffer no delusions about my value to the army, I still have to make the effort again."

Particularly galling to the restive War Bird were reports of the adventures of Jake Stanley and Larry Callahan, who were both now full colonels and were playing active roles with the 8th Fighter Command headquarters in London, Jake as chief of staff and Larry as intelligence officer.

Despite a festive day of celebrating an Army-Navy "E" award won by The Springs Cotton Mills, Fort Mill seemed isolated and dreary. "My social activities have been nil . . . Frances is busy running a house with no servants and very little heat, but her main job is nursing me. . . .

"I have no plans except to try and stay quiet until this stomach gets better or worse. I get my exercise pacing the floor, and every time a plane flies overhead, go out and kick myself around the house."

Sonny had graduated from Culver with honors and was now, having reversed himself, attending Princeton. He demanded his father's permission to enter the army. Elliott would not hazard a guess at his son's future. "He's too like me to be predictable," he said. To the boy's pleas Elliott replied that he was too young and inexperienced to lead men in battle. He sought to reason with Sonny: "You can hardly doubt that I am sympathetic with your attitude . . . *why* do you think I joined the army last June. . . . This war is not like a term at school. . . . This is your last chance for an education." In the midst of this letter, Elliott was forcibly reminded of the irony of his plea and interrupted his argument: "Miss Williamson is writing this for me. She says it is unnecessary for me to dictate because she can get out the files of 1915 and just send you copies of letters that Father wrote to me. . . .

"Get it out of your head that your mother or I are trying to stand in your way, and I hope you can make up your mind to get as much education as you can while you can. You will be a better soldier for it and that is what we all want." Sonny acquiesced and finished his year at Princeton in engineering. Anne graduated from Chatham Hall in Virginia in 1943, worked in the mills that summer, and prepared to enter Smith College in the fall.

When, after the end of the school year, Sonny enlisted in the air force and proved himself an apt student, Elliott was outwardly delighted, but his continuing frustration over his own failure to get into action only increased when the boy began pilot training. "To have him flying, while I am sitting on the ground, is just about to kill me."

Even so, Elliott was determined to have Sonny taste frontline action before the war ended. In June 1945, when his son was ferrying B-17 bombers within the United States, Elliott wrote to his friend, General Caleb Haynes, at 1st Air Force headquarters, "While I have never asked any favors for him . . . I am anxious that he get a chance at combat when his time comes, and that he not be sidetracked." He hoped that Haynes would take Sonny to the Pacific theater with him, but the war ended before this could be done.

Sonny was discharged from the air force in September 1945, and, at his father's suggestion, enrolled in Georgia Tech's school of textile engineering. Elliott's hope was that the boy would return home to prepare for directing The Springs Cotton Mills.

Elliott envisioned a new kind of company that Sonny could lead into another era of growth, for he was no longer content to produce grey goods for the converters' market. He intended to finish his own cloth for such products as sheets and pillow cases. Elliott made plans to build a huge new bleachery, which would be the cornerstone of a transformed consumer products company. Sonny would inherit a more profitable company and a far more complex one and in his maturity should become the most successful owner of The Springs Cotton Mills. It was not to be.

Lancaster civilians were treated to displays of aerial warfare that spring, but few people were surprised. Elliott had assembled a small air museum—a collection of surplus military planes: two BT-13 Vultee trainers, B-17, B-24, and B-25 bombers, a P-51 fighter, and a helicopter. On weekends the Colonel practiced aerobatics once more. The two old Vultees wheeled and dove through the sky in fierce dogfights as the Colonel took on first his company pilot, Cecil Neal, and then Sonny. The tortured whine of the motors filled the air as the aging ace dove after his prey, plunging recklessly upon his victims. However they veered from his path, Neal and Sonny were helpless before the Colonel's phantom guns, for he hung tenaciously to their tails, a few yards to the rear, and could not be shaken off.

Despite his old-fashioned ways, Neal thought, Elliott was a superb pilot, though he never qualified to fly modern planes on instruments: "He flew full throttle, and when he landed he simply pulled everything off . . . but he was good at the old-style dogfighting." One day Neal managed to get the better of the Colonel:

> After he'd taken on Sonny for a while, I fought with him, and when he dove down on my tail, I used the prop on him. I just pulled it back and lost speed and the Colonel zipped right past. Oh, he fumed. "You guys don't play fair," he said when we got down.
>
> But he would try anything, and he was really good at aerobatics. I'd heard the tales of how he flew under the Buster Boyd Bridge and others, and I saw him fly between the chimneys at the Kershaw plant, using them as pylons. I tried that and backed off—I'd get just a wing

in there between the stacks and peel off. I measured the distance and found they were only sixty feet apart.

Finally Elliott bought a Navy glider and planned to have one of the old trainers tow him up for a flight over Lancaster. Cecil Neal warned Sonny, "If they try to tow the glider, you keep your ass out of that BT."

"You Navy guys are all old men," Sonny said.

The Colonel was listening but made no comment.

Neal also warned Sid Mahaffey, the experienced pilot who managed the airport, that the heavy, underpowered BT-13 had a tendency to spin to the right and should not be used to tow gliders. Mahaffey had told Elliott several days earlier that he had never flown a BT-13, but Springs had reassured him. "That's all right. We'll go and pick up Sonny. He knows how. He's instructed in them." Mahaffey had then agreed to the experiment.

Mother's Day, May 12, 1946, was clear and bright, with a steady breeze that cooled the heat of the sun—perfect flying weather. The Colonel and Sonny left Fort Mill before noon and flew to Lancaster for the gliding experiment. Mahaffey met them at the airport with John Taylor, who had flown gliders and C-47's in combat and was then working for a car dealer in Lancaster.

Cecil Neal was out of town, but he had anticipated this experiment and discussed it with Mahaffey. "Sid was an excellent pilot, but he was hard-headed and wouldn't listen to advice. He had a five-hundred-foot nylon cord for a tow rope—he didn't seem to realize how much it would stretch. A mechanic made a hook in the company shop—it was a four-and-a-half-foot hook and should have been no longer than three feet. A shorter hook would have improved the rig and shifted the center of gravity. But the C.A.B. approved the hook as it was, and things seemed to be o.k."

At about one o'clock Mahaffey climbed into one of the trainers with Sonny as his passenger. Taylor took over controls of the glider. Elliott sat to Taylor's rear, where he was to call off readings from the altimeter and the air speed indicator as they rose into the air. It was the Colonel's first flight in a glider, and he was unaccustomed to instruments of naval calibration.

Mahaffey chose the shorter of two runways, because the southwest wind was blowing across that strip. He planned to climb to eight hundred feet and release the glider, which would land on the longer runway.

The plane started from the rear of the glider, at the foot of the runway's five-degree slope. Mahaffey gunned his engines and zoomed past Taylor and Elliott. The nylon cord stretched slightly and dragged the glider for a few yards rather than snapping it cleanly into the air in normal fashion. Still, they were airborne within a few seconds and rose rapidly above the adjoining golf course. The Colonel began calling out air speeds to Taylor, "Fifty. . . . Sixty. . . . Sixty-five. . . . Seventy. . . . Altitude two-fifty. . . . Three hundred." With his gaze fixed upon the instruments, Elliott saw little of the plane ahead of them, though he did glance forward several times. The flight seemed to be progressing normally.

Mahaffey had given the agreed-upon signal for a turn by dipping the plane's nose but then began a slow descent to his left. Taylor realized that the only hope for the trainer was to release the glider, though the trainer had lost too much altitude to provide a safe release. There was a jolt as Taylor hurriedly cast loose the tow rope. Elliott could not see it, but the plane had gone into a spin at about two hundred feet and plunged into a grove of trees, where it burst into flames.

Taylor tried to nurse the glider toward a landing in the open, but it lacked altitude and crashed into the tops of some pines, shearing off its wings. The fuselage then crashed heavily onto a road. Though the light ship was completely wrecked, both passengers emerged, the Colonel dazed and bruised, Taylor painfully speared by the splinters from his plywood seat. They ran toward the plume of heavy black smoke in the distance but were too late. Sonny and Mahaffey were burned beyond recognition. (The remains were identified from dental records.)

Despite his injuries, Elliott's first thought was to return to his wife. He ran back to the airport about a mile distant and climbed into his Waco, having somehow summoned the will to make the brief flight home despite the nightmare vision of the burning wreckage. Several people begged him not to attempt to fly, but he persisted. "I've gotta go and tell Frances," he said. In Fort Mill he hurried from the landing strip to the house, eager to find her before someone called her with the news. He never forgot the moment in which they met. He wrote to an old friend a few days later:

"When she saw me come in alone she screamed and my ears will always ring with that scream and the sound of the crash. But she took herself in hand and has never asked a question. I have not told her anything."

Elliott paid tribute to the stricken Frances: "My wife has set me such an example of courage that I cannot fail to carry on. . . . As for me, I am still trying to work. But I have a tendency to start feeling sorry for myself and then I break up and have to go off by myself and kick myself back to sensibility. I catch myself cadging sympathy. . . . If ever a tough son-of-a-bitch is required at the helm it is now and you can't bawl out a competitor or fire a subordinate and then burst into tears yourself."

In fact, Springs went back to his office the day after the crash, grimly resolved to cling to his business routine. Eunice Hite, his telephone operator, recalled, "He was all strapped up and he leaned to one side as he walked . . . obviously in pain." The operator handled "about a thousand calls" that Monday: "The Colonel didn't take any of them. People called to ask if the Colonel's son had really been killed. They couldn't believe it. And people called about the funeral. They asked me everything—did the Colonel want the casket draped with a flag? All the details. It was a terrible day." Men of his staff noted that Elliott drove himself harder than ever on this day and afterward, as if striving to forget the tragedy for which he blamed himself.

Eunice Hite was struck by the change in the Colonel. "There was no fun in him after that, not for a long time—years." His daughter Anne said, "Sonny's death did something to him. He never mentioned his name again. And no one mentioned Sonny to him."

Springs wrote to friends in a vein of bitter remorse he did not share with his family: "Since May of 1917, I have watched men crash and burn. Then followed the hearse . . . a last toast. . . . It's been sad but I could always see that was inevitable and carry on. This time it's different. To make me see my only son crash and then stand by the plane helplessly—must have taken the best brains in hell to arrange . . . I don't know how it happened. Nothing was wrong mechanically. . . I know the plane didn't stall. I could see the BT clearly and I know the tow rope was clear. The motor did not cut out. The BT did not cut us loose." He reasoned that the pilot must have collapsed from a heart attack or seizure and prevented Sonny, who had been a BT instructor for almost a year, from taking the controls. This was only a theory. The actual cause of the crash was never determined.

Billy Bishop called from Canada to offer his sympathy, and Elliott replied, "You have no idea how the sound of a voice or the touch of a hand can bring comfort in a time like this. I haven't had a shock like this since Mac Grider went west and both times I had to be along and be helpless."

To Samuel Hopkins Adams, who wrote soon after the crash, the Colonel said, "I know I am dreaming because reality could never be this tragic, because no real woman could ever be as brave as Frances. I know I am dreaming because everything is in slow motion, and because my heart doesn't beat and my hand doesn't shake."

Cecil Neal never mentioned gliders to Elliott again, and for about a year the Colonel did not fly—until he borrowed a plane from a Charlotte friend and had Neal fly him and Frances to West Palm Beach. He had made plans for a new airport at Lancaster but now dropped them.

Though Springs could not bring himself to speak of Sonny for many years afterwards, his wife was able to do so. She talked of his loss with several intimates and made subtle efforts to rid her husband of his burden of guilt and enable him to speak of the tragedy. Robert Amory, a Springs sales executive who made occasional visits to Fort Mill, was always given Sonny's bedroom by Frances—in the hope that Elliott would enter it to talk with their guest. Springs never entered the room. At Elliott's insistence Sonny's grave in a Fort Mill Presbyterian cemetery was marked with an airplane propeller. Frances apparently made no objection at the time.

Anne felt a marked change in her father's attitude toward her after Sonny's death: "I felt like everybody was looking at me all of a sudden, and Dad began twisting my arm to do things his way. I felt that they'd never really noticed me before." Anne withdrew from college and married Hugh William Close, Jr., of Philadelphia, a graduate of the Wharton School of Business at the University of Pennsylvania. Close had planned to enter the advertising field and only yielded to the pleas of his father-in-law to begin working in the New York sales office of Springs. Elliott soon persuaded the young couple to move to Fort Mill. During these negotiations, Close recalled, Springs was merely insistent: "He never could come out and say, 'I need you'—though he had realized when Sonny was killed that he needed someone to succeed him."

Close came to admire his father-in-law, but their relationship was not an easy one. Bill had survived World War II in the Pacific as a lieutenant aboard the aircraft carrier *Franklin*, the most battered ship in U.S. naval history. Elliott irritated him with a slur at their first meeting: "Carriers are obsolete."

He also put Close to work at menial tasks in the mills, in much the same way Leroy Springs had once prescribed for him. He required him to learn the most basic steps of the cotton mill process, grinding cards, fixing looms, and doffing spinning frames. Close also worked longer hours than anyone else in the company and was driven so hard that he once complained to Earl Crenshaw, who was one of Elliott's most respected executives.

"I come to work at 6 A.M. and work until 6 P.M. while all the others get off early."

"You'll have to talk to your father-in-law about that," Crenshaw said.

Crenshaw commented later, "Elliott was tough on Bill, but he liked him—he was just trying to teach him the business."

Years afterward, looking back on these days, Bill Close agreed. In retrospect he felt only gratitude: "The Colonel treated me better than if I had been his son. He did make me work for everything, and because of that I learned the business. But I wasn't a surrogate son. Not at all. We weren't on a buddy-buddy basis. He had few friends like that."

After enduring his indoctrination, Close joined a small management training group and within a few years became an efficient mill executive. Winning approval from his father-in-law was not easy. Bill once entered Elliott's office with an idea for improving the manufacturing process of the mills. After he had outlined his scheme with a burst of enthusiasm, Springs handed Close a small volume from his bookshelf.

"Read this and come back," he said.

The book was entitled *Logic*.

The Closes lived in the railroad car *Loretto* for a few months—until Anne became so pregnant with her first child that she was unable to move about the tiny kitchen. Anne declared firmly that though they must move into a house, she refused to live near her parents. But Elliott was both persuasive and adamant and began building a house for them in the backyard of the White homestead. Anne battled her father over the design and construction of the house and scolded her husband for supporting Elliott against her. Close recalled later, "Building that house was tough. The Colonel thought of himself as an architect. I tried to be neutral—50 percent for him and 50 percent for Sis. I was always in the middle."

Despite her love and admiration for her father, Anne retained lifelong memories of his shortcomings as a parent: "Daddy always had his own way. . . . He was very manipulative and domineering. I had to say 'Wait a minute!' when he would intrude into my affairs, and then he would back off. I guess I was like him in some ways. My husband would give in to him, and when I asked him why he let Daddy push him around he'd ask what difference it made—but we did end up living right behind the big house, where I didn't want to be."

Joe Croxton, the new company architect who was assigned to design the house on an emergency basis, was also drawn into the protracted controversy. He rushed through the foundation drawings on his first day at work, and Elliott approved them without consulting Anne. Croxton never forgot the experience of building the house under Elliott's direction.

Springs insisted upon four-foot doors and resisted Croxton's advice that they were a foot too wide—appropriate for hospitals but not residences. Elliott said firmly that the doors in his house were four feet wide but called Croxton the next day. "Forget those doors," he said. "I measured mine. You're right."

"Next he wanted a bathtub placed under a window," Croxton said. "He insisted it was there in his own house. I knew that arrangement wasn't possible, since the adjoining commode would need a twelve-inch clearance and there wasn't enough room. I made the Colonel sit in an office chair and placed a box where the end of the tub would be. He then agreed that he'd been wrong."

The process continued until the house was finished.

The completion of the house did not end the Colonel's role in its destiny. Long afterward he intruded upon his daughter's prerogative by making unexpected alterations and additions. One day Cecil Neal flew an out-of-town trip to pick up Anne who had been away on a brief visit. They passed over Fort Mill on their way to Myrtle Beach, where she was to meet her family. "Want to see what the Colonel did to your house today?" he asked.

Anne saw that a wooden patio covered with translucent fiberglass had been extended from her house toward the swimming pool. "She didn't say a word," Neal recalled. "But when we got to the beach she scalded her daddy to a fare-thee-well. She told him to get that thing off her house and to never touch the place again. The carpentry crew had to work over the weekend to tear down the patio."

Frances Springs, who usually maintained a ladylike silence, occasionally resisted her husband's authoritarian ways. When she overheard Elliott and his sales chief Bob Amory arguing over some fact, she intruded in an effort to force her husband to admit for once he was in the wrong. The ever-confident Springs, proud of his powers of memory, insisted that Amory was mistaken about the birthplace of some prominent person.

"How much will you bet?" Elliott asked.

"Five dollars," Amory said, "but you're wasting your money. I know I'm right."

Frances broke in. "No, Bob, make it $500 and make him pay."

It was only now, after many years of postponement, that Elliott built the finishing plant which was to revolutionize his business. He would no longer produce raw cloth for the trade but would bleach, dye and print, and finish his own goods, adding fashion and performance finishes—and earning higher profits. He would also cut, sew, and package his own sheets

The proud father poses with twelve-year-old Sonny Springs and a huge gobbler he bagged on his first wild turkey hunt. Elliott circulated the photo among his friends. Such efforts by Elliott to establish a camaraderie with his son failed; as a young teenager the rebellious Sonny twice ran away from home.

Sonny and Anne Springs in their late teens. Reared by a governess, they saw little of their parents in early years. Anne recalled that she never dined with her mother and father until she was twelve years old. Relations between Sonny and his father were reminiscent of those between Elliott and the grim Leroy, and Anne felt that her father took little notice of her until Sonny's death.

The yacht Springmaid, *formerly the DuPont vessel* Marmot. *As one of three partners who owned the luxury craft during the early 1950s, Elliott used it occasionally in Caribbean and in Florida waters but protested that he never enjoyed life aboard because his guests were "people who never do anything."*

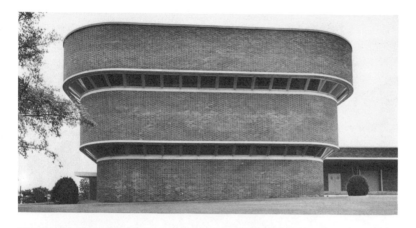

The striking facade of the executive headquarters building created by Elliott Springs in Fort Mill, South Carolina, with its "floating" walls and its glare-proof windows inspired by the design of the gondola of the German zeppelin Hindenburg.

Chairman Springs at his desk. The conference table is emerging from the floor, ready for his board of directors. Above the windows is a photographic panorama showing every foot of his 29-mile-long railroad line, the Lancaster & Chester.

Springs greets a radiant Gypsy Rose Lee, "Vice-President of Unveiling," at the dedication of the new Lancaster depot of the L&C. Springs is wearing a shirt decorated with his Springmaid beauty queens, and the celebrated stripper wears a gown of Elliott's "Harem Print."

Frances Springs was irritated by occasional visits of Gypsy Rose Lee to Fort Mill—particularly the one pictured here, featuring Miss Lee's troupe of beauties. Mrs. Springs, who reportedly left town in a huff, returned soon afterward.

A Miss Springmaid winner, visiting New York on a promotional tour, poses with a chauffeur and Elliott's stylish, custom-built Rolls-Royce town car. Springs sometimes took matters into his own hands during company beauty contests, overruled the applause meters, and revised the rules to choose his favorites.

$\mathcal{A}$ buck well spent on a Springmaid Sheet

This buck may look more like 47¢—which is what *most* bucks are worth these days. But not *this* "dearslayer." Any buck spent on a SPRINGMAID sheet gets you value of *100 cents* on the dollar— as any two smart squaws know.

Because they stand up so well to wear and washings and yet are soft and beautiful, any number of bucks couldn't get you a better sheet value. We sent them to an independent testing laboratory and, honest Injun, what happened to them would make Custer's Last Stand look like a Vassar Daisy Chain. First, they were washed 400 times—abraded 100 times warpwise and 100 times fillingwise.

That was equal to a whole generation of constant use! And those sheets came out looking like—you guessed it—a million bucks, with a lot more wear left in them, too! But don't take our word for it! See for yourself their luster and even yarns. And compare the "washability" of SPRINGMAID sheets and pillowcases with any other sheet on the market. We're betting plenty of wampum every time that you'll put your buck on a SPRINGMAID sheet—*and it'll be a buck well spent!*

SPRINGS MILLS, Inc.

The most famous of the Springmaid ad series by Elliott Springs was this example of double entendre. The idea reportedly was suggested by Dr. Robert McKay of Charlotte, Elliott's most intimate friend.

Beware the Goose!

During the war, The Springs Cotton Mills was called upon to develop a crease-proof cotton fabric. It was used with great success as a backing for maps, photographs, and other valuable assets. This fabric has been further perfected and made available to the ham hamper and lung lug trade.

Whether you are on Capitol Hill for business or pleasure bent, you need not eat off the mantel if you have your foundation covered with SPRINGMAID POKER, woven of combed yarns 37" wide, 152 x 68 count, in tearose, white, nude, and black, light and medium gauge.

If you bruise easily, you can face the future confidently with the SPRINGMAID trademark.

SPRINGS MILLS

200 Church Street • New York 13, New York

Atlanta   Chicago   Dallas   Los Angeles

SPRINGMAID *sheets, pillowcases, diapers, broadcloth, poplins and tubings*

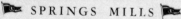

Springs found inspiration for his caricatures of Madison Avenue in unlikely places. Here he made use of a gibe at congressmen from the parody newspaper annual, The Bawl Street Journal. *Several of his ads featured special qualities of cloth he made for the armed services during World War II.*

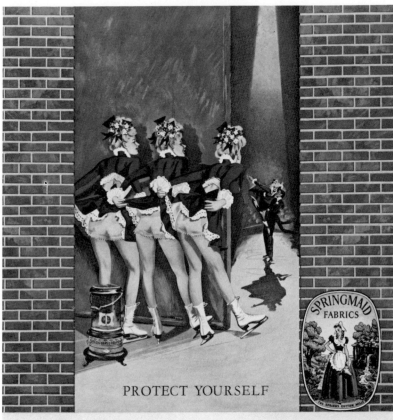

PROTECT YOURSELF

During the war, The Springs Cotton Mills was called upon to develop a light cotton fabric to be impregnated and made flame resistant. This was accomplished, and the fabric was used for airplane ground crews and carrier fire squads.

It is now known as SPRINGMAID KERPYR and is available to the ham hamper and lung lifter business as a combed broadcloth, 37″ wide, 152 x 68 approximate count, with a weight of 3.30. The finished fabric is sold in pink, white, nude, and dusty.

If you expect to attend a campfire picnic, a Fourth of July barbecue, scratch matches, or warm yourself in front of a crackling fire, be protected by the SPRINGMAID label on the bottom of your trademark.

SPRINGS MILLS
200 Church Street • New York 13, New York
Chicago   Dallas   Los Angeles

Coming soon . . . SPRINGMAID *sheets, pillowcases, diapers, broadcloth, poplins and tubings.*

Another jocular sales pitch, another all-too-obvious double entendre, and a further provocation to outraged readers. (Springs claimed that only six retail stores stocked his sheets when his ad campaign began—and that two years later, his outlets numbered about ten thousand.)

Elliott Springs, president
of The Springs Cotton Mills,
says he is prepared to make
everything shown in the picture.

BE PROTECTED

During the war, The Springs Cotton Mills was called upon to develop a crease-proof cotton fabric. It was used with great success as a backing for maps, photographs, and other valuable assets. This fabric has now been further perfected and made available to the torso-twister trade. After a convention, a clam-bake, or a day in the Pentagon Building, you need not eat off the mantel if you have your foundation covered with SPRINGMAID POKER woven of combed yarns 37″ wide, 152 x 68 count, in tearose, white, nude, and black, light and medium gauge. If you bruise easily, you can face the future confidently with the SPRINGMAID trademark.

SPRINGS MILLS

200 Church Street • New York 13, New York

Atlanta   Chicago   Dallas   Los Angeles

SPRINGMAID *sheets, pillowcases, diapers, broadcloth, poplins and tubings*

Using the same material, with a new and equally titillating drawing, Springs added spice to his appeal with the message on the right of the illustration. This ad drew hundreds of protests, many of them pointing out that "only God can make a tree"—a reference to the swirling autumn leaves that Springs had directed his artists to remove.

"My favorite
nite spot is a
Springmaid
sheet"

...says
Miss Gypsy Rose Lee,
prominent hostess
of New York
and Paris

Like so many aristocrats, Miss Lee finds SPRINGMAIDS a "must" for her guests. Those
favored leaders of fashion who share her hospitality are treated to the very finest of
bedroom appointments.

A gathering place for international society, Miss Lee's home, from breakfast room
to bedroom, is the epitome of elegant décor.

Living in the grand manner, Miss Lee has never felt it necessary to mingle with café
society. Her favorite nite spot is in her own home, a SPRINGMAID sheet.

SPRINGMAID
FABRICS

The Springs Cotton Mills
Lancaster, South Carolina   © 1954, The Springs Cotton Mills

*Queen Gypsy starred in several Springmaid ads, this one the most celebrated. Gossips
hinted that Elliott and Gypsy Rose Lee were lovers, an impression that Springs sought to
confirm.*

Miss Luella Gear, celebrated as a hostess to international society, blends the charm of the past with the convenience of the present.

"WE on the North Shore treasure our antiques fully as much as they do on the Cape or the Eastern Shore" modulated Miss Gear in the thrilling voice long since discovered by Hollywood and Broadway but now, thanks to her success on television, equally well known from Hollywood, Florida to Skagway, Alaska.

"My land dates back to one of the early Colonial periods. Cornwallis used to play games with the milkmaids here. My pool dates back to one of my early husbands. He used to play games with the mermaids here. My grandfather's chair dates back to Sitting Bull, and great-grandmother's bedspread was torn by George Washington's spur when he slept here. Nevertheless, the pool now has an electronic filter and is covered with polyethylene. Grandmother's bedspread is wired for diathermy but is yellow with age, and looks it—lying on top of my new Springmaid Sheets, which are bleached Whiter Than White*. Why do I use them? Don't be silly—I can't afford to use anything else. Colonel Springs is a lousy bridge player and fancies his game, though he still thinks the McCampbell double means business—textile business. He does not approve of gambling, so pays off in sheets. I wish that the Motor Moguls would take up Monopoly or the Boat Barons would take up Backgammon. These sheets wear forever, and it is my feet that need help now.

"Grandmother's diamonds are yellow too, but you need white diamonds these days to splash around Long Island and you find the same thing is true of sheets. Whether she favors the traditional or the modern approach, the clever hostess will find the 1957 whiteness of Springmaid Sheets essential to the attainment and maintenance of her proper position." *Trademark

The popular veteran actress Luella Gear, with whom Elliott was alleged to have had a long-standing affair, also appeared in more than one Springmaid ad. Springs made at least one substantial loan to Miss Gear.

Elliott enjoys some of the mail provoked by his ad campaign, most of which protested his risqué copy and illustrations. Some observers felt that Springs added to the furor by writing some of the more sensational letters himself. Many of these plaints were published in his amusing book Clothes Make the Man.

Elliott Springs at the age of fifty-seven, six years before his death. It was typical of his tireless campaign of merchandising that his jacket matched the plaid cover of his office chair. Controls at his desk operated virtually everything in his office, from lights and sliding panels to the retractable conference table.

and pillowcases in a large new sewing operation. Undeterred by warnings of disaster from important customers, competitors, and his own employees, Elliott began constructing a huge bleachery. He called the plant Grace in memory of his mother.

When Elliott proposed the plant to his board, Director Waddy Thomson, the former Treasurer, was shocked. "Do you realize you are asking us to approve an outlay of $8 million when all of the mills in the company are not worth more than that?" Springs pressed on, undeterred, even in face of rising costs that increased his investment in the bleachery to $15 million, much of the excess due to Elliott's frequent changes of plan. He visited the site and more than once ordered foundations torn up and moved in a series of hasty expansions during actual construction.

As another of his executives said, "Grace was his only big gamble. He usually hedged his bets. He complained about the cost for years afterward, but when I told him it was a bargain, he agreed." In any case the huge new facility, equipped with the most advanced machinery, was pressed toward completion. Elliott was resolved that the restructured company should be one of the most modern, and profitable, textile corporations in the world.

Springs sought a finishing executive in his characteristically oblique manner. Herb Mathewson, the general manager of Union Bleachery in Greenville, South Carolina, got several messages through salesmen that Elliott wanted to talk with him, but he resisted. "I'd heard he ran a one-man show and would let no one do anything on his own," Mathewson said. "I thought I couldn't get along with him. When Waddy Thomson finally asked me to see the Colonel, I agreed." Mathewson was soon in charge of Springs finishing.

Otherwise, Elliott imported only a chief dyer, chief bleacher, chief finisher, and two chemists. Springs employees made up the rest of the staff. "It was the most cooperative bunch I ever saw," Mathewson said.

Springs installed his sewing room as an adjunct to the bleachery in typical fashion. He walked into one of his plants and without preamble told his manager, Conway Still, "I've ordered 350 sewing machines. They'll be here in a few days. I want you to set 'em up so we can make sheets and pillowcases and tablecloths and napkins." Elliott left without further comment.

Still was astonished:

Hell, I didn't know how to start one of the things. I'd never seen one. But we struggled until we learned how to make 'em work. I hired somebody who knew a little about sewing and we started training our people. That was about a year before the bleachery opened, and by the time it was in operation, we had moved the sewing machines over there and were soon in production.

I was able to get that done because the Colonel gave me the idea at the start that there wasn't much to it. And left me with the choice of going back to him to ask how to do the job—which I was very reluctant to do—or to go ahead and put the thing over. He knew how to handle people. You would break your back to accomplish what he wanted. It might require us to work day and night, but we were glad to do it.

Herb Mathewson, who knew Elliott's reputation for volatility, was at first unsure of his new boss, and Springs did little to reassure him. When the two drove out to the bleachery, Elliott halted Mathewson at the entrance. "Let's go back," he said. "I can't look at that white elephant today." Later, Elliott visited the plant only occasionally and explained to Mathewson, "I'm too old to learn the finishing business. You take care of it." The explanation seemed reasonable enough, as the new chief of finishing said: "It was entirely different from what he knew of textiles." Still, Mathewson and other Springs executives surmised that the real reason for Elliott's reluctance to enter the plant was unspoken—the searing memory of the loss of Sonny, for whom the new operation had been conceived.

But, as Mathewson said, the bleachery was a success from the start: "We never ran part-time at all. From the beginning we poured sheets out of the sewing room. . . . And Elliott kept all of his promises to me. He let me run my own show. He never bothered me. There was never a cross word between us. The guys in the plants, who had so much trouble with him, couldn't understand our relationship."

Mathewson discovered that gossip about Elliott's reputation as an insatiable despot was false: "I thought he would be shooting people down, firing them. But he was a pussycat if I ever saw one. He never fired people who were up to their jobs. I know of only three men in management who left Springs in my day. One of those was injured, and one of those fired was turned out because a vice-president insisted he must be fired. Elliott finally agreed to the firing—but then he got busy and found the guy a job."

Mathewson and Springs developed a close relationship, though they did not meet socially. They lunched alone each Friday, and their talk ranged far afield. "He'd talk and talk, about everything but business—

wine, religion, art, anything. He had catholic tastes and knew a lot about everything."

With the opening of the bleachery, Elliott complained that he could not expand his staff rapidly enough to meet the challenges of new products and complex new processes. "However," he said, "the bleachery is coming into production at just the right time." The building had paid for itself within a few months of its completion. Waddy Thomson conceded, "I wasn't very keen on the move. But . . . it came at a time when people were starved for goods in that period after the war. Elliott was a miracle man. He outsmarted the converters by knowing his customers and what they wanted."

Elliott was also proud of the new plant: "Our sheets have been horribly mishandled in the past . . . at every bleachery in the United States, and the finish varied from coarse sandpaper to greased cellophane. . . . If anybody wants to laugh about the most expensive bleachery in the world, that is their privilege, but our finish looks the part. Comparing any other sheet with ours is like mistaking a pawnshop for Tiffany's window."

Elliott prepared for the new venture of merchandising his goods by purchasing a building at 200 Church Street in New York City and establishing his own national sales force. He then set out to make his "Springmaid" trademark a household word in the nation. He was aware from the start that he must accomplish this on his own, and though he began with only the faintest idea of how it should be done, he plunged into the task without hesitation.

XIII / "You Can't Go Wrong on a Springmaid Sheet"

In December 1946, impatient with the conventional work of his New York advertising agency, Elliott took this phase of marketing into his own hands. Neither the Springs textile organization nor American huckstering would ever be the same again.

"Your advertising needs pepping up," Springs complained to his agency. "We have had too many pictures of horses with some very tiresome text . . . to prove that the horses are thoroughbreds, and so are our sheets." He also protested that a Springs ad showing "a girl in a high-necked nightgown with long sleeves in bed . . . had been running continuously since Cleopatra had herself wrapped in a sheet [actually a rug] and delivered to Caesar."

Someone had offered him a series of inane cartoons "showing two goateed characters sitting by the levee, sipping mint juleps and discussing the merits of Springmaid sheets in Negro dialect. They think the Springs Cotton Mills need a Southern background." He had chased these ad men from his office. "I gave them a two-minute start," he said.

The Colonel realized that the basic problem with advertising was universal. "Now, you are not the only outfit which is lacking in originality," he assured his man in New York. "Many advertisements are an insult to a second grade IQ and are just as dull as yours." He acknowledged that cotton fabrics were "inherently uninteresting" to consumers and that the textile industry needed stimulating—even shocking—advertising techniques.

Elliott's assault upon staid and tasteless American advertising was set off by a *New Yorker* cartoon that caricatured ads for perfume. "When the editor couldn't stand the smell any longer, he printed a cartoon showing a girl shopping at the perfume counter with four children tugging at her skirts. She is toying with a bottle labeled LA PASSION, and the salesgirl is holding her head and shouting, 'For heaven's sake! NO! Madame!'" He cited another *New Yorker* parody of "fanny girdles that promise every-thing"—a cartoon of "a dowdy lady with a figure like a butterball in a corset shop struggling to get into one of the ultra-streamlined models. A very, very chic saleslady is standing by with her fingers to her ears in case of an explosion." Inspired by these ideas Springs conceived a campaign to burlesque American products and manufacturers. He wrote his agency, "Now, why can't we combine the ridiculous with the sublime and get something worth while out of it? We'll take a typical sexy ad and revise it into a cartoon."

As a central theme he resurrected a slogan he had sought to persuade his father to use twenty years earlier: "You can't go wrong on a Springmaid sheet."

Within a week he had outlined a series of lampoons of the foundation garment industry, launching a decade of hilarious mimicry that provoked both cries of outrage and gales of laughter and raised Springmaid sheets to the status of a national institution.

Springs began with specific suggestions to his agents:

"Here is a rough idea for such a series to run only in the sophisticated magazines. So, take it, toss it around, and refine it. But don't milk it." His ideas featured unlikely applications for fabrics Springs had produced for the military during the war.

Water-and-wind-resistant fabric for the "front support and rear guard business" could be illustrated by a wind-blown girl on a street corner, her skirts out of control.

A young lady at a party "being pinched surreptitiously by a gentleman behind her" could ignore the assault while the pincher grimaced in pain— her protective shield a tough, crease-proof fabric woven by Springs.

Another fabric offered protection through impregnation with "Jungle Smells" that once foiled Japanese troops during World War II—and could now defy problems of body odors in peacetime: "dancer's diaphoresis, ballerina's bouquet, rhumba aroma and skater's steam." Another antidote: sheets "impregnated with chlorophyll."

The best efforts of his New York agents to produce ads from these germs exasperated Elliott: "What I wanted was a subtle picture of a girl with her skirt agitated by the wind. You send me down a picture of a girl with her skirts blown over her head like she was standing over an air jet at Coney Island! It's about as subtle as the Can Can. Try again."

A month later: "The new sketches . . . are not even close. I want the ad . . . so designed that people . . . will think it is serious. I want it to appear as if we are just imitating our competitors, and really trying to sell sheets with cheesecake.

"A lot of dumb bunnies will then write in and bawl us out for being vulgar and stupid. Then some people will take a second look and catch the burlesque, and be very proud that they're so smart. They'll think they are the only one to get it, and write and tell us about it. That is, if we do a good job. But these last sketches will just make people think that we forgot to pull down the shade."

Springs dismissed his agency and hired a new man, Hill Wolfe, as advertising liaison in his New York office. His search for a creative agency was prolonged. Some firms declined the Springs account after reading Elliott's proposed campaign: "They . . . are scared of it," Wolfe reported. "They don't know what to do about art work and don't think any magazine will run our text." One ad executive said flatly, "We'll have nothing to do with such a campaign."

Elliott finally found an agent in Erwin, Wasey & Company, but his war with magazines raged on. The advertising trade magazine *Tide* reported problems: "Putting the media list together was no routine chore, since the arrival of the Colonel's copy usually sends the chosen publication into a spasm of conferences. . . . Springmaid's agency . . . admits that most of its ads have to go through publications' top echelons; often as far as the publishers themselves."

Despite such opposition, Elliott began his campaign in May 1948, in nine magazines including *Esquire, Fortune,* the *Saturday Evening Post,* and the *New York Times Magazine.* He won national attention immediately. *Time* reported that "such lusty ballyhoo . . . startled high-necked readers of *The New York Times.* . . . It also drew a shocked cry of 'bad taste' from *Advertising Age* and protest from the *New Yorker, Life* and other magazines which refused to run other Springmaid copy." *Tide* declared that Elliott's campaign failed "to achieve the fundamental objective of all product advertising—to sell goods. . . . Agency men who have seen the copy are most upset (90%) by it; advertisers are two-to-one against it."

But in Lancaster, the reading public was being heard from. A deluge of mail threatened to overwhelm the resources of The Springs Cotton Mills and the local post office as well. Elliott was equally delighted with the furious responses of offended readers and the enthusiastic praise of those who cheered him on.

To continue the campaign Springs bought drawings of sexy, half-dressed girls from New York artists and wrote his own copy to accompany them. Some of the best-known illustrators of the day began to work with him—James Montgomery Flagg, Rockwell Kent, Russell Patterson, Arthur William Brown, Varga, and Petty. One of the early "second-hand" cartoons he bought, from *Esquire*, was a Fritz Willis sketch of a young woman jumping rope, her skirt at the customary Springs-style high post and her bosom in delicate balance as it strained a low-cut blouse. Elliott found an appropriate clipping from the *Bawl Street Journal*, the mocking annual parody of the financial trade, which warned that congressmen were among the nation's most notorious girl-pinchers: "Any young females subject to bruises should wear at least two thicknesses of girdles before venturing on Capitol Hill. A chest protector would be valuable in a pinch."

Under the caption "Protect Your Assets," Elliott offered his celebrated "Poker" cloth, a crease-proof material developed during the war as backings for maps. Now, Springs assured American women, "If you bruise easily, you can face the future confidently with the Springmaid trademark." The same copy was used under the caption, "Beware the Goose," illustrated by one of Elliott's shapely, long-legged models standing in a pond, staring in distress at an aggressive mother goose.

As the campaign flourished, Elliott turned from ads for his "specialty" fabrics and began to market sheets. He prospected for ideas among employees, competitors, and friends. Some of the most striking of his ads were originated by his friends. A memorable early example was proposed by his friend Dr. Robert McKay: "What would you say to this—an Indian lying on a sheet, about half-dead, with a pretty squaw just leaving him? You could call it 'A buck well spent.'" Elliott needed no more. He soon had McKay's idea rendered by an artist—the buck collapsed in a hammock made from a sheet, looking as if he had been run over by a Conestoga wagon and the luscious departing squaw regarding him with a smile of satisfaction.

"A buck well spent on a Springmaid Sheet," the ad proclaimed. "This buck may look more like 47 cents—which is what *most* bucks are worth these days. But not *this* 'dearslayer.' Any buck spent on a SPRINGMAID sheet gets you value of *100 cents* on the dollar—as any two smart squaws know."

This spoof became a sensation. Elliott and his friends created variations upon it until the theme became rather threadbare, but in the process entertained themselves and a growing audience. Elliott's first spin-off from this ad was titled "How to Make an Extra Buck"—a scene in which a sexy Minnehaha, reclining in a canoe powered by a sail made of a

Springmaid sheet, skims past another canoe powered by two handsome bucks, one of whom is preoccupied by a beautiful squaw lying amidships. Minnehaha, with a wave to the salivating paddler in the bow, asks "Why push with a paddle when you can lay alongside a SPRINGMAID sheet?"

"Hereafter," the copy continued, "this Buck will be ballast for Minnehaha. . . ."

"How to make a buck for a banquet" was a sketch of an almost nude African maid luring a sailor from his sheet-powered raft to an ambush laid by cannibals whose pot and cooking utensils are in evidence. "I'm sure you can improve on that," Elliott wrote, "there's the start." It was also the end product, for the New York experts added only some brief copy, with the final line: "For everyone, from the man-eaters below the equator to the nose-rubbing Eskimos, knows he can't go wrong on a Springmaid sheet."

The most inspired nonsense in this series was an impromptu creation sketched on the back of the menu of a Palm Beach restaurant by the cartoonist "Zito," with whom Elliott and Frances and friends were dining. Zito's sketch depicted cannibals boiling a pot of water before "a very ripe blonde tied to a tree." A small black messenger was seen dashing to the spot. Elliott's roar of delight greeted the caption proposed by his friend, Tod Belfield of Pennsylvania: "Hold everything! The chief wants breakfast in bed."

The *Woman's Home Companion* played into Elliott's hands by refusing to publish his now-famous "Buck Well Spent" ad until it was redrawn so as to place both feet of the comely squaw on the ground, rather than posing her in the act of descending from the hammock. "Why are you so upset?" Elliott replied. "The only explanation I can think of is that you were disappointed in love by a ballet dancer and have developed a Freudian neurosis, which makes you allergic to any gal who raises one foot even high enough to rest it in a hammock." He declined to have the picture redrawn—and obscure the point of the ad.

This incident gave Elliott opportunity to test his inspiration for a remarkable by-product of his ad campaign—the Acousticot Bed. "If you won't take the squaw," he told this editor, "how about this one? I promise—no cheesecake. It's just a photograph of a bed with a lot of gadgets on the headboard like a lot of these Hollywood beds you see advertised in all the ritzy magazines. That's all—nobody in the bed."

The Acousticot was an all-purpose bed equipped with every luxury of which he could dream, a spoof on the American love for gadgetry. He had his bed built in the company shops and added improvements as reactions from an amused public stimulated Elliott's creative powers. Magazine ads depicted a huge bed in contemporary style, with Springs standing along-side in a Springmaid shirt. The copy was simple: " 'I tested sixty models,' says Joe Gish, our Undercover Agent, 'and there was not one single case of insomnia due to sleeping on Springmaid sheets.' "

The bed boasted an acoustical center board, to enable either occupant to snore without distracting the bedfellow. Soundproofing was so com-plete, in fact, that headphones were supplied for intercommunication, radio, and television. "Not even a hogcaller can arouse the occupants for breakfast, so a special set of high-frequency gongs is provided for rev-eille." Creaking slats and springs were avoided by use of foam rubber and a pulsating mattress.

There were also air-conditioning controls, hygrostat, thermostat, and aerostat, a sprinkler safety system, an electric razor, slot machine, movie projector and screen, a ship's bell, "turn and bank indicator," perfumer control with choices for mountaineers ("fragrance of spruce and sour mash"), Southerners ("mint and smoked ham"), or, for those who yearned for the tidewater towns, "the smell of fresh fish and decayed aristocracy."

Elliott appeared on Dave Garroway's popular television show to pro-mote the bed and then sent the Acousticot on a cross-country tour of department stores where it was offered, in jest, at a price of $3,500.

The Acousticot drew the appreciative laughter Elliott had anticipated—but a show in New York attracted some customers whose reaction brought the joke to an unexpected end. Staff members of the Ethiopian Embassy felt that the Acousticot would be an ideal gift for Emperor Haile Selassie and ordered one shipped home. No record of comment from the Lion of Judah, nor of the bed's subsequent adventures, has survived.

Delighted by private responses from readers, Elliott intensified the uproar by publishing complaints in a new book, *Clothes Make the Man*. Some suspected that many of these protests might have been concocted by Elliott himself, but his files reveal that all were genuine cries of anguish from readers who denounced Springs as a degrading influence upon American mores. Elliott published scores of these without comment:

"I am through with Springmaid sheets. . . . They are very fine but I prefer—after all these years—to deal with decent people."

"I should think a man in a big business like you would watch out for what goes in these magazines under your name. Some of the awfullest things are said about using sheets and all. It looks like whoever writes your advertising does not have a spark of decency left. I would advise you to look into it very soon."

"Your copy stinks, and in my nostrils it causes your products to stink . . . simply vulgar."

A woman in Louisville, Kentucky, incensed by a Springs ad, declared, "I am not a fanatic . . . I read current fiction, see Broadway plays . . . and consider myself a fairly normal human of twenty-seven. Advertising is a dignified and useful art. You have degraded it. . . . May I suggest that you get a new advertising head?"

A housewife from Bigelow, Minnesota, was offended by Elliott's sale of copies of the ad, "A Buck Well Spent." She wrote, "I am sure your sales must have increased. . . . It has certainly put your fabrics into the limelight and I suppose many have sent their quarters for pictures 'suitable for framing.'

"But today great leaders of the world are deploring the fact that so many homes are ruined by divorce. It is alarming to see our inward decay creeping upon us. Does it mean nothing to you that you are helping this flood of immorality along? This ad encourages indecency, adultery, and divorce. I plead with you to think for a moment about the God who said, 'Thou shalt not commit adultery.' "

Elliott was particularly pleased by a letter from the president of a small denominational college in New York state who charged Springs with promoting "loose morals, drunkenness and gambling" among American youth, which, he pointed out, needed little encouragement:

"In 1945 there were 95,000 illegitimate births recorded . . . nearly 50% to girls between fifteen and nineteen." This critic also cited the Kinsey report on sexual behavior and added: "The American home is facing a blackout with 25% of marriages ending in divorce." The protester sent the offensive ad and a copy of his letter to the sternly moral journal *Evangelical Action*. Springs went to unusual lengths to help the cleric publicize this outburst.

Though his campaign was a great success, the Colonel was frustrated by the technical difficulties of shepherding ads into print. Communication with New York in such complex matters became a nightmare. He set up his own studio in a vacant mill house in Lancaster. Buddy Montgomery, a young local photographer who became his one-man staff, never forgot the years of hectic activity that followed:

> He tore out the interior of a house and set up an old iron bed, an orange crate and a rickety bedside lamp, and that was our stage setting.
>
> The Colonel brought in twenty-five or thirty girls, one after the other, to pose in and around the bed. He liked to pick out the Springmaid girls himself, too. He went through the mills to find the prettiest ones, and then he'd dress them up in nighties or whatever he had in mind, and I'd pose them and shoot them.
>
> You could see it was his creative outlet. He was enjoying doing something that no one else had done, and doing it in-house with a boy photographer.

Montgomery understood the problems of communication between the Colonel and New York.

"He changed his ideas about every picture at least twice a day, so it was almost impossible for him to work with an agency. He drove them crazy. So he worked at home, and when we got the pose he wanted, he'd send it to New York and let them take it from there.

"He would get a basic idea and I would go to work. But he didn't want me to change anything—not even the least detail. 'Don't think,' he told me. 'I pay you to work. I think.' You did things his way."

Montgomery's patience was often tested by the Colonel's quest for perfection. On one occasion he made two thousand photographs for an ad posed by Springs himself. "He simply changed his mind. He would send those pictures to all kinds of people and get comments, and then we'd shoot again, over and over, until he was satisfied."

One example of Elliott's personal intrusion into the ads became a favorite with readers—though its impact upon sheet sales may have been minimal. He chose a drawing of a pretty girl with panties visible and bosom overflowing her blouse, with autumn leaves swirling about her—an ad rejected by several magazines. The copy promoted one of Elliott's old standbys, crease-proof fabric for underclothing. Elliott instructed his agency to revamp the ad to include a new joke calculated to outrage the guardians of public morals: "Take the same picture and remove the girl's shoes, bracelet and necklace. Take out the autumn leaves. Put in a pool to explain why she is barefooted. Then, put a box inconspicuously some distance from the text reading, 'Elliott Springs, President of The Springs Cotton Mills, says he is prepared to make anything shown in the picture.' " The ad (complete with autumn leaves) appeared in *Collier's* August 28, 1948. Though laughter was the general reaction, there were enough complaints to delight the Colonel.

The National Better Business Bureau scolded Elliott for debasing American morals with his gag: "We, of course, assume that you had neither the intention nor the desire to have the readers . . . get the impression that the copy was to be interpreted literally. However, since the courts have ruled that the public has the right to interpret advertising literally, it seems to us that . . . your advertisement is very likely to draw criticism upon advertising. . . . We respectfully ask whether you would not be willing . . . to make the slight modification of the phraseology necessary to clarify the copy."

Elliott had no intention of "clarifying" the copy for the "National Busybody Bureau," and he was highly amused by the suggestion of a reader from Milwaukee that Springs himself was unable to "comprehend the innuendo" his advertising experts had used. "The matter contained in your ads is so vile," this correspondent wrote, "that the Postmaster General will take an interest in suppressing them."

Many protesters were so literal-minded as to complain that Springs was challenging the Almighty in this ad. As he wrote his agency, "I told you to take out those autumn leaves. So far I have received 320 letters enclosing the ad and ending up with 'only God can make a tree.' "

The Colonel did not hesitate to insert himself into his campaign under other pretexts. He once announced, "Elliott White Springs is not a resort but an author. The confusion arises because SPRINGMAID sheets are known as America's favorite playground."

In one of his satirical "Men of Distinction" testimonial ads he posed in a cape of Springmaid Girl material, a low-crowned derby hat that recalled early vaudeville comics, and his back-support brace worn outside shirt and trousers. He also wore sunglasses with red and green lenses and shoes with red and green vamps. He stood beside a Buick disguised as a Stutz Bearcat (with Russian license plates) whose fog lights were also in red and green, with a dog sporting one red and one green eye. He perpetuated this zaniness by ordering six pairs of shoes with the red and green vamps and wore them for years with his bizarre costumes.

Elliott also posed as a fisherman (with arm in cast and sling and two black eyes) and as a big game hunter, with a preposterous elephant head overhanging his living room fireplace.

Springs stirred a fresh furor with his protest of the innate vulgarity of American culture in an ad depicting four familiar cleavages—a quartet of women in poses emphasizing the need for more effective brassieres. In the group, which he offered without comment, were well-known entertainers of the era—Dagmar, Marilyn Monroe, Dorothy Kilgallen, and Faye Emerson. The spectacularly busty Dagmar created some problems. She demanded $1,500 to pose for a later picture, which Elliott felt was excessive for "an hour's work," but he agreed, adding, "I'm sorry I can't get to New York to fit the blouse." When she learned that the caption for the ad was "We put the broad in broadcloth," the model demurred on the ground that her dignity would be at risk.

Elliott's expose of the great American bosom drew prolonged response. A particularly vociferous protest, as Springs reported it, came in a telephone call from a New York lawyer who represented brassiere and corset manufacturers—"The Foundation Federation."

"This business is intimate, but it's dignified," the lawyer told Springs. "What's fun to you is bread and butter to our manufacturers. You must discontinue that ad at once."

"If I'm really hurting the business I'll stop at once," Springs said disarmingly, "but I believe I'm helping."

"Why refer to our industry as 'the bust bucket business'?"

"I'll gladly use another name."

"What do you have in mind?"

"I'll use something from your manufacturers' own ads."

"I can't be responsible for all their ads," the lawyer said quickly.

"Why, then, do you want to be responsible for Springmaid ads?"

The lawyer threatened an injunction.

"That's all right with me," Springs said calmly. "In fact, I'll pay the legal costs—but of course I'll have to bring my model into court."

The lawyer slammed down the telephone but called again within an hour. "I've studied your ad—I just want to say the girl's skirt is not high enough to show off her panties to best advantage—and why is she wearing no bra?"

"She's wearing one, all right. It's made of our new camouflaged material."

After a pause the lawyer said guardedly, "Could you send me a sample?"

"Soon," Springs reported, "we were talking like old friends and this bird asked whom we used as public relations counsel."

"We don't have any."

"I'd like to apply for the job."

Springs declined his application.

Elliott resorted to historical precedent to justify burlesques of contemporary ads featuring testimonials from leaders of American society. "Everybody has gotten a little annoyed with the testimonial type ad," he wrote Hill Wolfe.

> I believe Queen Victoria originated this particular racket whereby the Royal Family gets paid for endorsing a hair tonic or a shoe polish, but in this country it has reached the low point of snobbery whereby American purchasers are asked to imitate any little tramp who happens to be temporarily bedded and boarded by Royal appointment . . .
>
> Let's get out an ad using the best points of the English and American system. The copy will read:
> "I LOVE SHOW PLACES," says MRS. MARTIN MCMARTIN ST. MARTIN III, "ESPECIALLY SPRINGMAID SHEETS."

He added a few lines of slapstick copy with the claim that "other large users" of his sheets included the Countess of Skavinsky Skivar, Fraulein Lilli Marlene, Miss Belle Watling, and Mademoiselle D'Armentieres. But these were only the beginning. He invoked the names of Lady Chatterly, Belle Boyd, Mercedes Benz, Sadie Thompson, Lady Fauntleroy, the Infantas Casablanca and Torquemada, Scarlett O'Hara, and Nell Gwynne.

Springs suggested imposing houses or institutions as backgrounds for the series—"Dundreary Castle or the Breakers." One result was that lawyers for the Reformed Presbyterian Church threatened suit after he published a photograph of one of its retirement homes in an ad. Elliott's response revealed no remorse: "Please introduce them to the firm that is going to sue us over the Junior League ad, and tell them both, if they will wait a few weeks, they will have plenty of company."

Elliott's favorite weapon in this campaign was Gypsy Rose Lee, who became a star of the satirical ads so disturbing to the dull fellows of Madison Avenue. She seemed to welcome this new role as the bogus queen of society. Gypsy had come into Elliott's life to help promote the L & C railroad. His fun-loving friend Agnew Bahnson of Winston-Salem,

North Carolina, brought the stripper to Elliott's attention as a devoted rail fan who kept models of famous trains in her cellar. Elliott invited her to dedicate the Lancaster & Chester's new depot in Lancaster and named her the line's "Vice-President in Charge of Unveiling." Gypsy arrived with her six-year-old son, Erik. Frances Springs, who was not pleased, saw to it that the visitors were housed in the railroad car, *Loretto.* Gypsy rode in a parade through Lancaster and captivated a large crowd. After her introduction by Springs, Miss Lee seized a gilded hatchet ready to sever ropes and release an enormous sheet which covered the facade of the new station.

"You don't mind if I take off my gloves?" she said. "I can assure you that will be all."

The crowd sighed. Gypsy whacked the cords and unveiled the new building and clambered into the cab of a diesel engine with Erik and clowned for photographers. Elliott asked her to take the throttle for a brief run.

"What's a throttle?"

"That's something that when you pull it, something happens."

"Oh, yes. Like a zipper."

She jerked the throttle, and the engine surged ahead.

Despite the 102-degree heat of the day, Miss Lee appeared to enjoy the ceremonies. It was the first of several invasions of Fort Mill and Lancaster by Gypsy, some of them with reinforcements of show girls from her troupe—but her most popular role in collaboration with Springs was his advertising campaign.

On one of these visits Miss Lee posed for a memorable ad while sitting in a bathtub in Elliott's home, as the smiling proprietor stood nearby in full dress. In this case, at least, Miss Lee's image was not her own. Buddy Montgomery recalled, "When I made those pictures, Gypsy no longer had such a great body so I superimposed her head over the body of Mavis Funderburke, a Miss Springmaid Beauty Contest winner who did have a great body."

Gypsy appeared in the series caricaturing testimonial ads as "Mrs. Julio Diego, charming collector of modern art," as "Princess Napoleona Buonaparte," and other characters of Elliott's imagination—but she usually appeared as herself. She posed *en négligée* on several fashionably dressed beds, smiling broadly, or giving her audience a wicked wink as she declared, "My favorite nite spot is a Springmaid sheet." For the cause, she went to such lengths as to lift a sheet from the spikes of an Indian fakir's bed, to illustrate some of Elliott's outrageous puns: "I'm going to spike a rumor" and, in a second version, "That's no way to spike a roomer."

Elliott made occasional use of older friends in the campaign, one of them the actress Luella Gear with whom he apparently had an enduring romance. Miss Gear was posed beside her Long Island swimming pool, confiding to the public that she had used Springmaid sheets "since cotton became fashionable. Why shouldn't I? They didn't cost me anything!" She maintained that Elliott was a proud but inept bridge player "who paid off in sheets rather than money."

Miss Gear remained his friend until near his death; he seldom missed one of her Broadway openings and was usually among the first to go backstage to congratulate the star.

The provocative series of "endorsements" by his assorted celebrities continued over the years, most of them devised by Elliott himself. When the American star Gussie Moran shocked the sedate world of tennis by appearing at Wimbledon in short skirts that revealed her lace-trimmed panties, Elliott immediately featured her in his ads. She posed with his custom Rolls-Royce on a New York street minus a slip with panties of a Springmaid design fully revealed.

There was also the sultry red-haired singer Connie Russell, who had just released a recording of the tune "Don't Smoke in Bed." The temptress was pictured in bed, gazing at the reader and cooing, "I love these slow-burning Springmaid sheets."

In 1949, when his campaign was still young, Elliott developed a gag about a bowlegged bride whose hopes of happiness lay in her other charms. For months he sought in vain to have New York artists draw such a girl's legs for him. "No! No! No!" he once wrote his New York agency. "I said a bow-legged girl! The sketches show girls with bandy legs, corkscrew legs, bench legs, piano legs, spindle legs and the Arc de Triomphe. But not one good pair of legs slightly bowed. I don't want a caricature. . . . bend her legs slightly outward, or forget the whole thing." Elliott then "trained" a homegrown artist from Spartanburg, Wales Turner, who produced a winsome drawing of a windblown bride, revealing a pair of bowed legs that delighted Elliott. He sent the picture to New York and suggested a caption smacking of an old poolroom joke: "A Bride Must Have a Chest Full of Sheets and a Soul Full of Hope."

The punch line for his copy read, "So, a bride's platform for a happy marriage should be to forego hemstitching and monograms, which show wear first, and put only the right thing on her SPRINGMAID sheets. Then she will have sheets for her grandchildren, and grandchildren for her sheets." Later, in his book *Clothes Make the Man*, the picture was captioned "A girl's best friend is her chest."

Clarke Olney, a literary critic who had praised *War Birds*, dismissed Elliott's ads as beneath the notice of serious readers. "Springs' crusade to debunk advertising is no doubt commendable, but there are times when he seems to go too far." Olney felt that such phrases as "bust buckets," "bosom bolsters," "lung lifters," "ham hampers," and "hip harness" displayed poor taste as well as alliterative skill and an eye for the picturesque: "Of course, it *is* a matter of taste rather than morals, and probably harms no one; moreover, it undoubtedly gives Colonel Springs—and many of his readers—a modicum of pleasure. And unquestionably it has brought the Springmaid line its share of business."

Elliott took delight in reporting that his ads had indeed brought a dramatic surge in profits. He wrote to a New York columnist who questioned the value of the ads, "When we started our campaign, we had six customers using the Springmaid label. We now have over ten thousand stores in every state and every province who display our sheets . . . and we can't keep up with the demand." He conceded that other factors contributed to his new prosperity, especially the efficient new bleachery, which by the spring of 1953 was turning out seven million yards of cloth weekly. New machinery in his renovated plants had also aided the surge in business, and his standards of quality were part of his secret: "Even our competitors admit that we make the best cloth in the market."

Within a few months the ads and the restructuring of Springs Mills had transformed Springmaid sheets from an unknown brand into one of the most familiar American textile products. Elliott soon overtook Cannon Mills, a traditional leader in the field, and for many years led the nation in production.

Elliott was alert to every nuance of the campaign that might affect sales. One magazine declined an ad captioned "Bundling without Bungling," in which a baffled colonial couple inspected a bed divided by a bundling board installed by the girl's parents. Springs protested that this advertisement had drawn more than ten thousand letters from earlier readers. *Liberty*, he noted, increased its circulation by 180,000 with the issue that carried the bundling ad. Many of these readers, he said, wrote of "how much they enjoyed the ads, and hoped that we would continue to give the hotfoot to hucksters who mix a little dirt with colored water and claim that it does everything."

Still, he was not a cocksure ad man: "My grandfather and my father before me ran this business for sixty years on the mousetrap theory, and it must have worked pretty well. They never spent a nickel on advertising. I am not sure that I was wise to change that policy." But he claimed that, once he had begun, he was virtually forced to continue his campaign. At the end of each year, Elliott said, he tried to halt the ads but was overruled by a public clamor: "Every time there is a pause our customers write, wire and telephone insisting that I give them more of the same, and quickly."

He published calendars featuring his ads and sent them to customers. When the Springs calendar failed to appear in January 1953, he was "deluged with complaints from all over the world." In response, Elliott hastily assembled a new calendar that appeared belatedly in May and silenced the howls of his audience.

By the summer of 1953, the campaign had gained such momentum that most leading magazines were eager to share the limelight. When he learned that a new series had been accepted by the *New Yorker*, *Newsweek*, *Woman's Day*, *McCall's*, and the *Ladies Home Journal*, Elliott feigned distress: "Our show must be slipping! Those magazines run only very dull ads." His confidence was restored, he claimed, by *Life*, *Collier's*, the *Woman's Home Companion*, and the *Princeton Alumni Weekly*, which were "still able to recognize a threat to the sanctity of womanhood, and rejected them indignantly."

This pattern continued. These four publications were still holding out when Elliott launched his series of ads featuring "leaders" of high society. This time they were joined by *Life*, *Newsweek*, *Harper's Bazaar*, *Time*, *Collier's*, and several newspapers including the *New York Times*, the *New York Herald-Tribune*, and the *American Weekly*.

Other editors also resisted Springs.

He once concocted an ad based on a none-too-subtle pun on the name of Polly Adler, a celebrated New York madam whose memoir, *A House Is Not a Home*, had become a best-seller. Elliott's ad depicted "Polly Adullah" as she flew through the air on a sheet, calling down to the reader, "I love to navigate on a Springmaid sheet." This scene caused nervousness among editors of *Vogue* magazine, who insisted that he change the name "Adullah" to "Abdullah"—diminishing the risk of a libel suit but rendering the ad obscure and virtually meaningless. Elliott pointed out that *Vogue's* current issue included such advertising art as "a grown lady sitting in a tub naked to the navel, and a portrait of Dorothy Kilgallen endorsing plated tableware. Polly Adullah won't do either. I had rather just skip the whole thing." He placed the ad elsewhere.

The assault on Madison Avenue continued with new salvoes each month. To maintain his production of double entendre, Elliott devised such illustrated hoots as a female circus midget performing a high-wire act on a taut sheet held by clowns: "You Can't Stretch a Good Thing Too Far," the ad declared. Another depicted an elated company of volunteer firemen onto whose outstretched sheet a pretty model was falling from a burning building. The rhymed text was the work of Elliott's staff poet-attorney, A. Z. F. Wood, but had a distinct Springs flavor: "We love to give the gals a treat and catch them on a Sprigmaid sheet. We make them, Sir—and that's no jest. The sheets, we mean, they'll pass the test."

In fact, Elliott seemed to devote most of his working hours to his jousting with the hidebound world of advertising. He and Wood spent happy evenings devising new soft-sell schemes for Springmaid sheets by rewriting words to such old ballads as "Who Threw the Overalls in Mrs. Murphy's Chowder," "Abdullah Bulbul Ameer," "She'll Be Comin' Round the Mountain," and "I Took My Harp to a Party." (Elliott's suggestion for transforming the last: "I took my sheet to a party, but nobody asked me to lay.")

At this time Elliott produced his book, *Clothes Make the Man*, a volatile mixture of his short stories (which changed with succeeding editions) and some of his elaborate jokes—but chiefly he told the story of his ad campaign and its results. He promoted the book in much the same spirit he had given to his ads:

"Elliott White Springs, President of The Springs Cotton Mills, has written another book . . . which was indignantly rejected by every editor and publisher who read it. So he had it printed privately and sent it to his friends for Christmas. After they read it, he ran out of friends, so there are some extra copies. It contains a veritable treasury of useless information, such as how to build cotton mills, how to give first aid on Park Avenue, and how to write advertisements."

On other occasions the book was offered in a "35 cent pocket edition," a "head-whirling book" that included "the possible solution to three of New York's most famous unsolved murder mysteries, his sizzling letters and short stories, plus how to lose friends and write advertisements."

The critic Clarke Olney felt that this "hodgepodge" of a book contained "some of the very worst" of Elliott's early stories, "which, unfunny and tasteless in the 20's, are even more so today." Olney believed that Springs's literary reputation suffered from this publication.

But Elliott was not only enjoying himself. He was also a tireless merchant now that he had found a stage. He combined pictures of Springmaid ad girls into a "Harem Print" and sold shirts of this material. The girls also appeared in calendars annually—and in decals and reprints—all sold through the ads themselves.

To give his campaign a new dimension, Elliott tracked down the amusing spoofs of classical paintings made by his late friend, Grace Drayton, whose kewpie doll drawings had been used earlier in Campbell Soup advertising. There was soon a series of Springmaid ads including Drayton illustrations with the smirking kewpie posing as Mona Lisa or other celebrated subjects of Da Vinci, Rubens, Van Dyck, or Gainsborough.

The furor over Elliott's unorthodox advertising continued until his death, for he persisted until he had seen the Springmaid name become a household word and company sales nearly double in a decade. His campaign was praised as "one of the most cost-effective in the history of advertising"—a success won despite the growing popularity of man-made fibers. Springs was one of the few companies that flourished by producing finished cotton goods of high quality.

The Colonel was also entertaining himself and his friends, quite apart from the practical results of his efforts. *Fortune* commented,

> Springs has fun with his advertisements. By now nearly every literate American is acquainted with the Springs Mills ads—the willowy, leggy, abundantly busted girls scantily attired . . . a burlesque of . . . the advertising business as a whole. . . .
>
> All of the cries [of protest] have served only to impress the general public forcibly with the Springs Mills trademark, exactly the intent of Springs' campaign. . . . An unreconstructed business rebel, he has gone ahead, selling, competing, producing, and having a good time. Making money, for him, seemed to be a by-product of having a good time—which is probably the reason he makes a lot of money.

Springs was hailed as an influential pioneer by Professor of Marketing James D. Taylor of South Dakota, author of numerous cases for Harvard's Intercollegiate Case Clearing House. "Springs was a forerunner of the school of advertising that seeks a dramatic contrast with contemporaries," Taylor wrote. "With so much competition, having something to say is not enough. An ad must be memorable and relevant to the brand. . . . Ads should entertain, not bore. . . .

"Springs did achieve what he attempted. . . . One wonders if any other type of ads could have gained these objectives."

In later years, though he was given scant credit in the history of American advertising, his campaign was taught in numerous college courses, and the influence of his Springmaid ads lingered for a generation.

In the wake of Elliott's unique campaign, American advertising lost many of its inhibitions, and Madison Avenue never again took itself quite so seriously. The exhausted Indian brave, the alluring sex symbols, Gypsy Rose Lee, Marilyn Monroe, Dagmar and company—and the parade of saucy pinup girls—had not performed in vain.

XIV / "This Is Small Enough for the Colonel to Decide"

ypsy Rose Lee visited Fort Mill several other times, and Frances Springs was at first amused. One evening when the striptease queen was a guest for dinner in the White homestead, Mrs. Springs invited Anne and Bill Close and their friends, Mary and John Hallett.

Mary Hallett recalled the subtle undertone of humor provided by Mrs. Springs—who had privately sent Anne and Mary pairs of flamboyant sequined panties with a suggestion that they wear them for the occasion. "It was a memorable evening," Mrs. Hallett said. "Gypsy was a good conversationalist, was quite ladylike and beautifully dressed. But Anne and I enjoyed it mostly because of Mrs. Springs's delicious sense of humor."

Once more, at least, Elliott invited Gypsy to visit without notifying Frances. The guests arrived in a large touring car—half a dozen strippers, Gypsy and her son, Erik. There were also four cats, for whose benefit a bathroom was spread with newspapers. As one friend remembered it, Frances was appalled. Elliott ate supper in Lancaster that night, apparently to avoid his wife's wrath. This precaution was unnecessary, because Mrs. Springs left for Charlotte, apparently in a huff.

Thereafter Elliott's relationship with Gypsy continued only in New York, where he saw her with some regularity. His telegraphed congratulations on the opening of a new Broadway show ended with the promise: "I look forward to seeing you every week."

There was gossip of an affair between Elliott and the stripper, and Elliott probably encouraged such reports. He sometimes went to great lengths to create an impression that he was a lady-killer. (In hope of shocking his callers he kept a life-size cutout of a scantily clad Marilyn Monroe in the toilet of his private office.) Springs and Miss Lee were certainly congenial and had mutual interests. Elliott admired her resourcefulness, showmanship, and business acumen, and especially the literary abilities revealed in her mystery novel, *The G-String Murders.*

Righton Richards, Sonny's former teacher and coach, retained an impression that Frances was offended by Elliott's relationship with other women: "Elliott had dated Rhetta Blakeney, from Camden, years before, and he liked to go to the races in Camden and play cards and drink all night with a crowd. He often went without Frances."

In any case Rhetta Blakeney and Frances Springs were intimate friends. After one domestic spat in the Springs household, the two women left town together—Frances evidently seeking to irritate her husband. Elliott seized the opportunity to fare forth on his own. He telegraphed Larry Callahan: "Frances has left for Bermuda in a four-motored dudgeon. Worse than that she has taken Rhetta with her. Luella Gear is opening in New York in a new musical show called *My Romance* on Tuesday. I have met the chorus, and there are some fine *bridge players* among them [italics by author]. I think I will fly to New York Friday in my single-motored dudgeon and investigate the matter further. Do you care to join me? We can visit Lu over the weekend."

Such outings by Springs must have been brief at this time, for he was unusually busy at home. Spurred by the growth of the company he built a new headquarters in Fort Mill, one of the most remarkable industrial structures in the country. Planning for this had begun in 1936 after his return from Germany, where Elliott had seen the ultramodern offices of the huge chemical firm, I. G. Farben.

He began his fruitless search for an architect by sending his engineer, E. W. Scruggs, to see Frank Lloyd Wright. Scruggs was taken aback by Wright's demands: "You understand that when I design a building I design everything, including furniture—and I won't touch it if you are going to build under contract."

"How do you ever get your work done?" Scruggs asked.

"I have no time to argue with contractors when I want to change a line here or there, or even tear down a wall after it's built. Build with day labor and supervise it yourself."

Scruggs reported to Springs, "You don't want Wright."

"Why not?"

"You're too much alike. We'd never get the damn thing built. He's out of the question."

Elliott turned elsewhere. One distinguished New York firm designed a nine-story tower crowned by a massive statue that Springs rejected as inappropriate to the setting. He also eliminated an all-glass design as too hot for the South Carolina climate, and for various reasons he spurned the sketches of other nationally known architects including Eero Saarinen.

Elliott and several of his executives, Scruggs among them, had a memorable final session with one of these firms. The architect presented drawings of an imposing building surrounded by a moat, with a separate building for the Colonel's office at the end of a winding drive. Springs was attracted to the idea, but the visitor offended him during the conference. "Now, Colonel," the architect began, "you know all about textile manufacturing and we know nothing. And we know all about architecture and you know nothing."

Elliott rose abruptly. "Pay him off, Scruggs," he said quietly and left the room.

The architect was incredulous. "What did he mean?"

"Just what he said," Scruggs replied. "You'll never do business with Springs." He did not trouble to explain that the Colonel would brook no challenge to his knowledge and expertise, whatever the field—or that Elliott considered himself a competent amateur architect. The firm was paid for its preliminary work, and its crestfallen partner left town.

Elliott developed a plan of his own by importing two designers from the Atlanta engineering firm of his friend Chip Robert. These men worked for weeks developing numerous plans, all of which Elliott rejected. At the end of a month, when Springs turned down the best of their designs, the Roberts men told Scruggs they were going home.

"Just give it one more try," Scruggs urged. "If he rejects this you can quit and I'll stay on with it. Let's just turn the building upside down and make a few changes so he won't recognize it."

This plan was taken to Springs a few days later. "Exactly what I wanted," he said brusquely. "Build it."

"It was exactly the same plan he'd rejected," Scruggs said. "It was just turned upside down and with its windows slanting inward. Those windows sold him—they reminded him of the *Hindenburg*'s windows."

The building which emerged was without precedent. Its two floors were "successively overhanging," and the exterior walls were suspended from the roof, rather than supporting it—which allowed windows to be set at an inverted angle to bar direct rays of the sun. Exterior walls, floors, and ceilings were independent of each other, and interior walls were movable partitions. There were teak floors, aluminum window sashes, and ceilings of soundproof panels. The exterior appearance of this huge contemporary building was so skillfully rendered as to maintain the harmony of the small-town setting—despite the presence of the late nineteenth-century home of Elliott's great uncle, John White, which stood just across the street.

Elliott added a few touches of his own to the final plan. To save space, so he said, he ordered a concealed conference table for his office which rose through the floor at the push of a button.

Elliott also had lively skirmishes with interior decorators. He called in a celebrated firm from New York, but when presented with its design said sharply, "There's nothing here I couldn't buy in Macy's basement." Elliott pretended that the cost of the building exhausted his budget for furnishings, so he proposed that the furniture be made from old mill machinery and parts. He recorded the ensuing reaction: "This was a shock to everyone, and the engineers, architects, decorators, and furniture manufacturers shouted that this would desecrate a beautiful building and make them the laughing stocks of their respective professions. The president announced that an empty office building would make him the laughing stock of his respective profession, and the estimates for furnishings would make him the laughing stock of his respective banker."

He fitted out the entire huge structure with furniture made from old mill equipment and machinery. He had his staff members design pieces from junk stored in his warehouses: an 1800-pound loom, a spinning frame, a stitching machine, and some motor supports all became sofas; a bobbin and a roving can were made into a lamp; a yarn frame was used to build a desk; spools, rolls, cones, creel boards, shuttles, crankshafts, all went into the bizarre furniture of the new building. Rugs were made of discarded Sanforizer blankets. Bale cloth burlap now covered the walls. Even flower pots, ashtrays, cuspidors, and a hand-dryer in his restroom were made from obsolete mill equipment. The result, as A. Z. F. Wood reported in the *American Weekly*, was furniture "so graceful and practical that it made [15,000 opening day] visitors gasp."

The president's office was an oasis. Despite the junk-pile furniture, the decor was dignified, and Elliott's desk was equipped with controls to raise the directors' table from beneath the floor, open and close the 120-foot drapery screen which gave him privacy—or expose blackboard charts and graphs. There were also controls for radio, television, lights, telephones, recording machine, and film projector. His secretary's chair was equipped with a vibrator.

Elliott found himself with a blank space around the walls of his office, some four feet high and 120 feet long, and for this space he proposed the installation of a photographic mural of his 29-mile Lancaster & Chester Railway. Despite the insistence of aerial photographers that this was an impossibility, Springs sent Cecil Neal aloft with the well-known photographer Elliott Lyman Fisher. They flew up and down the line until Fisher had worked out the scale and photographed the varied landscape along every foot of the track—villages, mills, fields, and woodlands. When several experimental mountings of the prints failed to satisfy the Colonel, Fisher colored each of his enlarged color slides by hand. One hundred and eighty lights illuminated the slides from the rear, giving them a three-dimensional effect that reminded one viewer of "seeing the curtain go up at the Metropolitan." At last the master of the L & C had spread before him the complete panorama of his cherished little railroad, which he could now inspect at any hour of the working day.

The novelty of the bizarre furniture wore off within a few years, and it was replaced. But in the meantime Elliott's appetite for detail remained insatiable, and his staff suffered for months before he was content with the new building. He had false windows installed in some of the windowless offices "to prevent claustrophobia." One of these treatments was a three-dimensional photograph of a mill clock tower, so realistic in appearance that Elliott had a real clock installed in the pictured tower to carry out the illusion. He had the hours tolled by the sound of a mill whistle rather than a chime. Realism was further enhanced by tiny puffs of smoke which rose from the mill stacks.

Other defects drew Elliott's attention. E. W. Scruggs was bombarded with memos from the President's office:

"You will remember that I specified thermopane glass. . . . Well, I have news for you. The engineers knew better. . . . The result is that when the heat comes on, there is condensation. . . . You can't wipe the windows without taking them apart."

A few days later he wrote:

I left the cooling and heating systems to the engineers. . . . Well, I have news for you. Yesterday, eighteen of us went into the Conference Room, the temperature was about seventy-six. An hour later it was ninety. . . . There is not an office in the whole buiding with a thermostat. And since the air ducts and radiant heating pipes are set in solid concrete . . . to remount and wire up . . . we would have to tear down the whole building. Well, it's an idea at that. There's one thing you can do. Come up here with a sledge hammer and knock a hole in the Conference Room wall and install an exhaust fan.

And again:

You will recall that the windows were set at an angle so no direct sunlight . . . would come through. . . .
   The engineers miscalculated by five degrees. For the last week the sun has been getting low enough to shine through the back windows.
   I have consulted with my astronomer and find this condition will last from December 9 to January 21. I have consulted with the building superintendent and find that . . . it will be impossible to install blinds or shades. . . . Of course we could paint them, but that would cut out all the light. The only solution is to equip all the personnel with adjustable dark glasses.
   My congratulations to the engineers!

It was a rare occasion when Elliott lost control, but one such incident was reported during his struggle to perfect the new building. When he proposed a project to Engineer Scruggs and was told it could not be done, Springs strode furiously down the hall, his face livid, shouting, "It's my damn company and I'll run it any way I damn well please." After he had recovered his poise, he returned to work as if nothing untoward had happened.
   The movable table in Elliott's office was also a source of trouble for the engineers. Long after the elevator platform was installed, mechanics were called virtually every Monday morning to adjust or make repairs. They were baffled by the recurring malfunctions until Elliott confessed that he permitted his grandchildren to play with the apparatus on weekends, pretending that they were raising his board of directors into sight or abruptly consigning it to the depths.

Despite such episodes, Joe Croxton, the company architect, became devoted to Springs. "I found that I really missed him when he went away. Things got dull without him. He got ideas from all over. His mind was always whirring—you could almost hear it."

Elliott's pride in his managerial ability bred cunning in Croxton and other executives, who went to great lengths to convince him that he had actually originated proposals they hoped to put into action. The architect habitually included at least three minor errors in drawings he presented for Elliott's approval—realizing that he would never accept a proposal without raising some objection. For years, as Croxton anticipated, Springs pointed out the obvious errors incorporated for his benefit and then accepted the work. Croxton finally learned that Elliott had been aware of the ruse all the while when he declined to inspect one drawing and said, "Just make those three changes of yours, Joe, and go ahead with it."

Croxton was asked to design a new wing for the White homestead including a facility Springs called a Nataborium (evidently combining "natatorium" and "arboretum")—an indoor swimming pool within a greenhouse filled with tropical plants. "He was a stickler for detail," Croxton recalled. "When I put a brown pelican in a mural in his nataborium, he had first to make certain the bird was native to Florida." When Croxton rendered in flaming red the bloom of a vine he had seen at Biltmore House, Elliott asked him to drive to Asheville and confirm its color.

Springs saw in a magazine a photograph of the diving tower and slide of a swimming pool aboard the new luxury liner *Andrea Doria*. "I want that," he told Croxton. "Fly to New York and get photographs right away."

The architect discovered that the ship was scheduled to sail at 5 P.M. of that day, but he telephoned a New York photographer who hurried to the docks. "The ship was about to sail and the poor guy went through hell. The pool area was roped off, it was raining—and he got poor photographs. I finally got what the Colonel wanted from one of my friends in New York.

"When we got the slide drawings and built the thing, I told him it would last no more than twenty-five years—the base would collapse."

"What do I care what happens twenty-five years from now?" Springs asked. "I won't be around."

Croxton frequently found himself driven to achieve "impossible" goals by the uncompromising Colonel. On one occasion when he was entertaining board members of the Southern Railway in his home, Springs belatedly conceived of a bronze plaque to remind his fellow directors of the spectacular profits reaped by investors in the railroad's stock.

"I want a bronze plaque by the swimming pool to show that the Southern paid for the pool and the building," Elliott told Croxton. "Here's the wording: 'Springs Nataborium, Courtesy Southern Railway.' Then add this list of my stock purchases and sales and profits. I'll need it by this afternoon." Croxton realized that it would be virtually impossible to cast the plaque in the allotted time—but, thanks to emergency aid from the company's expert machinists and artisans, Croxton placed the plaque on the wall just before guests arrived. Mrs. Springs came by and read the inscription. "But you've misspelled 'natarborium.' "

"Well, this is how the Colonel spelled it."

"But it's wrong."

When Springs saw Croxton he asked if the plaque was in place. "Yes, sir," Joe said, "but your wife says it's spelled wrong."

"Nataborium?" He chewed his nails. "That's my word. I made it up and I'll spell it any damned way I want to."

A few weeks later Springs asked Croxton to repeat the process for directors of another firm whose stock had been profitable for him—American Foil Company. "Make me another plaque, Joe, like the other one." He added, with a sheepish grin at Croxton, "This time put an 'r' in natarborium."

Some of Elliott's most cherished projects were originated without warning like bolts from the blue. He returned from a trip to New York where he had seen an attractive corporate cafeteria and insisted that his plants be equipped to serve meals to employees in the same way. "I want nice green salads and fresh vegetables and fruits and melons spread out on ice. And the best food we can supply for balanced meals—no more of those old soft drink wagons in the mills. . . . Damn those pink cakes and soda water. Who can live and work on that junk?"

As usual Elliott sought someone to operate the system by the unique guidelines he was developing for his mills. By intuition and without regard to her lack of previous experience, he chose Righton Richards, very likely because he had admired her freewheeling methods as Sonny's football coach. Her career as a food handler had been limited to a brief stint as overseer of a small school cafeteria, but Elliott invited Righton to establish and operate thirteen company cafeterias.

He invested heavily to make the cafeterias attractive, but Elliott did not intend that they become social centers. He installed high tables and used no chairs—thus forcing his employees to stand, rather than loiter over meals. He also insisted that there be no bells on the cash registers. "My people would hear those things ringing every time someone paid for a meal and think, 'He's paying me with one hand and taking it away with the other.' They'll think I'm making a fortune here." In fact, he lost money on the cafeterias but considered them good investments in improved employee morale, health, and attitudes toward management.

To insure a high-quality milk supply, Springs had the milk from his own dairy processed in Charlotte, specifying a butterfat content in excess of commercial standards. But on occasion he could not resist bargain purchases. A food consultant retained to study the new system reported that Miss Richards was a hopelessly inept manager: "She has cases of applesauce stacked on counters, crowding the pantry and warehouse and every other available space." This visiting expert was surprised to learn that Elliott himself was to blame. Springs had bought a freight-car load of applesauce because of its low price, a supply that lasted for years.

This consultant also observed Elliott's habitual attention to details. He once found Miss Richards making hamburgers in four sizes. "Colonel Springs is going to inspect them and choose the size he wants me to serve," she said. The visitor could hardly believe his eyes when "A fellow in an outlandish getup came in, peered at the hamburgers through his half-moon glasses, chose one size and walked out—and that was Colonel Springs, the owner of the entire chain of mills!" The Colonel put his stamp of originality even on the hamburgers—they were made in squares and served on square rolls, perhaps the first of their kind.

Once she had established an efficient food service, Miss Richards was thrust into a totally new field. Despite her protests that she knew nothing of journalism, she became editor of the company's employee newspaper, *The Springs Bulletin*, and, as a sideline, served as official chaperone to Springmaid beauty contest winners on their annual trips to New York.

As a result of such varied service, Miss Richards became one of Elliott's few confidants in Fort Mill. "I could talk back to him and get away with it," she recalled. "He talked over all kinds of things with me—even religion." Elliott broke his silence on Sonny's death years after the tragedy when he said somberly to Righton, "I let the time pass without letting Sonny know how much I loved him." (This admission did not seem to render him more affectionate toward his spirited daughter with whom he was frequently at odds.)

Elliott also made candid confessions of his relationship with his father to Miss Richards. "He thought Leroy was the meanest man in the world," she recalled. "I doubt that he really loved him. He seemed to resent most the way his father used his power over people. Elliott said that Leroy would do nothing for his employees until he was forced to it, and his son felt that they deserved better and he tried to give it to them when he took over the mills."

Miss Richards regarded Elliott as an ideal mill owner. "I don't think that he was ever unfair to anyone, even to Lee Skipper in their terrible fights."

Springs also admitted Miss Richards to his inner domestic circle, which was almost without precedent. He sent her to his home one day to act as a companion to his wife because, he said, she was lonely. On another occasion when wives of mill executives were invited to the White homestead for some social event, Elliott sent Righton to coach Frances, who was acquainted with few of the local women whom she was to entertain: "I was supposed to tell her who they were."

The most popular event among the entertainments Elliott provided for his employees was the annual Springmaid beauty contest, for which he devised elaborate rules. The contests, he felt, would provide opportunities to the young women who spent their lives working in the mills. Elliott sometimes cheated outrageously to help his favorite contestants. He installed an applause meter to gauge the crowd's approval, but as master of ceremonies he once overruled the meter and named as queen a pretty girl who had finished in second place in the judgment of the audience. Anticipating an argument, he crowned his favorite hurriedly and then went home. One of his rules barred married women from the competition, but Elliott changed one contest so that a charming young matron could win. On another occasion he declared three winners rather than one, in order to include his choices as queens—and he once went so far as to improvise a prettiest redhead contest to insure victory for another of his personal favorites.

Winners of these contests were sent to New York for a few days of interviews, photography sessions, public appearances, and tours of shows and night clubs. These mill-town beauties went in style, with a substantial purse of cash and new wardrobes. After being settled into a suite at a luxury hotel, they were driven about the city in Elliott's custom Rolls-Royce to pose for a celebrated artist, to dine in night clubs, give interviews, attend baseball games and plays.

To avoid gossip, the queens rode northward by train with a chaperone—usually Miss Richards—and Elliott followed later. But he accompanied the girls on their rounds in New York and enjoyed singing with them at such tourist attractions as Bill's Gay Nineties Saloon or watching celebrities at fashionable clubs like 21, the Stork Club, and Toots Shor's.

Elliott once accompanied Righton and Miss Springmaid to New York by train. The trio departed from Fort Mill earlier than scheduled, leaving behind Frances Springs, who had planned to join the party. Mrs. Springs caught the next train and without her husband's knowledge registered in his hotel, the St. Regis. The next day Elliott took Righton and Miss Springmaid for a ride in the Rolls. "He just careened down the streets, as fast as he could go," Righton recalled. She begged to be put out so that she could take a cab, but Elliott merely laughed. At that moment he saw that they were being followed by a Rolls driven by his friend Paul, a professional chauffeur from whom he regularly rented limousines in New York. Paul's passenger was Frances, who was obviously determined to overtake her husband. After a chase through the heart of the city, during which Paul tried to force Elliott's car to the curb, Frances at last gave up the pursuit—evidently when she had identified Miss Richards as one of her husband's companions.

Elliott later upbraided Paul, "I'm going to fire you."

"What else could I do?" Paul asked. "She's your wife. I had to do what she told me."

Elliott's idiosyncrasies made him more interesting to his lieutenants, whose study of his behavior was unceasing. Employees on lower levels also kept a careful watch for his comings and goings. One woman recalled: "You never could tell when or where he'd turn up. He wore those rubber-soled shoes and it was hard to hear him when he left his office and came down the hall. The only sound he made was a little 'sss-sss-sss' as he walked."

His employees were also at a loss to predict where Elliott's attention would focus next. He kept a constant watch for signs of waste and inefficiency and issued frequent pronouncements designed to save money, however small the amount. He was not always successful.

When he saw a crew mowing the lawn at the home of a plant manager, Elliott said nothing to his manager but ordered all the company's mowing equipment sent to the salvage warehouse. Grass soon grew tall and unkempt except at the executive offices, where the lawn was tended by a crew from the golf course. When grass became unmanageable in one area Elliott brought in a few sheep to keep the area tidy. He was forced to remove the flock when visitors complained of slipping on the manure, and his insurance agent threatened to raise rates.

But it was the insects who lived in the knee-high tangle of grass and weeds surrounding Springs plants that frustrated Elliott's campaign for economy and efficiency in lawn care. Clouds of small green grasshoppers poured through the windows of the Fort Mill plant, which was not air-conditioned. The insects struck lighting tubes, fell into the whirring machines, choked rollers, and halted operations. Plant manager V. A. Ballard demanded that the company engineer send a mowing crew at once.

"I can't do it. Orders."

"If you don't do it, I'll rent equipment and have it done. Those damned grasshoppers have closed us down."

The engineer then agreed to send help but added, "You've got to send a note to Colonel Springs explaining why you had to cut grass, and send me a copy."

Further complications arose. Cotton lint caught in the rank grass and created a fire hazard. When fire hydrants were finally concealed by the grass, the ever-alert insurance agent ordered the lawn at the Lancaster plant cut once more. This experiment by Springs was over, but he persisted in making others.

He entered the personnel office one morning and asked, "Who's that black woman who washes plant windows at the Fort Mill plant on Saturday afternoons?"

"That's Maggie. She's the only one who does that."

"Well, she should have had something more important than window washing to do, if she had to work overtime. And I know those five supervisors who were watching her should have been doing something else.

"And find out who the man was who was sweeping in front at the same time. By Monday I want a list of all employees who are being paid overtime."

Pam Freeman, his beleaguered personnel man, had three calls from Springs on Monday, pressing him for the list of overtime employees. Freeman produced it only at 3 P.M., after several clerks had culled the records of 12,000 employees. Freeman remembered the incident for many years. "Just by observing a minor operation, the Colonel began his full investigation of nonproduction overtime work. He meant to eliminate that entirely. He couldn't stop all of it, but he did save hundreds of thousands of dollars by investigating the practice.

"That simple, direct method was the heart of his managerial system. He made mistakes, but not very often. It was that kind of close personal attention to detail that made him the best operator in the industry."

Despite his reputation as a superior executive, many more of Elliott's important decisions were decidedly impromptu in nature. When he decided to expand his Fort Mill plant by 25 percent, thus creating the world's largest sheeting mill, Elliott began the project without notice to his general manager, plant manager, or even his chief engineer. Several of his younger executives, conspiring with Bill Close, worked diligently to revise his irrational one-man approach to management, with some success. But nothing could deter the Colonel from making decisions on the spur of the moment. During the expansion of the Fort Mill plant, he drove past the construction site and saw that though the walls rose high on all sides, one corner was missing. Elliott approached a foreman.

"What's the trouble here?"

"We haven't figured the final corner yet."

Elliott sighted the lines of two walls and ground his heel into the earth. "Put it right there," he said.

As a result, that corner in the completed plant was not square, leaving wasted floor space where no machinery could be placed.

Elliott's unflagging attention to company affairs enabled him to react quickly to eliminate other forms of waste and inefficiency. He encouraged a certain independence in operations by plant managers but once found that lack of communication invited fraud. An employee who tended a machine in one of the Chester plants suffered a back injury and claimed that he was permanently incapacitated. After he was awarded total disability benefits for life under the Workman's Compensation program, this man was employed by another Springs plant in Chester, where he again claimed these benefits—and was upheld by government agents, who rejected the Springs protests: "You hired him again—you should have known what you were doing." In an attempt to prevent a recurrence of such fraud, Elliott created an integrated clearinghouse for new employees and made one of his executives responsible for all hiring.

Elliott was also decisive in his campaign against other forms of inefficiency. He had sought to centralize clerical and payroll operations and eliminate numerous jobs then scattered through his various plants. His older executives resisted this suggestion, and Elliott consulted Pam Freeman of the personnel department, who not only assured him that the consolidation was feasible but gave him details of the wasteful routines followed by timekeepers in his plants.

Elliott then ordered the payroll and other clerical work concentrated at

Lancaster. He supported his order with such an array of details that, as Freeman recalled, "He left them shaking their heads. Managers never knew where he got his information. He was a genius in his own right, with astonishingly broad knowledge, but his secret was in his preparation—he sought out experts and grilled them, picked their brains—and then he could dazzle people with the extent of his knowledge. I've heard doctors say he knew more about medicine than any layman they ever knew—and a food systems expert who came here left Elliott's office saying that he'd learned more about food handling than he'd ever known."

Elliott's methods of dealing with personnel problems were singular. One of his executives habitually shouted into telephones to the distress of the Colonel, whose ears were highly sensitive. Elliott sought relief through indirection. He appeared in this man's office one day and called the telephone company. "I want you to send over and repair the phone on this extension. It sends too loud a signal—it's deafening everyone who gets on the line." The hint was too subtle. The uncomprehending offender continued to bellow messages to his unseen victims—and then disappeared, one of the rare Springs employees who was fired during Elliott's era.

Elliott's passion for secrecy in business affairs became legendary. One director who was also a key executive recalled that he never saw a financial report during his seven years on the Springs board. He had heard rumors that Elliott had passed brief, single-page reports around the table at earlier board meetings, "But he always took back the sheets and never released figures."

Springs was even more guarded where outsiders were concerned. On one occasion he sought to borrow money from an Atlanta bank and refused the routine request to present a financial statement. When pressed, Elliott simply took from his safe a large bundle of cotton receipts (the equivalent of cash) and sent them by his personnel chief to Atlanta, where they remained in the bank's vault until the loan was retired.

Even the social life in the White homestead was frequently affected by Elliott's last-minute decisions to have guests for luncheon or dinner, usually friends from nearby Charlotte. Charles Crutchfield, a Charlotte television executive, recalled that Elliott would telephone him about six o'clock and invite him and his wife to come down to dinner with Bob and Claire McKay. "There were usually three or four couples, and they were great parties. Elliott was a superb host, but he did have one odd habit. After dinner he would sit in a corner and read a magazine, concentrating intensely, and wouldn't speak to the rest of us until we left."

Elliott sometimes exhibited a lack of consideration for his wife. He invited General Omar Bradley to visit Fort Mill without advising Frances. Bradley landed at Columbia, where Elliott was to meet him. When Bradley called the Springs home, Frances was none too hospitable. She told the General that she knew nothing of his visit and said she was certain that Elliott was not expecting company. Springs met Bradley in Columbia but did not take him to his home.

The unstable relationship between Springs and Lee Skipper continued its raucous course over the years with periodic outbursts of temper between the lifelong friends and associates. Skipper ate lunch at odd hours until Elliott finally forbade him to do so. "Irrespective of your complete disregard for your own stomach" he told Lee, he must have lunch between 12:30 and 2:00 P.M. Springs explained: "This organization has got to function between 9 in the morning until 12:30 and from 2:30 until 5:30, if we are going to have any cooperation and concerted action."

In another typical sally, Elliott wrote Lee, "In spite of your bad disposition I'm going to raise your salary. But if you backslide and start picking fights with the rest of the organization I'm going to cut it. Beginning with July, you'll get $1200 per month." (This was soon increased to $2400 and beyond as Skipper's value to the company became more obvious.) In response to his periodic raises, Skipper deprecated his role as chief of production, which was, in fact, crucial to the success of the mills. "I don't know why you do this," Lee wrote to Elliott. "I'd work just as hard for the company without the raise. Really, your generosity exceeds all bounds. I'll do all in my power to warrant this. . . . As to the bad disposition, I must have been born with it and a leopard cannot change his spots but I am trying to curb any unusual temper I may have. Please don't be too hard on me."

Elliott and Lee Skipper, who had quarreled throughout their careers in the mills, finally parted in 1948. "The only reason I've kept him," Springs told a friend, "is because he's the best general manager in the world at getting work out of his hands." An observer, however, noted an odd tug of war between the two: "Lee would scold the workers and have everyone hard at it, but Elliott would go into the plants right behind him and tell the hands not to let Skipper worry them—playing Mr. Nice to Lee's Mr. Tough. But then Elliott would call his supervisors together and tell them they'd have to get more out of their workers. Those two buttinskies kept the Lancaster plant in an uproar for years."

Relations between Elliott and Skipper finally became so strained that they communicated by written messages carried by a black courier who drove a small car on frequent trips between the mills and offices. At one point Springs wrote to Skipper: "Try to remember that these mills are mine, after all." Skipper also apparently irritated Frances Springs, for she insisted that her husband dismiss him.

Elliott acted at last. "I'm going to give you an ultimatum," he told Skipper.

"No," Lee said. "I'm giving you one. You're like a child. You go behind me and soothe the workers after I've gotten them straightened out, and I quit."

"You aren't quitting. You're fired."

Soon afterward Springs called an issue of the company's preferred stock in which Skipper had been investing for years. Righton Richards recalled the climactic scene in this conflict of wills: "Lee was as mad as a hornet when Elliott called in that preferred. And just to show off he piled his stock certificates in a rickety old wheelbarrow and rolled it into Elliott's office, bangety, bangety. Mary Williamson and I were the only ones who'd admit to having seen that. Elliott didn't think it was a bit funny and pretended later it didn't happen, because everyone enjoyed the story so."

Though forced to resign and to sell his stock, Skipper seemed to remain on good terms with Elliott, for Lee was restored to the Springs board in 1953 and continued to be a valuable consultant to management for many years. Skipper also continued to accumulate Springs common stock and eventually owned more than 35,000 shares.

Righton Richards remembered, "Elliott would have liked to have taken Lee back, but he couldn't have faced Frances if he had done so."

There was no apparent diminution of Elliott's energies as he entered his sixties. Other leaders of the textile industry recognized the threat of increased Japanese imports when the Eisenhower administration announced liberalization of its foreign trade program in 1955, but it was only Springs who responded with the instincts of a born propagandist and controversialist. *The Springs Bulletin* greeted news of the latest Japanese import invasion as a catastrophe with grave implications for the American future:

DECEMBER 7, 1941—WASHINGTON FAILS TO ALERT U.S. NAVY

SEPTEMBER 10, 1955—WASHINGTON FAILS TO ALERT U.S. TEXTILES

Two photographs accompanied the headlines, one of U.S. battleships wrecked in the attack on Pearl Harbor—the other of an unidentified textile mill lying in ruins. Elliott's protests were no more effective than those he had made during the New Deal era, but he made himself heard in a way that influenced the views of the Southern textile industry for a generation.

Ludicrous aspects of American business procedure also continued to draw Elliott's eye, even in his own plants. Despite his affection for loyal employees he was aware that many of them sometimes loafed on the job. Elliott once asked the author Carl Sandburg, after a tour of a Springs plant that was operating at full speed, "Did you see any of 'em working? Did you?"

His employees became accustomed to his wry comments on such matters. This solemn memorandum once circulated through the company without further explanation:

To: All Department Heads
Subject: Death of Employees
    It has been brought to our attention that many employees are dying and refusing to fall over after they are dead. This practice *must* stop.

On and after November 16, any employee sitting up after he has died will be dropped from the payroll. . . . Because of the highly sensitive nature of our employees and the close resemblance between death and their natural working attitudes, investigation will be made quietly. . . .

If doubt exists as to the true condition of the employees, extend paycheck as test. If employee doesn't reach for it, it may be reasonably assumed that he is dead. . . .

In all cases, a sworn statement by the dead person must be filled in on special form W-17 1/2. . . .

Twenty-five copies will be made; one is sent to each department, three to this office, three will go to the deceased . . . to eliminate further identification of the corpse before burial. The remaining copies will be filed alphabetically, numerically, by date, right side up, with two copies left for misfiling.

Elliott White Springs
President

Elliott also issued "regulations" to be observed by his employees in dealing with him—a list which Springs workers realized was not to be taken as a joke:

Never lie to me. I can usually detect a liar. If I ask a question and you do not know the answer, say "I don't know." Do not beat around the bush and try to make me think you know. No one can possibly know everything.

Do not stand up when I enter your office. I am not a female nor the President of the United States. . . . If you call on the phone and I answer, don't say "Who's this?" . . .

Speak softly on the phone when talking to me. Don't yell. I have sensitive eardrums. . . .

You have every right to disagree with me, but don't argue the point.

When I ask you to do something for me and say "There is no hurry, just when you can find time," don't believe me. I will probably be back within an hour.

Be brief, just give me the details. I have some Department Heads who, if [I] ask them the time, want to tell me how to build a watch.

Despite such serio-comic badinage, Elliott's pride in his enterprise and in his workers seemed to increase as he grew older. He had a sentimental feeling for those who had remained faithful to the company over many years. His stockholders, he claimed, were still the original ones or their heirs—and most of his employees stayed with him throughout their careers. Shortly after World War II he reported that 2,162 workers had been with the company fifteen years or longer, that 700 of these had been on the job for twenty-five years and four of them for fifty years.

Springs was proud that "99 and 44/100 per cent" of his employees were descended from early settlers, just as he was. He had convinced himself that these people were the nation's chief reliance in times of crisis:

> They fought with Braddock on the Monongahela; they killed Ferguson at Kings Mountain; they went with their Cousin Andrew Jackson to New Orleans; they went to Mexico for Cousin James K. Polk; they flung the gauntlet at Cousin Abe Lincoln, and they refused to be reconstructed by Cousin Andrew Johnson; they joined their North Carolina and Tennessee cousins in the Thirtieth Division to break the Hindenburg Line; they saddled Halsey's white horse at Tokyo; and they are ready to take on a Joe Stalin or anyone else who attempts to exploit them. Every spinner could be a Colonial Dame, a D.A.R., or a U.D.C., if she wished. They have never lived anywhere but Lancaster, York, and Chester Counties, and each family still owns a farm, and expects to return to it when wages go down and cotton goes up.

Not only did hourly workers spend long careers with Springs, turnover on the administrative staff was so low, a personnel manager recalled, that only three new people were hired during one year, and two of these were former Springs employees returning home.

The broad-scale program of benefits for employees launched by Elliott in the postwar era became a model for the industry: free insurance, free golf course, low-cost hospital care, a credit union, attractive cafeterias, cheap automatic laundries, camps for Boy and Girl Scouts, college scholarships for children or dependents of employees, and an enormous recreation park near Lancaster (with a bathing beach, a merry-go-round, bowling alleys, roller skating rink, baseball field, a steam-powered miniature train, archery range, an amphitheater, and shuffleboard courts). New, modern housing was available near the plants at rents below cost—in the late 1940s six-room houses, some with fifteen-acre farms attached, rented for thirty-six dollars per month. In later years, houses were sold to employees on easy payroll deduction plans. Such programs did much to diminish the threat of unionization or the wooing of Springs workers by other mills, but Elliott went far beyond the level of benefits offered by his competitors, and his innovations had a marked effect upon worker morale.

Springs employees were not always quick to respond to Elliott's largesse. When he built an oceanfront resort for them at Myrtle Beach, South Carolina, his workers at first showed little interest, because they were unaccustomed to holidays at the beach. They were finally enticed there by weekend rates they could not resist—one dollar per day per person including meals. Guests at Springmaid Beach found a large vacation retreat with a capacity of eight hundred and excellent food service. They also found an example of the Colonel's passion for efficiency. The buildings were built of concrete, even the beds (equipped with foam rubber mattresses), so that the place could be thoroughly cleaned within a short time.

When Elliott felt the need for fuller insurance coverage for his employees to replace the system of self-insurance then in use, he acted in characteristic fashion. He called in his treasurer, Bill Medford.

"Medford, start an insurance company—and let's call it Kanawha."

Without further orders, even as to the fields of coverage Elliott had in mind, Medford formed a general insurance company based in Fort Mill to serve the needs of Springs employees—a small firm that became increasingly profitable.

Medford came to appreciate Elliott's abilities, "He was the smartest business man I ever met. If I'd been able to afford it, I'd have worked for him without salary, just for the association. He had a truly probing mind and was a superb decision-maker. You could get an answer from him at once—he'd hardly ever take more than a day or so to think over a problem. He had a great advantage over most textile owners—he knew every tiny detail of his business and almost all of his people, intimately."

Another executive, James Bradley, a former bank examiner imported to head Elliott's Bank of Lancaster, had a similar experience. When he was summoned to the Colonel's office without warning during his first days at work, Bradley went somewhat apprehensively.

Elliott did not look up from his desk. "Bradley, what do you know about prefabricated housing?"

"Not a thing."

"Find out what you need to know and come back and tell me about it tomorrow."

Bradley spent most of the next twenty-four hours investigating and reported to Springs that he had found some surplus prefabs at the naval base in Charleston.

"All right," Springs said. "I want thirty in the next three months." Bradley was dismissed without further discussion. He recalled, "I knew nothing else, no suggestions about price or where he wanted the houses placed. And I didn't ask. He expected me to figure out the details. I simply went and did as he said, and the houses were ready for occupancy by the deadline. Many of his staff people were afraid of Springs and had to wait to be told everything they did. These were the people who felt that he was unwilling to delegate authority."

Jim Lasley, Herb Mathewson's successor as head of the finishing plant, recalled, "When the Colonel told you something, you just didn't ask him what he meant. He thought you should know. Employees just took orders and, if they weren't clear, talked it over among themselves. There was a saying in the company that if the Colonel broke wind while using the phone, the guy on the other end would say, 'Yes, sir.' "

James Bradley learned that despite his rather colorful reputation as an author, aviator, and advertising man, Elliott was inflexibly conservative in all business affairs—at least in his later years. "He hedged everything. Even late in his career, when he operated on a grand scale, he bought cotton futures to nail down the price and fix his costs on all large orders for goods. He had a cautious approach toward stock market investments— and he made lots of money in stocks. He built up a conservative, diversified portfolio, chiefly in blue chips and government issues—he owned few textile stocks at the time I knew him. He was a long-term investor—no in-and-out trading for him."

Elliott's daughter corroborated this estimate, "Daddy did do imaginative things and moved boldly on them—like the Springmaid ad campaign and stocking up on grey goods in the 30s, and the timing on the bleachery investment. But mostly he was a business man of the old school. All other Springs men were gamblers. Uncle Eli once cornered the cotton market— and my grandfather Leroy was a terrible gambler. The family was known for that trait. But so far as I knew, Daddy was not a gambler."

Anne Close also perceived her father's other qualities in candid fashion: "Daddy could be patient and kind, but I felt that he was making an effort at such times. He was restless and never relaxed. He bit his nails and paced constantly. . . . I felt he was a very closed person. And even his sense of humor was not spontaneous or revealed in conversation. It was sort of contrived and written, not spoken. In later years he had a small group of close friends, but I think he didn't enjoy social life."

The complex Springs was also idealistic, devoted to the highest standards, motivated by pride of heritage, position, and accomplishment—and was yet so modest and self-effacing in personal matters that he disdained expression of obvious sentiments. At once flamboyant and subtle, uninhibited and reserved, he could be courtly and charming as well as forbidding. Despite his cultivated tastes, his writing, though vigorous and vivid, was usually undistinguished and frequently descended to the level of coarseness or slapstick comedy, and his behavior was often marked by gaucheries. In all, as his contemporaries perceived, he was a man whose personality defied analysis.

His friend and employee Julian Starr commented that Elliott sometimes fastened enthusiastically upon new people, but soon, when he had learned what they had to say, lost interest and dropped them unceremoniously. "His mind was so quick and he was so perceptive that he could often finish a sentence you had begun—most disconcerting."

Elliott was unpredictable in his dress. For twenty years or longer he wore an old brown sports jacket and a pair of patched pongee trousers that dated from the 1920s. He kept in his office an even more ancient and disreputable green jacket, which he often donned before meeting some salesman or other caller to his office. He also liked to startle people by appearing in his Sherlock Holmes outfit, complete with an Inverness cape and deerstalker hat. (On occasion he wore an ancient low-crowned derby of the type worn by the Weber and Fields vaudeville team.) He sometimes wore shoes with one vamp dyed red and the other green.

Still, he had fastidious taste in clothing and frequently berated his New York tailors about minor errors: "Every pair of trousers you have cut for me has had to be taken in at least an inch and a half and I think you would be as tired of this as I am." And: "The white shantung coat would fit a man comfortably who had a 39-inch waist and looks like a maternity jacket on me." He kept two wardrobes of formal clothing, one of them in his New York hotel room, and this included tail coats and an opera hat. Springs continued to wear army uniforms on special occasions—white serge in summer and khakis in cooler weather.

Elliott's most intimate friend in his later years was Dr. Robert McKay, a distinguished urologist from Charlotte, whom he called "The Plumber." McKay, an enthusiastic fellow prankster, was a huge man of some three hundred pounds who, unable to climb in and out of automobiles of the day, drove an ancient—and roomy—Chevrolet. The car listed sharply toward the left after years of bearing the doctor's bulk in the driver's seat, but McKay clung to the old vehicle in desperation, and it was kept in running condition by mechanics in the Springs shop. After one of these regular overhauls, when McKay drove off for Charlotte, Springs notified state police that the car had been stolen and gave the doctor an opportunity to test his powers of persuasion. Springs and McKay were also intellectual companions and rivals. Both had studied Greek (the doctor the more seriously) and both were familiar with the Bible. In attempts to best each other, the two occasionally resorted to late-night telephone calls—at 2 or 3 A.M.—demanding translation of some obscure Greek phrase or Biblical passage.

As a philanthropist, Elliott was of major importance to his region, but his contributions were made on his own terms, and he resisted agents of various causes who begged his aid. Fund-raisers who invaded his office with visions of large donations were greeted courteously but firmly. Elliott asked his secretary to bring in his check book.

"Oh, no, Colonel. We simply want to know how much you will pledge."

But Elliott was insistent. "I'll attend to it right now," he said. "I know you need to make your plans."

He invariably wrote a check for five dollars for each worthy cause. As a result, few people realized how generously he supported local causes, usually in anonymity.

Despite his best efforts, the Colonel was never able to eliminate the yes-men in his company. Harold Bagwell, manager of the Kershaw plant, once criticized a mill village house that Springs offered for sale. "Colonel, that's the worst house I ever saw. We'll never sell it."

"Bagwell, I designed that house myself. One of the first things I ever did here."

Bagwell did not pause. "Like I say, Colonel, that's the finest house I ever saw. We'll sell it right away."

"You really mean it?"

"I'll sell it or I'll buy it myself."

Springs laughed aloud, one of the few times an employee ever heard him do so. Plant Manager V. A. Ballard recalled that the Colonel seldom laughed at anything, in fact. "He smiled at times, but he always seemed distant and lonely to me. But he could get to you and make you want to do for Springs—he could work through us—any of us."

Though sycophants usually enraged him, Elliott's manner did not encourage independence of spirit in his managers. As his personnel chief, Pam Freeman, said, "People weren't exactly afraid of the Colonel, but they were apprehensive when dealing with him. You never knew what he had in mind. He commanded—not demanded—loyalty. He was a winner and all of us knew it and were glad to be part of his operation. People seldom challenged his decisions."

A vice president, Bill Summersby, once held a meeting of the eleven Springs plant managers to discuss a current problem and, after debating for an entire morning, led the group to a unanimous decision. Summersby then telephoned Springs and explained what the conference had concluded.

"Yes, sir, yes, sir," Summersby said and hung up the telephone. "Well," he told the plant managers, "the vote was eleven to one and the one has it."

Elliott's decision was final, and there was no further discussion.

Elliott rarely played golf, but he appeared on the company course with some of his executives now and then, usually dropping out after one or two holes to return to his office. His officers were not always happy to see him come, for in the case of a lost ball the Colonel would halt play until it was found. "It wasn't so much the cost," V. A. Ballard said. "It was the inefficiency of the thing that vexed him, and so he would hunt and hunt, wasting our time. Then one of the fellows would drop another ball, on the sly, to satisfy him, and only then could we go on to the next hole."

Earl Crenshaw, an expert production executive in the field of spinning cotton, presented a unique challenge to Elliott's standards. Crenshaw was of great value to the company, and when he left Springs for another mill in a nearby town, Elliott made a rare gesture by offering to treble his salary if he would remain. Crenshaw refused. "If I'm worth it now, why didn't you pay me that before?" He returned to Springs seven years later, after many enticing overtures had been made to him. Someone asked Elliott why he wanted Earl back. "Because he's not a 'yes man,'" Springs replied. But a few months later, in a heated discussion of production problems, Elliott told Crenshaw sharply, "You don't have to be a 'no man' *all* the time."

Though he valued Crenshaw as an unusually talented technician, Elliott accepted his counsel most reluctantly. He could not resist the temptation to stock inferior cotton when it was offered and occasionally, rather than pay for the standard 1 1/8-inch staple cotton, bought 7/8-inch staple at a discount of fifteen dollars per bale. This cheaper cotton caused trouble when it was used in one of the plants, and Crenshaw took Elliott to the idled machines, hoping to convince him that his discount shopping was false economy.

"You can't mix these lengths of cotton and draft them out on these machines," Crenshaw said.

Temporarily persuaded, the repentant Elliott instructed his cotton department: "From now on Crenshaw is the cotton expert. Buy what he tells you to buy."

But after two or three months of trouble-free production, Elliott succumbed once more to the lure of cheap cotton and the disruptive process was repeated.

A competing mill once tried to lure Crenshaw with a then-princely salary of $60,000. He reported the offer to Elliott.

"You're not going to get it."

"Well, you're going to pay me sixty, then."

"I'll raise you but I won't pay you sixty."

The competing offer was withdrawn. "We can't hire you after all," the competitor said. "The Colonel says no and he's our friend." Crenshaw confronted Springs angrily and charged him with spite, but remained in his job.

Soon afterward, when Springs again interfered in the cotton-buying process (and incurred a loss of $350,000 on a single transaction), Crenshaw resigned once more and withstood pleas by Elliott's emissaries, who telephoned him until 2 A.M., begging him to reconsider—all in vain. "My leaving was mostly my own fault," Crenshaw recalled many years later. "I wanted to do things my way, and Springs people had to do things Elliott's way, even if it was wrong." But Crenshaw realized that Elliott's motive was always to get the most from every employee and every machine. "If you tried it his way and it didn't work, then you could explain and he would accept it. He would simply test everyone who worked for him and, as a result, you never knew whether he really meant all that he said."

Crenshaw, who found a new job in Chattanooga, Tennessee, met Elliott some years later at a convention in Florida. Springs sought to persuade him to return to Fort Mill.

"I won't say I'll never work for you again, Colonel, but I'll be hungry before I do. I had an ulcer all the time I worked for you."

Elliott turned aside the rejection and ignored the implied criticism: "Oh, I can cure ulcers," he said. "I got two of them when I was in school."

Crenshaw merely laughed and they parted.

Springs remained a resourceful and astute executive who commanded the respect and attention of competitors. He foresaw a strong demand for wider cloth in the 1950s and took bold action to win market dominance. His mills were then the world's largest producer of cotton cloth, but the Colonel seemed to know through intuition (his own or that of some veteran employee who was subjected to periodic grillings) that the market would soon demand more of him.

As usual, he wasted no time. Without preamble, he ordered one hundred of his forty-inch looms from Lancaster sent to the company shop for conversion to a width of fifty inches and began producing wider goods. The new cloth created a sensation and demand was so strong that Springs's output set new records, and competitors were hard put to catch up with the Colonel. By the time other major mills were offering cloth in fifty-inch widths, Springs had gone to sixty-four inches and was stretching his lead in the market place.

Temporarily, at least, Elliott led a more active social life during the 1950s after he bought an interest in a ninety-seven-foot yacht, the *Marmot*, formerly owned by Lammot DuPont. The luxurious, diesel-powered vessel slept eight passengers in comfort and carried a captain and an eight-man crew. Though he protested that he might be unable to afford it, Springs paid $40,000 for a one-third interest in the yacht. His partners were his old Culver schoolmate Fritz Holliday of Indianapolis, and Tony Hulman, owner of the Indianapolis Speedway. Upkeep of the vessel was costly and Holliday welcomed Springs as an investor. Characteristically, Springs bought a share of the *Marmot* through one of his corporations and planned to write off some of the cost as a business expense.

Elliott felt that his friends would enjoy cruises from New England waters to the Florida Keys and the West Indies. Larry Callahan, he said, particularly wanted to be a yachtsman, though "I do not know why because he knows only one blonde who looks good under a yachting cap, and she already has a yacht."

He joined the New York Yacht Club, and for several years spent many pleasant weeks aboard the boat—which, with the consent of his partners, he rechristened *Springmaid*. Friends and customers joined his cruises along the Inland Waterway or to Nassau, Jamaica, Haiti, and Cat Cay, Florida. In August 1950, he took the boat on the New York Yacht Club annual cruise out of New London, Connecticut, then chartered her for a month, took her back to South Carolina, and returned her to Florida for repairs before the winter season. He was an openhanded host, frequently entertaining employees and offering the vessel to friends for vacations.

One day when the boat was tied up at Cat Cay, Elliott and Frances and their guests, the Robert McKays and Mr. and Mrs. H. K. Hallett, of Charlotte, were having cocktails on the deck when a pretty, scantily-clad black girl walked along the pier. Hoping to get a reaction from his wife, Springs dashed down the gangplank and chased the screaming girl from sight. When he returned an hour or more later, Frances was awaiting him behind the door of their stateroom with a shoe in hand. She struck him on the head with the metal-tipped high heel, and the prankster was taken to a hospital emergency room for stitches in his scalp.

With the instincts of the Dutch tradesmen of his ancestry, Elliott sought charters for the yacht when the partners were not cruising. When Captain Eddie Rickenbacker lost his chartered yacht in a fire at Beaufort, South Carolina, Springs telegraphed the aging ace of World War I, offering the *Springmaid*, which was then conveniently docked at nearby Georgetown, South Carolina.

Though he protested that he was not an accomplished yachtsman, he was a fearless one. One season when the *Springmaid* was not available, he chartered a top-heavy seventy-footer designed for commuting to New York City over Long Island Sound. Elliott and Frances welcomed two couples aboard in Miami—Bob and Claire McKay and Jake and Maxie Stanley, and the party retired, with orders to the captain to leave port at 8 A.M. on the run to Cat Cay, near Bimini.

Storm warnings were issued during the night but Frances, unaware of the danger, appeared on the deck at 8 A.M. and ordered the captain to put to sea. The vessel was soon in trouble, the yacht pitching and rolling in a gale. China and glass crashed, and the passengers held on for their lives. Mrs. McKay clung to a stanchion with closed eyes, praying. Frances Springs lay in her bunk in terror, refusing to leave even when Elliott went below to warn her the boat might capsize.

After an hour or so, when he noticed that the boat was making no headway, Elliott relieved the captain, who was hysterical, and unable to hold the wheel. Elliott took over and eventually sighted Cat Cay, where he raised the island by radio and summoned a boat to lead them through the reefs to safety. Once inside he returned the wheel to the captain.

Soon afterward he went below to Frances. "What do you think the captain has done now? He's run aground."

"Thank God," Frances said fervently.

Elliott used the *Springmaid* less frequently as the years passed. He once told one of his executives, "It bores me to death. I don't enjoy that kind of people, anyway, they don't *do* anything."

The partners chartered the yacht more frequently as the years passed and finally sold her after the death of Fritz Holliday.

During the postwar years Elliott gave full rein to his affection for automobiles, which was almost obsessive. He was not merely a devoted owner-driver; he was a part-time mechanic for most of his life. In addition to the beloved Stutz Bearcat of his final days at Princeton, he also owned a "big pink" Master Stutz and, among others, a Winton, Isotta Fraschini, Detroit Electric, Pierce Arrow, Auburn, Cord, DeSoto, Cadillac, Jaguar Mark VII, Mercedes Gullwing, Volkswagen, Buick, Chrysler, Aston-Martin, Corvette Stingray, and three Rolls-Royces.

He spotted a New York street peddler driving a Rolls that had been converted into a pickup truck and bought it at once. This vehicle was actually a Rolls front mounted on the body of a Dodge truck—"sired by Rolls and dammed by Dodge," Elliott said. He had the truck restored in the mill shops, drove it briefly, and used it in publicity photographs.

Another Rolls, a sedate sedan, was used by Frances. The third, a custom-built Phantom II town car with open front, was two feet longer and six inches lower than standard models. After using it to haul Springmaid beauty queens and advertising models in New York for four years, Elliott offered the car to Governor James Byrnes of South Carolina as an official ceremonial car:

"It was built by Darrin in Hollywood for the Countess di Frasso. She had to leave the country hurriedly. . . . It is much too good for the ordinary citizen . . . ideal for parades and would undoubtedly impress any visiting dignitary. . . . You have only to fill it with oil and water once a year and you can leave it connected to the gasoline pump. . . . This is the only one of its kind in the world and I have never seen it fail to steal the show." Byrnes accepted, and the imposing limousine did official duty in Columbia for several years.

Elliott seldom missed a New York automobile show and was prowling through one of these in 1953 when he saw, and carefully inspected, a prototype of the new fiberglass Corvette. He offered to buy it off the floor and left a blank check for the purpose but failed to get the prototype. Instead, he was sent one of the first production line models.

The new sports car, powered by a straight six-cylinder engine with three carburetors, created an sensation in Fort Mill and on nearby roads. But, as the research chief and company photographer Skeebo Martin recalled, the Corvette was merely another of the Colonel's passing fancies. "It rode like a truck, and he didn't like to ride in it. He took it on short trips and about town for a while and had his picture made in it and then turned it over to me, to drive around to the various jobs. I didn't like it either. Its leather seats smelled like a cow pasture."

Springs later sold it to Joe Chatman, a special sales representative for Springs in New York. Chatman drove the car for years, sometimes in fast sports car competition. He traded it to General Motors for a new Stingray in 1963—and Elliott's old Corvette, restored to its dazzling original glory, was displayed at the World's Fair in Seattle and in several automobile shows.

Another favorite car was an antique Detroit Electric, bought for $800 and expensively restored in the company shops. For several months Elliott chauffeured his executives in the electric to the *Loretto* for their regular luncheons but tired of its silent, sedate pace. After a year or so of disuse the car was advertised for sale at $1,500, an exorbitant price at the time. There was no response to the ads for some months, but at last a New York collector telephoned to say that he would appear in Fort Mill the next morning with a cashier's check for $1,500. Only then did Elliott decide that he was unwilling to sell the old car.

"How do I know who you are? Are you trustworthy? I must have cash." The buyer remained calm under all insults. "I'll bring the cash," he replied. Springs was forced to acquiesce and thus lost one of his favorites.

Skeebo Martin once showed Elliott an advertisement featuring a Gull-wing Mercedes 300 SL, which had a rated speed of 140 miles per hour. "I can't afford it," the Colonel said. "And I sat in one of those in New York, but it's no good for me. I couldn't get in and out of the front seat—the salesman had to help me out." About a month later one of the new Mercedes models was delivered in Fort Mill, and Springs drove it briefly before turning it over to Martin. "His wife must have gotten after him for driving too fast on those roads to Myrtle Beach because he drove it only a few times."

To Elliott, the appeal of fine automobiles was their performance rather than appearance. He apparently drove at breakneck speed all his life. A durable South Carolina legend, which exists in several forms, has it that Elliott made an early attempt to reach an understanding with policemen about his high-speed driving: an officer allegedly halted Springs for speeding on his way from Fort Mill to Lancaster and said, "That will be five dollars." Elliott paid promptly. "Here's ten dollars," he replied. "I'll be back this way tonight, and this way we'll both save time."

Elliott made several visits to the King Ranch in Texas, where he hunted with his friends the Klebergs and was so impressed that he stocked several areas of his lands near Fort Mill. He also bought a Jeep and equipped it with all necessities for hunting, including radio communication with his home, so that he could call for food or fresh dogs. One friend recalled that Elliott and some of his hunting companions baited the airstrip near the White homestead and rode up and down, perched on the Jeep's outriggers, "blasting everything in sight." His most frequent companions were John Morehead, H. K. Hallett, and Dr. Robert McKay of Charlotte, all inexperienced hunters.

Elliott's grandchildren had now become a major interest of his life. Anne and Bill Close had seven of their eight children during Elliott's lifetime, and Anne in particular was determined that her father would not spoil them. She imposed restrictions upon him—he was to visit her house only with her permission and could take gifts there only rarely. But Elliott was not to be denied. He kept watch on his daughter's house, and when she and Bill were away, usually in the evenings, he descended upon the children to entertain them and to take gifts.

Despite these problems, Anne recalled, "He was wonderful with my children. He often read to them from mythology or made up stories of his own. He was very close to them." He also took them fishing and on brief jaunts in and near the town—"things he never did with his own children," his daughter said.

Family regulations forbade the children to beg their grandfather for gifts or favors, but all of them knew that he kept packages of Juicy Fruit chewing gum in his pockets. Crandall, the firstborn, with the business instinct that later made her a capable executive of the Springs Company, which manages family holdings, devised a way to circumvent the rule. Rather than mentioning gum, she would ask, "Do you have something in your pocket a little girl might like?" She was never refused.

One evening when Elliott and Frances had guests in their home, Elliott rose abruptly and left the house without explanation—he had felt in one of his pockets a gift intended for a grandchild and hurried to Anne's house to make the presentation.

Elliott frequently surprised Anne and Bill with expensive gifts, which they usually refused. They declined to accept automobiles, which he offered at Christmas for several years. When her father installed a television set in her house, Anne ordered it removed—she did not intend to expose her children to the medium.

Frances Springs also enjoyed a close relationship with her grandchildren. Her namesake, Francie Close, found her own way to circumvent family rules and wheedle forbidden soft drinks. The little girl often found her grandmother in the large den of the White homestead, where she wrote letters or played solitaire. Since she could not ask for soda pop, Francie approached "Giggie" and merely panted audibly until she was permitted to have a drink.

Francie recalled years later, "She had the air of a real lady and the presence of a woman who was in charge of her house. She had a fine sense of humor, though it was always quiet. She was very good to us. She used to hire me to wrap her Christmas gifts for her. I often played gin rummy and backgammon with her, and she was good at backgammon—her father had been a champion player.

"I remember Giggie's saying to me once when I blurted something about religion, 'There are three things you don't talk about, Francie— religion, politics, and sex.'

"That may have been about the time I told Pop (my grandfather) that he was going to hell because he didn't go to church—an idea I had gotten from Tony Dehler.

"I remember he paused a little and said, 'Well, we all go to Heaven. It just takes some people longer than it does others.'"

Anne Close was now to lose a major battle in her campaign to shield her children from great wealth. In the mid-fifties, when he belatedly began to investigate tax problems which would arise at his death, Elliott was forced to the realization that his family might someday lose control of the Springs textile empire. He had earlier separated his several charitable foundations from the mills and was apparently content with that move. In extended consultation with an Atlanta law firm, he was at last convinced that though his liquid assets were not enormous, he had accumulated a fortune of some $200 million—and that he must take steps to shield it from ruinously heavy death taxes.

Attorney Herbert Elsas found Elliott to be a difficult client. "He was always courteous but was impatient with complexities. He wanted a one-page explanation—and when I completed my study of the Springs empire, including the various companies and the charitable foundations, I found that the situation was complex indeed."

Elsas created thirty-year charitable term trusts to be financed from Springs Mills dividends—trusts which would benefit the people of the mill communities while remaining under control of Anne Close and her husband. The bulk of the remaining funds would pass to Elliott's grandchildren after a maximum of thirty years. Elliott's wife and daughter had already been provided for. In actuality the charitable trusts were fully funded through increased dividend payments far in advance of the maximum term, and the Springs fortune passed to Elliott's grandchildren much earlier than had been anticipated.

Springs left his grandchildren equal amounts of money but insisted that the grandsons be given preference in assuming control of the mills and other enterprises. He resisted the advice of Elsas that the girls receive equal treatment and seemed to enjoy the prospect of rivalries among his grandsons. "Sure, they'll fight among themselves," Elliott said. "And the stronger one will come out on top."

He fell into a series of arguments with Elsas over the plan. "He fired us several times," Elsas recalled. "But his people kept after him, especially Bill Medford, the treasurer, and he came around at last."

After lengthy negotiations with the Internal Revenue Service the plan was approved, the trusts were created and funded by large gifts of Springs Mills stock in August 1959. The granddaughters were given equal status with their brothers only years later, after protracted efforts by Anne Close resulted in a court order. "No grandson had the temerity to object," Elsas said.

Anne Close was dismayed by the prospect of her children's becoming multi-millionaires when they reached the age of twenty-one, but her objections went for naught. The realities of tax law forced her to acquiesce, because the control of the family mills was at stake.

Some 20 percent of the funds was dedicated to aid the people of the communities and, at Anne's insistence, a large portion of this money was spent to improve public schools in the mill towns. The estate plan provided a rich legacy for people of the region for many years and at the same time enabled Elliott to pass on to his heirs the fruits of his labor, courage, and ingenuity.

XVI / "The Real Man Is
Somewhere between the Lines"

Only company executives who worked with him daily realized what stress Elliott placed upon himself by his compulsion to give personal attention to all details of his business. George Harris, a key employee who left Springs to become head of Dan River Mills in Virginia, urged Elliott to delegate some of his authority, "The constant drive and the strain of the highways will surely get you in time. Your responsibilities are too great to take the risk of a physical breakdown . . . I hope you will learn to allow others to help you more. I know the affectionate desire to do this is in all your men, but obviously they are not going to think as you think in all matters and do at times appear to you to be 'going to hell in a hack.' Give them a chance and in their own way they will work out your problems probably just as well, and with much less fatigue to you."

It was in vain. Elliott could not break the habits of a lifetime and these may have hastened his death.

Though he continued his ceaseless activity, Elliott's health had deteriorated steadily since the end of World War II. For ten years he had suffered from spastic colitis and other gastrointestinal ailments, and he had also survived "three episodes of chest pain" that could not be diagnosed by X-ray. Some of his troubles, his doctors concluded, might have been linked to an attack of hepatitis in 1922. Elliott himself traced much of his discomfort to the artificial section of duodenum inserted in 1924, though diagnosticians found that the implant functioned normally. Elliott's own colorful versions of his ailments amused his friends, if not his doctors, for, despite his preoccupation with his medical problems, he treated them as a series of jokes.

He developed pneumonia and pleurisy near the end of 1952 and, after passing through three Charlotte hospitals and the care of numerous doctors, maintained that he had not enjoyed himself so much for the past ten years, since his bout with amoebic dysentery and pellagra. "I was given shotgun prescriptions . . . by all the medicos from the Army doctors in Atlanta to the herb doctors in Boston. I added the white of an egg and lived on them for a year."

Elliott now traveled between hospitals and medical specialists so frequently, in fact, that he bought an ambulance in order to "travel at my own expense." He also reported that one of the anesthetics used in his treatment was "truth serum"—and that Frances had banished his nurse and sat by his bed for three hours: "She had been opening my mail since I have been sick and had a lot of questions. . . . She also had accumulated considerable curiosity for the last thirty years about this and that, and had some doubts about the answers she had previously received. . . . She had a field day, and has sent for wholesale catalogs of mink coats. . . . Hereafter, when we have guests for a dull evening, she says she is going to stick me again with pentathol and everybody is going to have a hilarious time."

At various times Elliott claimed that he had lumbago, arthritis, and sciatica, all brought on by ptomaine poisoning. He suffered for years with "the same illness that killed Tex Guinan," the celebrated nightclub hostess, not to mention a hiatal hernia, "the same thing that afflicted the Pope and Red Skelton." He also reported bouts with pneumonia, "secondary anemia," a sacroiliac strain, abcessed throat, and a raging rash that was cured by gentian violet, which, he claimed, pleased him so much that he took it internally to clear up his ulcers.

Of a later illness he wrote, "Doctors in New Orleans diagnosed me with everything from trichinosis and gallstones to schizophrenia and senile dementia . . . the culture from one ulcer produced monilia parasoccharomyces, a condition so rare they want to stuff and mount me for the Smithsonian." The prescribed treatment of large doses of arsenic, he claimed, would "kill or cure in 17 days. You can get even money either way."

He reported results of an automobile accident in 1954: "I have three busted ribs, a ruptured diaphragm and a bruised lung. I am on my back, on a diet, on the wagon and on the verge of frustration."

At least one of his doctors concluded that Springs was a hypochondriac, "the worst neurotic that God ever made." Events were soon to prove the inaccuracy of that charge.

One doctor asked Elliott: "Tell me something about your sex life."

"I'm modest. I'd prefer to just give you a list of references."

"Then," Elliott recalled, "he got out my old X-rays and papers and found where the surgeons had turned me over to a psychiatrist. The psychiatrist's report said that I was incurable. He asked me how I got well, but, by the look on his face, I knew what he wanted to ask was, 'Did you get well?' "

Another physician baffled by Elliott's complaints once read to him a chapter from a textbook that "gave all my symptoms."

"What's the treatment?" Elliott asked.

The doctor closed the book. "There isn't any," he said. Then, according to Elliott, "He suggested that I give up my business, turn my affairs over to a trust company and move to Florida . . . buy a corner lot with southern exposure in a good segregated cemetery. Then I should rent a cottage nearby and be patient."

Elliott studied another medical book on his own and diagnosed his condition as "non-tropical uncomplicated sprue, a malabsorption syndrome or pellagra, caused from antibiotics." At least, he claimed, that "suits my symptoms just as well as that other chapter."

Elliott wrote soon afterward, "I have taken the treatment for sprue for a month and think I am really improving, even though I did not have sprue. The doctors are now trying to find another disease I haven't got so they can treat me for it."

By the spring of 1957 Elliott's condition had worsened. He complained continually of discomfort in his upper abdomen, a condition that remained undiagnosed despite his visits to numerous doctors. There were other problems. A prostate operation in 1958 revealed abnormalities but no malignancy, but there were increasing signs of serious illness.

Still, few of his associates realized that Elliott's health had begun to fail. His message to stockholders in the spring of 1959, though not a triumphant one, revealed him in an ebullient mood:

> In 1958 we produced 11 percent more pounds, sold them for 6 percent more dollars, and earned 8 percent less than in the previous year.
>
> I have no excuses to offer for this. Some of my competitors increased their production of alibis last year as much as 35 percent. Maybe I sold our goods too cheap. It is always our policy to take care of our customers. Maybe we put more quality into our goods than the price justified. . . . Maybe I did not gamble enough in cotton with your money. I have always tried to avoid this. . . . Textile executives always promise their stockholders a rosy prospect or keep their mouths shut. I am keeping mine shut.

He said he wished that the profit-sharing plan of his employees were larger but added, "an enterprise that nets only 7 percent return on its depreciated capital can hardly be considered to have a profit to share." Still, he said, he recommended an increase in the program for 1959, because "incentive is the life of capitalism."

At the end of 1958, which was to be Elliott's last full year as chief executive, The Springs Cotton Mills had net assets of $138.5 million, compared with $13 million in 1933, an increase of more than 1,000 percent during the twenty-seven years of his leadership. Though only seventh in size, they led the American textile industry in profitability. Sales were $163 million, more than nineteen times the level of 1933. There were now 13,000 employees, an increase of slightly less than 150 percent, and the payroll was about $40 million. Spindles had increased from 300,000 to 836,000 and looms from 7,500 to 17,800. With the help of the new Grace finishing plant, Springs was the world's largest producer of sheets and pillowcases.

Progress during his years of leadership had been spectacular. Dividends had been paid quarterly for twenty-eight years, and the original shares had been split on a basis of eighteen for one. Elliott had increased earnings steadily and spectacularly. During the troubled years of the early 1930s, he managed a profit of 9 percent on sales after federal taxes, which averaged only 12 percent—and in 1958 a respectable return of 7 percent on sales was achieved even after corporate taxes of 52 percent.

Production for the second week of October 1959 set a new record for The Springs Cotton Mills—more than ten million yards of cloth.

But Elliott was forced to leave the enjoyment of these advances to others. He apparently sensed that the increasing pain he was suffering denoted a fatal illness. The realization that his life might be approaching an end drew him closer to his wife. In the late summer of 1959 the two of them took an unprecedented brief vacation by driving to a Linville, North Carolina, resort for an overnight stay. Soon afterward, when he complained of continuing abdominal discomfort, he was taken to a Charlotte hospital, where he underwent surgery on September 2, 1959.

His internist, Monroe Gilmour of Charlotte, brought Elliott the prognosis soon after the operation: the surgeon had discovered terminal cancer of the liver and pancreas, which had spread to nearby areas. Elliott had only a few months to live.

The doctor noted that Elliott's steady gaze did not falter in the face of this shocking report: "He was very calm and matter of fact." Even in this moment his first thoughts were of his business. "It's a satisfaction to me to know that Bill Close is so well trained to carry on the mills," Elliott said.

He asked to see Close.

"It's not very good news," he told his son-in-law. "We've got to make plans. And I want you to tell Frances and Sis."

Soon afterward he wrote to his friend Harry DeButts, president of the Southern Railway, in his usual jocular vein, though he made no attempt to conceal the seriousness of his condition: "They opened me up like an Idaho potato.... My chest no longer looks like a backgammon board because I now have the Cross of Lorraine on it. They did a cholecysso-gastrostomy on me.... I am, therefore, the only person connected with the whole Southern Railway system that has two artificial openings in his stomach."

Elliott was taken home, where he was under the constant care of nurses for the first few days. He interrupted the medical regimen for daily meetings with his mill managers, reviewing the status of the business in detail—finances and plant, stocks of goods, cotton and sales prospects, and executive personnel. To his treasurer, Bill Medford, Elliott emphasized that he was leaving no debts behind him. "I have no obligations to anyone—friends, officers, customers or employees." The possibility of claims, however small, against his estate seemed to prey upon his mind. He repeated this statement to Bill Close.

Close was summoned to his bedroom at 6 P.M. daily, and the two talked for an hour each evening. "He went over all of his business deals and advised me on how they should be handled," Close recalled. "One of the last things he said in these talks was, 'If anybody says I owe them money after I die, just punch 'em in the nose.' He was serious. When I had one or two people try that, I threw 'em out."

Despite his weakened condition, Elliott insisted upon playing a role in his daughter's life. One day he walked the few yards to Anne's house with a tape measure to ascertain the proper dimensions of a dining table he was ordering for her. She recalled the poignant visit for years: "He was terribly weak but he got down on his hands and knees and measured the dining room. He wanted to be sure the table would seat twelve people."

Elliott announced that the room was too short for a table seating five on each side and one at each end. "It will have to be wider than usual," he said. "I'll seat two at each end." The table was to arrive six months after his death, a perfect fit for the room and his purpose.

After about three weeks at home, when it was obvious that Elliott was growing worse, he prepared for a trip to the Sloan-Kettering Clinic of New York's Memorial Hospital. He had little hope of improvement in his condition. In fact, some of his friends felt that Springs left home only so that his grandchildren could not witness his physical deterioration and death—throughout his illness he had worn dark glasses to help conceal the ravages of disease. He now looked much older than his years, and he was already thin and wan, though his ankles were noticeably swollen. His yellow skin suggested that he was suffering from hepatitis, and his abdomen had expanded by two inches since his operation.

An ambulance arrived at the White homestead to carry Elliott and the company doctor, J. R. Reid, Jr., to the Charlotte airport. Elliott emerged from the house in jaunty attire, including a derby and spats. He walked slowly to the ambulance. Bill Close asked Elliott if he wanted him to accompany him to New York.

"What the hell for?" Springs snapped. "Who'll run things down here?"

But he changed his mind a moment later and asked Close to ride with him as far as Charlotte. Frances and Anne were driven to Charlotte to meet Elliott at the airport.

The ambulance moved northward out of town. Elliott stared at the countryside where he had spent so many years. "Good-bye," he said, as if to an old friend. He added, without a pause, "If I live until next spring I'm going to travel with Frances as she wants me to." From his prone position in the ambulance he could now see only the clear, brilliant blue of the sky. "Look at that sky," he said softly.

A few moments later he said, "Dammit, I'm going blind, and I can't read any more."

Dr. Reid, Frances, and Anne met them at the airport. Word of the trip had spread, and a crowd gathered at the outdoor boarding gate. The ambulance pulled up at the Eastern Airlines plane and the men prepared to have Elliott carried aboard on a stretcher. "No," he said. "I want to walk," and though his step was slow and halting he climbed into the plane without faltering.

Bill and Anne Close did not make the trip until later. Anne had recently given birth to her seventh child and remained behind to care for the infant, Derick. Elliott stretched out on the lounge seat in the rear of the plane, and Frances sat beside him. The plane took off at sundown, heading north into the twilight. Dr. Reid had dinner on the plane, but Frances and Elliott declined.

The plane arrived in New York about 10 P.M. Elliott was carried in a wheelchair to a limousine, and they were soon in their hotel, where Frances and Elliott ordered dinner; Elliott ordered cherrystone clams and lamb chops. When the food came, Elliott told the waiter the clams were not cherrystones, but he did not send them back.

The next morning he entered Sloan-Kettering, where it was discovered that he was suffering from myocardial disease as well as from the ravages of cancer. Doctors considered a liver biopsy but rejected it as too dangerous and began both radiation therapy and chemotherapy. Throughout more than two weeks of this and other supportive treatments Elliott's course was "progressively downhill."

Anne, who was trying to wean her six-week-old son, joined her mother in New York a few days later. She sat in her father's room on the night of October 14 and found him resting quietly. She and Frances returned to the hotel in the early evening but were called at 5 A.M. and told to come to the hospital immediately.

In the early morning of October 15 Elliott complained of difficult, painful breathing and soon afterward hemorrhaged massively from his mouth. He died quietly a few moments later, at 6 A.M., just two and a half months past his sixty-third birthday. Anne and Frances arrived a few minutes later.

An autopsy revealed that pneumonia was the immediate cause of his death, but also that the cancer had originated in the gall bladder rather than the pancreas and had spread to the pancreas and liver and a few lymph nodes, with "no evidence of distant spread."

The body was cremated, and the ashes were returned to Fort Mill for a memorial service. A throng of people, most of them Springs employees, lined the streets of the small town, three or four ranks deep, as the funeral procession passed. Many of them watched with tears in their eyes as the hearse rolled toward the Presbyterian cemetery, where Elliott's ashes were buried in the White family plot, near the graves of his grandparents, his mother, and Sonny. The airplane propeller that marked Sonny's grave drew poignant glances from mourners—but it was soon to disappear. Frances Springs had it removed within a few days.

A lengthy obituary in the *New York Times* marked Elliott's death as the passing of an eminent American but described Elliott as "the world's champion fun-loving business man." It also recalled the "leggy, scantily-clad girls" of his advertisements that "sometimes startled readers and brought down censorship from various publications. But it all seemed to be good for his business." The *Times* also mentioned his Christmas card hoax of a generation earlier, when he had posed his family as jeans-clad mill hands and inspired spirited protests.

An anonymous writer at Princeton, reporting the death of Springs to alumni, noted the large number of obituaries and wrote,

None . . . lengthy, detailed and anecdotal though many of them were—fully pictured the man thousands claimed to know, and few really did, let alone understood. . . . [He] was too complex, too much of an enigma and a paradox for any biographer to reveal all of his many facets.

Time alone will tell how lasting the imprint of the man who be-came a legend in his own lifetime. One thing is certain, though, without awaiting the verdict of time. If degrees were awarded for what you put into and got out of life, that of Colonel Elliott White Springs . . . would unquestionably be *summa cum laude.*

The men's magazine *Cavalier* recalled the combat record of "The War Bird Who'll Never Die." The article conceded that even his closest friends failed to understand this proud, sensitive, complex man: "There was swagger and color and daring to Elliott White Springs. . . . To some people he was a glory hunter, always calling attention to himself . . . a grandstand player, a show-off."

But, the article continued, one of his old war comrades denied this: "If Springs cared for credit and claimed every German that he downed, he would have been right up there with Rickenbacker. . . . Springs didn't care enough to bother."

Nor did Springs care much for the opinions of others: "He took life as he found it and enjoyed what he found. . . . Elliott White Springs will always be many things to many people. He was a show-off, or he wasn't; an under-rated ace or an over-rated one; a mill-owning tycoon or a neighbor to those who worked for him; a vulgar, crude advertizer or a man with a sense of humor who enjoyed kidding vulgar, crude advertizing; a scatter-brained playboy or a man of tremendous ability who refused to take his own accomplishments too seriously. The real man is somewhere between the lines of the contradictions."

"Many people laughed when they read his obituary," the magazine's editors said. "That was O.K. Indeed, the Colonel would have liked it. But those who knew Springs the Ace reacted in a different way. They are sure that he will live as long as men honor those who gave their all."

Notes to Chapters

Prologue: August 1918

This sketch is based upon *War Birds* and the letters of Springs to his parents, particularly those of July to November 1918. Additional material is drawn from Walter Musciano, "Never Another Ace Like Elliott White Springs!" *Air Progress* (November 1967): 49–76. In minor details the observations of Springs conflict with facts presented by historians of World War I, but his eyewitness testimony has been relied upon in this narrative.

The story of Elliott's spitefully scrawling "Here's looking at you, you old drunk" across the photograph sent to his father from France was told by John Roddey of Rock Hill, South Carolina, in an interview with the author, 29 July 1984.

Elliott's comments on aerial combat at the end of this section were written for *Pilot's Luck*, an anthology about World War I published in 1929.

Chapter I: "As Smart As He Could Be"

Elliott White Springs's family background is drawn from Katherine Wooten Springs, *The Squires of Springfield* (Charlotte, N.C., 1965) and from various newspaper articles in scrapbooks of Katherine W. Springs and the Elliott White Springs family. The shooting of John R. Bell by Leroy Springs was reported in the *Charleston* (S.C.) *News and Courier*, 28 June 1885.

The early history of the family textile operations is summarized in the house organ of the Springs mills, *The Springs Bulletin*, 30 July 1947, and in an unpublished manuscript history of the Springs mills dated 16 June 1967.

Elliott's traumatic experience at the death of his grandmother is described in an unidentified newspaper clipping of 1903 in the family scrapbook. His mother's death is similarly detailed in a clipping from an unnamed Charleston newspaper in the collection of Frances Close Hart of Columbia, South Carolina.

The diseases Elliott had as a child were recorded in his army flight physical for 1942, which was administered at Morris Field, Charlotte.

Springs himself described in *Clothes Make the Man* his encounter with the red-haired girl known only as "Auld Lang Syne." It is possible that he created the incident out of whole cloth, as the Springs corporate historian Louise Pettus has suggested, but in context, the story was convincing to this author. Elliott's boyhood adventures with other girls were based on letters from Elaine Baxter Carter, Savannah, Georgia, 20 October 1956, and Virginia Durham, Columbia, 5 July 1949.

Elliott's days as a sandlot baseball player were described to the author by V. A. Ballard of Fort Mill and by Elliott himself in a letter to H. F. Gibson, 1 July 1935.

The amusing tale of Captain Sam White and his stomach pump is from a letter from Springs to Dr. Robert McKay of Charlotte, 27 November 1958.

Elliott's career at Asheville School is based on his correspondence with his father and grandfather between 1908 and 1910, his report cards for the period, and the 1910 volume of *The Blue and White*, the school's first published annual. Elliott's writing at Asheville is discussed by Helen Vassy Callison in "The Literary Achievement of Elliott White Springs" (Ph.D. diss., University of South Carolina, 1974).

The years at Culver were recorded in Elliott's letters to his father; in the 1913 edition of *The Roll Call*, the school yearbook, especially p. 75; in Elliott's scrapbook of the period; and in Leroy's letter of 21 February 1911 to his son. Elliott's literary career at Culver is sketched in Callison, "The Literary Achievement," pp. 146–48.

Chapter II: "You're Abnormal Anyway"

Springs recounted his experience at The Johns Hopkins Hospital in a letter to his wife, 27 August 1921.

His years at Princeton, the period of his first maturity, are most vividly pictured in his correspondence with Frances: his abandonment of celibacy in a letter dated "Thanksgiving Day 1921," and his romance with Adahmaye and the wild parties that caused trouble with college officials, in a letter written 28 November 1921. His affairs with numerous women on the eve of his departure for war are recorded in his terse diary of 1917.

His story of his conquest of the "bit of fluff" from Nashville, Tennessee, and his father's discomfiture over the escapade is in an undated letter to Frances from Pinehurst, North Carolina (apparently written in 1922).

Elliott's role as Captain of the Princeton Drinking Team was described by Landon T. Raymond, class of 1917, to John Gates.

In their correspondence Springs and his father left a candid record of their increasing hostility. Elliott's letters of 3 March, 11 April, 28 April, and 15 May 1917 and of 6 June and 16 June 1918 are particularly revealing. Leroy's letter of 30 July 1917, a pause in the barrage of accusation and recrimination, is the most moving of their exchange: "Protect yourself . . . come home to us safe . . . I think of you all the time."

Official records of Elliott's performance at Princeton and in his first weeks as an army pilot are found in the *Nassau Herald* (Princeton, N.J., 1917), pp. 234–35; *Ten Years of Princeton, 1917* (Princeton, N.J., 1929); Springs's "Vertical Adventure," pp. 229 ff.; and Princeton University War Records, 22 April 1924. The university has no records of his grades—and the only references to his graduation "with honors" are in correspondence of Elliott and Leroy. Elliott wrote his father before commencement that he had won honors in psychology, and philosophy and ethics, but according to Louise Pettus, he listed his Princeton honors as having been in Latin, Greek, English, and psychology when applying to the air corps for reinstatement in the 1930s.

Elliott described his limited literary endeavors at Princeton in a letter to Dr. Clarke Olney of the University of Georgia, 29 April 1957. Springs revealed his lingering bitterness over Princeton's failure to recognize his gifts as a writer in a note to Dr. W. P. Jacobs of Presbyterian College, Clinton, South Carolina, 19 March 1936. Elliott's lack of loyalty to Princeton in later years was challenged by a class agent. The agent wrote, "Elliott, I don't like to speak so frankly but it is time you made a contribution . . . I don't think you are yellow but you certainly dodged my telephone calls" (1 November 1955). Springs's records, however, show $1,000 annual contributions from 1951 to 1955. He resigned from the Princeton Club of New York City in 1955.

Laurence Callahan's recollection of Springs as top sergeant of the aviation company is from Marvin L. Skelton, *Callahan, the Last War Bird* (Manhattan, Kans., 1981), p. 3 ff.

Chapter III: "That Select Company of Ruffians"

This narrative of the fledgling American pilots during training in England is a synthesis of numerous letters by Springs to his stepmother, Lena, from September 1917 through May 1918 and the account of these adventures in *War Birds*. The chapter presented a challenge to the author not only because *War Birds* blends fact and fiction, but also because Springs frequently expresses himself through the narrator (a role ostensibly filled by Elliott's friend Mac Grider). Comparison between the text of Springs's celebrated book and his contemporary letters, however, revealed remarkable agreement in most matters of importance.

A copy of the brief shipboard diary of Mac Grider, which was to become an object of controversy, is in the Springs Papers. Springs sent the original to the Grider family.

The sketch of Billy Bishop is from Ezra Bowen, *Knights of the Air* (New York, 1981), p. 132. Callahan's version of Bishop's recruitment of 85th Squadron, RFC, is cited in Skelton, *The Last War Bird*.

The vivid scene of the squadron's departure for France is based on Elliott's letter to Frances of 21 November 1921 and his earlier, less explicit, one to Lena Springs of 23 May 1918.

Chapter IV: "I've Got to Get Killed. I Can't Go Home."

Springs documented his adventures in France thoroughly—not to say exhaustively—in a diary, in almost daily letters to his parents (chiefly to Lena Springs), and in his flight log. The two chapters on his combat days in France are based chiefly on these. The striking letters to Leroy and Lena from this phase began on 1 June 1918 and continued until his departure for home in January 1919. They were almost certainly written with future publication in mind. All are in the Springs papers.

Other valuable sources are W. P. Taylor and F. L. Irvin, *War Diary of the 148th Aero Squadron: History of the 148th Squadron* (Lancaster, S.C., 1957); Elliott White Springs, "The Iliad of the 148th" and "Odyssey, 1918" (typescripts, 1927) and "War Birds" (typescript, 1926); Wiliam A. Bishop, *The Courage of Early Morning* (New York, 1965) and *Winged Warfare* (New York, 1967); Sholto Douglas, *Combat and Command* (New York, 1966); Edward H. Sims, *The Aces Talk* (New York, 1972); and Gwilym H. Lewis, *Wings over the Somme, 1916–1918* (London, 1976).

By far the most important of these printed sources is *War Birds* in all of its editions, 1927–66. The typescript (apparently the earliest surviving form) used by the author was said by Springs to have been limited to four copies.

Elliott's story of his first combat and his near-miraculous escape is cited in Skelton, *The Last War Bird*, p. 12.

Mac Grider's impressions of life in 85th Squadron's first base is from Skelton, *The Last War Bird*, p. 18, which cites Josephine G. Jacobs, ed., *Marse John Goes to War* (New York, 1933).

The sketch of E. C. (Mick) Mannock is based largely on Ira Jones, *King of the Air Fighters* (London, 1934); on Stephen Longstreet, *The Canvas Falcons* (New York, 1970), pp. 180 ff.; and on Bowen, *Knights of the Air*, pp. 164 ff.

Chapter V: "This War Isn't What It Used to Be"

Of several versions of Mac Grider's death in combat, the most significant is Elliott's letter to Lena of 20 June 1918, two days after his friend was shot down. *War Birds* offers no satisfactory account of Grider's death because Springs was forced to falsify the chronology of events in order to present his full story (Grider actually died on 18 June 1918, though *War Birds* records the event at an indefinite date—but after 27 August). Elliott's letter to Lena of 12 September 1918 confirmed Grider's death and burial by the Germans.

Elliott wrote of Billie Carlton's reaction to Mac's death and of Hallie Whatley's suicide to Nevil Shute on 31 December 1958. Musciano wrote in *Air Progress* (November 1967) that Springs was "tense and restless because he felt partly to blame for Grider's death. He volunteered for many solo missions and . . . destroyed several more enemy planes over the German lines which could not be confirmed."

The author found it difficult to account for Springs's combat victories with precision. Taylor and Irvin in *War Diary* credited him with becoming the squadron's first ace by scoring his fifth kill on 3 August 1918. Though this is accepted in the present narrative, official British and American records present a different version.

The Springs Papers include copies from the "R.A.F. Victory Log," which credits Springs with two kills (one near Merris on 18 June, one near Kemmel on 25 June). Springs was transferred to the U.S. 148th Squadron on 1 July, and his own subsequent combat reports show his kill of 3 August (near Ostend) to be his third.

Other victories are shown in his reports, copies of which are in the Springs Papers: 13 August (near Roye) and 22 August (near Velu, 10:10 A.M.). Thereafter, he claims credit for 6 1/4 other enemy aircraft, one each on the dates 22 August (5:40 P.M.), 27 August, 5 September, 20 September, 24 September, and 27 September. (The one-quarter credit was claimed during a patrol action on 15 September near Epinoy.)

Skelton in *The Last War Bird* follows neither the official records nor the squadron history.

The author of this volume, unable to resolve the conflict, accepted the Taylor and Irvin version of the date of Springs's fifth kill because they reviewed sources unavailable to him.

Springs himself, who might have been expected to furnish the most reliable account in his combat reports and letters to his parents, wrote to Lena: "I don't think anyone embarrassed me by asking me the number of planes I had until I reached Paris. I couldn't tell them because I don't know exactly . . . I think the British give me 12 1/4 but by American figuring it will be 14" (9 September 1918). Elliott's most striking comment on combat described his reaction to shooting down German aviators: "The first time it happened to me I was sick at my stomach for three days. The last time it happened, five months later, I did not even look down to see the end. I was fixing my glove" (*Ten Years of Princeton, 1917*, p. 230).

Chapter VI: "I Have No Use for a Wife"

Elliott's return from war was reported in a telegram from Lena to a relative, Mrs. J. M. Odell of Concord, North Carolina, 2 February 1919.

Springs telegraphed Callahan that New York's "fleshpots" awaited him and offered to send addresses of women in a dayletter of 26 March 1919.

Elliott's dalliance in New York during 1919 is amusingly recalled in a flurry of exchanges of telegrams and letters between Leroy and his son, beginning May 11 and ending in mid-December.

Elliott recorded his projected venture with Nordhoff and Hall in a letter to Preston Boyden of Chicago written 25 March 1927.

The official opening of Elliott's career in the mills is described by E. Lee Skipper in *The Springs Bulletin*, 17 April 1968, and this source was used in depicting some phases of the later relationship between the two.

Elliott's courtship of Frances Ley in Europe during 1921 is documented in his subsequent love letters to her, some two dozen of which are in the Springs Papers; a few additional ones from Springs to his fiancée (dated from 8 July through August) are owned by Anne Springs Close. Letters from Frances to Elliott in this exchange evidently failed to survive.

H. A. Ley's covert investigation of his prospective son-in-law is detailed in an unsigned report to Ley in the Springs Papers. Leroy's simultaneous investigation of Ley was related by Elliott to his friend William H. Grier, who recorded his recollection many years later (tape in Springs Papers).

The Leroy Springs–Charles D. Jones controversy is described in Elliott's letters to Frances, cited above. Additional material appeared in the *Lancaster* (S.C.) *News* over the course of many months, most completely on 31 March 1922.

The White homestead, built by Elliott's great-grandfather in the early 1830s, and restored and expanded by Elliott, is used today as a guest house by Mrs. Close and Springs Industries. The historic mansion was the site of one of the last meetings held by Jefferson Davis and his Confederate cabinet, in flight at the end of the Civil War.

The abortive sale of the family mills by Leroy Springs was reported in several regional newspapers, especially the *Charlotte Observer*, 27 September and 17 October 1923, and *The Southern Textile Bulletin* of Charlotte, 4 October 1923. Cancellation of the sale "by mutual consent" was announced in the *Observer*, 28 November 1923. Robert Amory recalled in an interview with Barbara Fenix, 27 May 1971, that Elliott urged his father to accept cash only: "He didn't trust Greene." The supposition is that E. F. Greene was unable or unwilling to meet this demand.

The award of the British Distinguished Flying Cross to Elliott by Edward, Prince of Wales, is described in Elliott's correspondence with the British Air Attache in Washington, 16 September 1919.

From Elliott's various accounts of his flight under the Buster Boyd Bridge, which suffered nothing in the telling, it is unclear when his plane arrived at the dedication scene—but his appearance was anticlimactic in any case. Two Charlotte aviators, P. R. Redfearn and Benjamin F. Withers, Jr., had flown beneath the bridge a few moments earlier.

Elliott's jocular, temporary name for his son, "Julius Caesar" Springs, was recalled by Anne Springs Close in an interview with the author.

Chapter VII: "The Biggest Smash"

The writings of Springs during 1925 are summarized by Julian Starr in the introduction to *Clothes Make the Man*, rev. ed. (New York, 1966); Clarke Olney, "The Literary Career of Elliott White Springs," *Georgia Review* (Winter 1957): 400–411; and most substantially in Callison, "The Literary Achievement." Elliott's later accounts of his work during 1925 are so varied as to be untrustworthy in detail.

The present narrative was drawn from Springs's files for 1925–28 and from interviews with Elizabeth Mack, Elliott's literary secretary. The files include extensive correspondence between Springs and the editors of *Blue Book, Colliers, Cosmopolitan, Liberty*, and *McClure's* (particularly with Arthur McKeogh). In addition, he wrote to officials of Dorrance, Doubleday (and received fifty-six letters from the publishing house in 1927 alone, often from Doran), Harper & Brothers, Henry Holt, and Houghton Mifflin. There is also correspondence with various agents, especially Carl Brandt of New York.

Of particular importance is the correspondence between Elliott and his father (letters exchanged between Fort Mill and Lancaster, some twenty-eight miles apart). Leroy expressed his anguish over the original version of *War Birds* both before and after *Liberty* published the book as a serial.

The Springs Papers include four typescripts of *War Birds* (in addition to numerous printed versions, six British, one Canadian, and one Australian). Springs said that the "original plates" were destroyed during the German bombing of London in 1940. The book was out of print for more than ten years.

The denunciation of Elliott by his father during a company board meeting is from an interview with John Roddey of Rock Hill, South Carolina.

Chapter VIII: "The Unknown Writer"

The controversy over *War Birds* between Springs and Mac Grider's family (chiefly Josephine G. Jacobs) is clarified by substantial files of correspondence in the Springs Papers. Mrs. Jacobs put her complaints most forcefully to Elliott in a letter of 25 May 1927. Elliott's correspondents on this matter included, in addition to Josephine, Marguerite (Mrs. Mac) Grider; Mac's sons, John and George; Mac's father, mother, and stepmother; Wilson J. Northcross, guardian of the Grider boys; and Emma Cox Smith, Mac's friend and banker.

Most important is Elliott's account of the genesis of *War Birds* to Preston Boyden, 25 March 1927 (as quoted in the present text). Elliott's letters to the editors of the *Memphis Commercial Appeal*, 19 October and 25 October 1927, are also revealing.

Though Springs conceded in his foreword to the 1951 edition of *War Birds* that Mac Grider was the diarist of the novel, he never made public his own role as author, de facto diarist, and hero.

Springs not only gave his earnings from *Liberty*'s serialization of *War Birds* and more to the Grider family, but also helped Mac's sons, John and George, enter Annapolis and followed their careers with interest. George commanded the celebrated submarine *Flasher*, which sank a record tonnage of enemy shipping in World War II; John served aboard a cruiser in the fierce battles for the Solomon Islands. In his brief diary Mac Grider had written, "I hope my boys will grow up to be good strong upwright [sic] men . . . go to college and make good friends and be accepted by the right sort of people."

Sources for cited criticism of *War Birds* include the following: Sidney Howard, *The Bookman* 65 (March 1927): 85; S. T. Williamson, *New York Times Book Review*, 23 January 1927; *Outlook* 145 (16 March 1927): 345; Arch Whitehouse, *Heroes of the Sunlit Sky* (New York, 1967), p. 5. Comments by the *London Daily Express*, the [London] *Observer*, and the *Yorkshire Post* appeared on the dust jacket of the Platypus (Australian) edition of *War Birds*. William A. Percy's appraisal is in the *Saturday Review of Literature* 3 (12 March 1927): 643.

To T. E. Lawrence, who later praised *War Birds*, Elliott complained that the book was "originally suppressed in England by the War Ministry as being unfit for consumption by the young pilots of the R.A.F."

Julian Starr's opinion that Springs was more accomplished as a salesman than as a writer is found in Callison, "The Literary Achievement," p. 58n.

Elliott's claim that he wrote the novel *Contact* in three weeks was made in a letter to C. C. Caldwell dated 15 June 1939.

The account of the shooting of Leroy Springs by Eldred Griffith is based on clippings, chiefly from the *Charlotte Observer*, in the scrapbook of Katherine W. Springs, and on Leroy's testimony.

Elliott begged his father to cease his reckless gambling in the stock market in striking letters of 16 December 1929, 8 April, and 25 June 1930.

Elliott's confessions of his failures to his father, made in a rare mood of depression, were written on 1 July 1930; his complaint that Leroy had shorn him of all authority in the mills is in a letter of 10 July 1930.

Mrs. Maxie Stanley discussed Elliott's extramarital romances in an interview with John Gates, 16 September 1981, and added other details in correspondence with the author. Earl Crenshaw described Springs's admiration of pretty women in his plants and his comparison of one of these with a companion in New York City.

Chapter IX: "Stay at Home . . . and Work Like Hell"

V. A. Ballard recalled in an interview that Elliott used the expression "stay home and work like hell" as a prescription for success in the cotton mill business. Ballard also recalled Elliott's ability to detect any threat to efficient operation from the sound of running machinery.

Springs recounted his trials as a neophyte industrialist in a formal statement to Internal Revenue officials dated 1 January 1934. Though designed to support his appeal for reduction of his father's estate taxes, the document is detailed and largely factual. This source was augmented by Elliott's explanatory letter of 18 September 1937 to D. A. Embury of the New York law firm Curtis, Mallet, Prevost, Colt, and Mosle.

Elliott's voluntary reduction of his salary was announced to company officials on 21 July 1933. His purchase of new and used machinery was described by Ballard, Charles Crutchfield of Charlotte, and others.

Extensive files of business correspondence in the Springs Papers illuminate Elliott's struggle after the death of his father, and his own letters of this period are remarkable for their colorful, irreverent spirit. Of special value were the following files (key documents are in parentheses): National Recovery Administration (H. H. Willis, South Carolina Chairman, to Springs, 26 February 1934; Springs to Willis, 2 March 1934); Cotton Textile Code Authority, New York, N.Y. (Springs to George A. Sloan, 13 August 1934); Cotton Manufacturers Association of South Carolina (Springs to William P. Jacobs, 8 April 1935); also Cotton Textile Institute; American Cotton Manufacturers Association; the Saco-Lowell Shops; Draper Machinery Corporation; Westinghouse, Inc.; Avondale Mills, Sylacauga, Alabama (Springs to Donald Comer, 16 October 1933); Southern Railway; Pennsylvania Railroad; and the New York, New Haven, and Hartford Railroad (Springs to F. A. Brainerd, 16 February 1934).

Elliott's complaints about Hugh (Ironpants) Johnson of the NRA were made to Pabst Goodrich of Milwaukee on 13 December 1933.

Labor strife involving the Springs mills in the early 1930s was described by Springs in an undated affidavit of 1934 in Lancaster County; in a telegram to

Robert Stevens of New York, N.Y., 6 September 1934; and by Cecil Neal in an interview with the author. A typescript of the undated and undelivered radio address by Springs is in the Springs Papers. Elliott wrote to Robert Stevens on 19 September 1934 that he canceled the address "to avoid stepping on the toes of some other mill Presidents." Waddill Catchings of New York reported to Springs on 9 October 1934 that President Roosevelt had read the proposed address.

Jake Stanley described the scene when Elliott told a crowd of his workers that he would respond to a strike by closing and taking his family to Europe.

Correspondence of interest for this period includes the following: Springs to *Time* magazine, 17 September 1934; Springs to Lawrence Stallings, 5 October 1934; B. M. Squires of the Textile Labor Relations Board to Springs, 24 October 1934, and Springs's reply, 29 October 1934. The role of Frances Perkins in the strike was described by Elliott to Waddill Catchings on 11 October 1934. Elliott's jocular appeal for help to Thomas Hitchcock, Jr., of New York was in a telegram dated 23 October 1934.

Earl Crenshaw remembered that Elliott kept a loom in the basement of his house to learn textile techniques but added, "The real basis of his success was at his supervisory level. He had the best technicians in the world."

Elliott's difficulties as a young executive are illustrated by his appeal to nearby banks for cash to meet his payroll. (He received $10,000 in twenty-dollar bills from the American Trust of Charlotte on one occasion in 1933.)

Chapter X: "My Ragged Individualism"

Sam Schwartz's reaction to Elliott's Christmas card hoax has been challenged as a figment of Elliott's imagination, but the letter of 30 November 1935 in the Springs Papers is genuine enough. It is signed "S. Schwartz," a textile manufacturer from Two Rivers, Wisconsin.

Elliott's clash with the machine manufacturer Clare Draper and the improvization of left-handed looms was described by Cecil Neal.

Anne Springs Close described her family's flight on the *Hindenburg*, and details (of uncertain reliability) were given by Springs to J. E. Dowd for an article in the *Charlotte News*, clipping undated, presumably September 1936. Other sources include Alec Waugh to Springs, 17 August 1936; Springs to Dora Hastings, 28 December 1936; Springs to H. A. Ley, 24 September 1936; and Springs to Admiral Charles E. Rosendahl, 18 July 1946.

Mrs. John Hallett of Fort Mill recalled visits from Frances Springs and her suppressed fondness for hotdogs.

The progress of the mills in 1938 is recorded in the annual report. V. A. Ballard recalled the work of the "mildew squad" in saving the cloth Elliott stored each year in order to keep his mills running. Wartime demand, beginning in 1939, consumed these stocks and made Elliott a very wealthy man.

It was Eunice Hite, former telephone operator, who recalled Elliott's promptness in the office and his daily routine of "playing with" his model train.

The restored private car, *Loretto*, donated by the Springs family, is displayed at the North Carolina Transportation Museum, Spencer, North Carolina.

The composition of the Lancaster & Chester's board of directors is revealed by the railroad's stationery, a typical example of Elliott's lighthearted approach to business and his shrewd grasp of basic principles of public relations.

The retraining of Springs as a pilot was recalled by his instructor, Walt Mallonee, in an interview with the author. Elliott's comments on the joys of flight—and his confession that he had lost his plane in New York—were made to C. C. Caldwell, 24 July 1939.

Elliott's trip to the Kentucky Derby in 1937 with Democratic leaders is documented in his correspondence with L. W. (Chip) Robert, Jr., 27 March and 2 April 1937.

Chapter XI: "I've Run As Far As I Can Go"

Elliott's attempt to go to Europe soon after the war began included a request to R. B. Shipley, chief of the Passport Division, Department of State, 26 September 1939. Springs's further efforts (and yearnings) to be posted to the war zone can be found in his letters: L. K. Callahan to Springs, 19 September 1939; Springs to Callahan, 10 April 1942; Springs to Colonel S. B. Horn, 25 October 1939; Springs to J. K. Stanley, 18 October 1941; and Dora James to Springs, 18 September 1939.

Elliott revealed his continuing poor health during the war in correspondence with Colonel Buxton, 16 February 1944; C. C. Caldwell, 15 June 1939; Jeremiah Finch of Princeton University, 5 December 1942; Dr. Edwin G. Zabriskie of New York, 4 February 1944; and General C. W. Howard, 24 January and 16 February 1944.

The 1942 army flight physical on Springs at Charlotte Air Base (Morris Field) lists his physical defects, illnesses, and injuries. He was then 5 feet 8 1/2 inches tall and weighed 165 pounds.

The army secretary who spoke so admiringly of Springs in later years was Lane Knox Yorke of Rock Hill, South Carolina. She did so in a letter to Walter Elisha of Springs Industries, 12 March 1985.

Springs was promoted to lieutenant colonel after he had left active service in 1942. The army acted only at the insistence of General Howard, his nemesis, and of Trubee Davison of the State Department. Elliott was called "Colonel" thereafter by friends and associates.

The estate of Lena Springs caused Elliott much anxiety. She had given some Springs mills stock to a New England foundation and her two brothers inherited the rest. Springs refused to purchase these shares at the prices demanded. His tax attorney, Herbert Elsas of Atlanta, reported to the author that he finally persuaded Springs to buy in the stock for the sake of his family's future.

Elliott's lengthy stay in New England mental institutions is described in his numerous letters and those of Dr. Robert Hiden and others at the Austen Riggs Clinic, Stockbridge, Massachusetts, to Frances Springs, July to September 1942. The most telling of these letters, Hiden to Frances Springs, 15 August 1942, pinpoints the childhood origins of Elliott's emotional problems. Bills from the two hospital stays are in the Springs Papers.

Harold Ley wrote his daughter, 27 August 1942, "It was quite a shock to me to learn that Elliott was . . . at Riggs but it didn't surprise me much for we had the feeling that he had been burning the candle at both ends."

Elliott described wartime conditions in his mills to his daughter, Anne, 2 May 1946; to Robert Amory, 7 July 1949; to General C. W. Howard, 24 January 1944; to George Harris, 9 February 1942; to Colonel G. E. Buxton, 12 March, 17 July, and 8 November 1940; and to Lieutenant Colonel Harold A. McGinnes, 18 November 1941.

Of Elliott's correspondence with Sonny that convinced the boy to enter Princeton for one year, the letters of 4 May and 30 June 1942 are particularly revealing of their relationship.

Chapter XII: "I Know I'm Dreaming"

The tragic death of Elliott's son Leroy in the glider-towing accident is revealed most vividly in Springs's correspondence as cited. The narrative also owes much to interviews with Eunice Hite and especially with Cecil Neal, a former Springs pilot, and to the affidavits of John R. Taylor, the glider pilot, and of undertaker Charles W. Holland of Lancaster, and of Ralph F. Jarrett, D.D.S., of Charlotte, who described the removal and identification of the two bodies. Newspapers of the region reported the accident. The author was unable to locate the official report made by the Civil Aeronautics Board.

Bill Close described his relationship with his father-in-law to John Gates in 1981. The building of the Close home was recalled by Bill Close, Joe Croxton, and Cecil Neal. Robert Amory recounted subsequent clashes between father and daughter.

Anne Springs Close, who spoke candidly of her family, conceded that she shared some personality traits with her father. She added, "Daddy wasn't easy all the time. . . . In fact, no two Springses can stay in the same room without fighting."

Of her mother's reserve and relatively isolated life in Fort Mill, Mrs. Close said that her father deliberately discouraged her mother's contacts with her relatives: "Daddy didn't want the Ley family here. She was his, and he kept her to himself."

Righton Richards quoted Elliott's friend Rhetta Blakeney as saying that Mrs. Springs was cowed by her husband: "Frances had plenty of sense; she's just not allowed to show it."

The building and early operation of the Springs bleachery were described by Herb Mathewson, James Lasley, and Conway Still. Elliott's long-frustrated plans to add a finishing plant are clarified by his telegram of 4 January 1934 to H. M. McCord of New York: "Under the code we cannot build a bleachery so have given up the idea."

Chapter XIII: "You Can't Go Wrong on a Springmaid Sheet"

The Springmaid advertising campaign of 1946–59 is the most thoroughly documented phase of Elliott's career. His papers not only include copies of all ads in various stages of development, but also extensive files of correspondence with his agencies and with his men in New York, Hill Wolfe and Joe Swan. These documents reveal the progress of his ads from conception to publication.

Springs publicized the entire campaign in his *Clothes Make the Man* (New York, 1950). A typical example was his version of the beginning of the offensive described on page 186 of this book. He disguised the recipient of his insistent letters in this case as "Joe Gatch" and later as "Joe Gish."

One of the first successes of the campaign, a cartoon depicting three scantily clad ice skaters warming themselves offstage, was used as the cover of *Esquire* for August 1946.

Callison offers a brief study of the campaign ("The Literary Achievement of Elliott White Springs," p. 115), and James D. Taylor of the University of South Dakota, placed Elliott's work in historical perspective in an essay for *Journal of Advertising* 11, no. 2 (1982). A brief, matter-of-fact account of the advertising blitz was left by Elliott's friend and attorney, A. Z. F. Wood, in a manuscript history of Springs mills dated 19 June 1967.

Criticism and commentary cited in the text on Springs's advertising campaigns are taken from *Printer's Ink* (3 December 1948), *Tide* (27 August, 10 September 1948, and 14 June 1950), *Fortune* (January 1950), and *Advertising Age* (7 December 1964).

Correspondence files with most of the magazines involved are in the Springs Papers. Resistance to these ads persisted long after the death of Elliott Springs. In 1975, according to Herb Mathewson, the *Wall Street Journal* declined to publish two of his old ads submitted by Bill Close on the ground that they might offend the public.

Interviews with the photographer Buddy Montgomery were of value in describing the production methods as well as the creative spirit of Springs, the advertising genius.

Elliott's claim that his outlets for sheets grew from six to ten thousand during the campaign was made to Lester Leber, a New York columnist, on 22 May 1953.

The story of the Acousticot bed was told by Cecil Neal, who built several models and shepherded them around the United States. The idea sprang from an illustration by Alexis de Sakhnoffsky in *Esquire*, but Springs expanded on this spoof of modern gadgetry for several months before losing interest.

The irate educator who objected to Elliott's ads was Dr. Stephen W. Paine, president of Houghton College in New York. Elliott made an elaborate defense of his purpose in a four-page reply dated 4 January 1952.

Original artwork from the campaign is displayed in the corporate headquarters of Springs Industries in Fort Mill.

Chapter XIV: "This Is Small Enough for the Colonel to Decide"

Miss Lee's visits to Fort Mill were recalled by Mrs. John Hallett, Righton Richards, and Bill Close. Close told John Gates on 28 January 1981 that Gypsy's appearances ceased when Frances Springs told Elliott firmly, "Let me know when she's coming again. I'm leaving."

Elliott's promise to Gypsy that he would see her weekly in New York was dated 12 October 1956.

The report that Frances had departed "in a four-motored dudgeon" was in a letter from Springs to Callahan dated 15 October 1948.

A few references to Elliott's purported involvement with women can be found in the Springs Papers. Among these is a query from Springs to Jake Stanley on 3 August 1939: "Do you, by any chance, remember a girl named Rosine? I cannot, but she has written . . . that she wants to . . . visit me and bring her child. . . . She seems to intimate that said child has a definite interest in me or I should have a definite interest in it. I cannot figure out whether somebody is about to put the bee on me, or whether she is mistaking me for Uncle Eli."

Another hint of Elliott's extramarital affairs is found in a letter from Representative James Simpson, Jr., of Chicago to Springs dated 27 November 1933: "You, Larry and I have got to get together in New York, as some very tasty packages might be developed. In fact, I have already gotten something that I think you two ought to see . . . Larry has ideas that a beautiful Spanish something he has found out here surpasses all else."

Elliott's loss of control, resulting in his tantrum in a corridor of the mill offices, was recalled by Eunice Hite.

E. W. Scruggs described the design and building of the new Springs mills corporate headquarters in Fort Mill in a 1971 interview with Barbara Fenix. Scruggs said that Frank Lloyd Wright, eager for this commission, wrote to Elliott several times in vain.

Other phases of the creation of the building were recalled by Palmer Freeman and Joe Croxton. Freeman was also the source of the stories about Elliott and the company's grass-mowing problems, the brash employee who collected twice for the same injury, and Elliott's impulsive choice for the location of one corner of a textile plant building that resulted in an irregular wall.

Freeman, among others, recalled Elliott's reluctance to join textile industry organizations and industry reaction to him: "There wasn't a man in the industry who didn't hate his guts but any one of them would have given his right arm to be able to run mills like he did and make the money he made."

Righton Richards recounted her experiences as a novice cafeteria manager for Springs in interviews with John Gates and with the author.

Earl Crenshaw recalled Elliott's secretiveness with his annual report as it was briefly passed around the table at a meeting of directors.

Working relations between Springs and Lee Skipper were described by Skipper's daughter, Mrs. Ann McAden of Columbia, South Carolina, by Miss Richards, and by Skipper himself in The Springs Bulletin, previously cited. Numerous file documents reveal Skipper's upward progress in the firm.

Chapter XV: "He Was a Very Closed Person"

Elliott's business methods as described in this chapter are based on interviews by John Gates with the late Bill Medford and on interviews by the author with James Bradley, James Lasley, V. A. Ballard, Earl Crenshaw, and Anne Close.

Elliott's relationship with Dr. Robert McKay and their penchant for pranks was described by Dr. Haynes Baird of Charlotte in an interview with the author held on 28 July 1984. Dr. Baird also recalled Elliott's imposition of a five-dollar limit on fund-raisers from charities who called at his office.

The yacht *Springmaid* was the subject of much correspondence between Springs and Fritz Holliday; Springs also frequently made the vessel available to friends and business associates. Charles Crutchfield recalled the story of Elliott's chasing the native girl and Frances's striking him on the head with the heel of her shoe. Maxie Stanley recounted the adventures aboard the yacht during storms.

The Springs collection of unusual automobiles was described to the author by Elliott's former associates Lunsford McFadden, Skeebo Martin, and Cecil Neal.

Springs made the gift of his custom-built Rolls-Royce to Governor James F. Byrnes in a letter dated 10 April 1953. Two years earlier, on 13 November 1951, Springs wrote Pacific Auto Rentals, a California limousine rental company, to see if they might be interested in purchasing it.

Charles Crutchfield described the hunting methods of Elliott and his companions used on his baited airstrip.

Herbert Elsas of Atlanta recounted his experiences as Elliott's tax attorney and described the tax planning of his estate.

Chapter XVI: "The Real Man Is Somewhere between the Lines"

George Harris warned Springs that the hectic pace of his life endangered his health in a letter of 23 April 1940.

Elliott's letter to Harry DeButts, "They opened me up like an Idaho potato," was dated 16 September 1959.

The summary of the growth of The Springs Cotton Mills during Elliott's tenure as chief executive appeared in *The Springs Bulletin*, 5 November 1959.

Springs elaborated on his endless ailments in much of his correspondence, particularly with Drs. Robert McKay and Monroe Gilmour of Charlotte. Dr. Haynes Baird of Charlotte, who recalled Elliott in an interview with the author as "the worst neurotic," treated him several times without the knowledge of his partner, McKay.

Dr. Gilmour, Springs's physician during the latter stages of his illness, described Elliott's condition during the treatment and surgery in Charlotte. Dr. J. R. Reid, Jr., The Springs Cotton Mills physician, recalled details in interviews with John Gates and Marshall Doswell. H. William Close related his memories of the final days. The autopsy was performed by Dr. Laird Myers of the Sloan-Kettering Clinic on 3 November 1959 and was transmitted to Dr. Reid on 21 April 1960.

Conditions in his mills on the eve of his death were depicted by Springs in his informal annual message to stockholders for 1959. The obituaries cited were in the *New York Times* and the *Charlotte Observer* on 16 October 1959.

The closing paragraphs of the book are from William E. Barrett, "Elliott White Springs: The War Bird Who'll Never Die," *Cavalier* (March 1969).

Index

144, 147, 150, 155, 160
—personality, 9–10, 17, 19, 20, 24, 26, 27, 29–30, 36, 38, 40, 44, 46, 48, 53, 54, 59, 81, 90, 91, 96–99, 134, 136–37, 147–48 and passim
—as philanthropist, 226
—precocity, 12, 13
—and railroads, 161–62
—recklessness, 7, 42, 44–46, 51, 58, 59, 79, 99–100
—relations with his children, 130, 145–46, 149–50, 156–57, 158–59, 175–80, 181, 212–13, 240
—relations with his executives, 90, 133, 139, 155, 167, 173, 181–85, 186–88, 198, 205–6, 218–19, 222–24, 227–28
—relations with his father, 7–8, 14, 16, 18, 20, 24–25, 26–29, 31–32, 34–35, 38, 61, 62, 76, 98, 102–3, 105, 116, 119, 127, 213
—relations with his grandchildren, 233–35
—relations with his grandparents, 12, 13, 14–15, 18, 19–20
—relations with his mother, 9–10, 127
—relations with his son-in-law, 180–81, 216
—relations with his wife, 99, 101, 103, 129–30, 145, 149, 156–57, 171–72, 178, 179–80, 182, 204 and passim
—secrecy, 147–48, 151
—and Springs Mills cafeterias, 211–12
—and Springs Mills Headquarters Building, Fort Mill, S.C., 205–9
—superstitions, 4, 45, 64
—as textile executive, 8, 135–36, 149–56, 167, 169, 172–74, 176, 183, 199, 210, 214–16, 217, 222–24, 238–39
—and textile machinery manufacturers, 152–53
—and textile trade organizations, 150, 152, 154
—wealth, 61, 76, 113, 132–33, 135, 137, 144, 154–55, 156, 157, 168,

224, 234–35, 239
—and women, 17, 19, 23, 25–27, 29–30, 32–34, 37, 40, 42, 43, 44, 49, 50, 52, 64–65, 76, 88, 96, 129–30, 165, 193–194, 195, 198, 204–5, 230
—and World War I, 3–8, 25, 27, 28–31, 33–37, 38–55, 56–70, 90, 95–96, 105, 156–57
—and World War II, 160, 162, 163–64, 165–69, 175
Springs, Frances Ley (Mrs. Elliott White), 91–98, 101, 102, 213, 214–15
—and alcoholism, 172
—background, 91
—health, 145, 171
—marriage, 94, 96, 98
—personality, 91, 98–99, 130–31, 145 and passim
Springs, Grace White (Mrs. Leroy), 9, 11, 13–14, 105
—death, 14
Springs, John, 11
Springs, Lena Jones (Mrs. Leroy), 21–22, 24, 26–27, 33, 35, 100, 128, 132, 133
Springs, Leroy, I, 7–131 and passim
—birth, 9
—death, 131
—as gambler, 10, 126–27, 132–33, 224
—grave, 131, 148
—and labor relations, 11–12, 92, 129
—letters to Elliott White Springs, 18–19, 21, 26, 34, 62, 112–13
—marriages, 7, 11, 24
—as merchant, 10
—personality, 9–12, 14 and passim
—and railroads, 11
—shot by employee, 125–26
—temper, 10–11, 93, 125
—as textile executive, 11–12, 98, 126
—and *War Birds*, 105, 112–13
—wealth, 10–12, 20, 93, 127, 131, 132–33
—work habits, 12
—youth, 10